# China's Agricultural Investment in Australia

This book critically examines the driving forces, discourses, and conflicts surrounding Chinese investments in overseas farmland, with a specific focus on Australia.

With growing amounts of finance channeled into the purchase of overseas food and farming assets, China has become a frontrunner in the global land rush. Unlike much of the existing literature that focuses on emerging economies such as Brazil or Africa, this book examines Chinese farmland purchases in the developed country context of Australia. Based on four years of extensive field work in Australia and China, it traces the encounters and interactions between investors, regulators, deal brokers, farmers, and eaters that shape the ways in which individual Chinese investment projects materialize in the Australian countryside. In contrast to conventional wisdom portraying China's overseas land rush as a state-led strategy to feed the Chinese population, this book reveals that Chinese investments in Australian farmland have been propelled by the intersecting interests of international finance and business elites looking to cash in on booming Chinese demand for high-quality, Western food products. This book provides a unique transnational perspective on China's overseas farmland purchases and shows how Chinese farmland investments produce uneven geographies of agri-food globalization that cut across national borders. Through the lens of China's agri-engagement in Australia, this book advances our theoretical understanding of the new types of power relations and dynamics shaping an increasingly multi-polar agri-food system.

This book will be useful to students and scholars of agri-food studies, Chinese studies and globalization with an interest in the global land rush and the shifting contours of the global agri-food system.

**Michaela Boehme** is the Deputy Managing Director at the Sino-German Agricultural Centre in Beijing, China. She holds a PhD in Global Studies from the University of Leipzig, Germany, and previously, she worked as an agribusiness consultant and analyst with a focus on China's agricultural transformation and its impact on the global agri-food system.

**Routledge Studies in Global Land and Resource Grabbing**
Series Editors: Andreas Neef and Chanrith Ngin,
*The University of Auckland, New Zealand*

This series presents and discusses 'resource grabbing' research in a holistic manner by addressing how the rush for land and other natural resources (water, forests, minerals, etc.) is intertwined with agriculture, mining, tourism, energy, carbon markets, climate change, and disasters. This series welcomes contributions from a wide range of inter-disciplinary approaches and on a global basis.

**Capitalism and the Commons**
Just Commons in the Era of Multiple Crises
*Edited by Andreas Exner, Sarah Kumnig and Stephan Hochleithner*

**Tourism, Land Grabs and Displacement**
The Darker Side of the Feel-Good Industry
*Andreas Neef*

**Agrarian Capitalism, War and Peace in Colombia**
Beyond Dispossession
*Jacobo Grajales*

**Land Grabbing and Migration in a Changing Climate**
Comparative Perspectives from Senegal and Cambodia
*Sara Vigil*

**Large-Scale Land Acquisition in Ghana**
Institutional Change, Gender and Power
*Kristina Lanz*

**China's Agricultural Investment in Australia**
Uneven Geographies of Agri-Food Globalization
*Michaela Boehme*

For more information about this series, please visit: www.routledge.com/Routledge-Studies-in-Global-Land-and-Resource-Grabbing/book-series/GLRG

# China's Agricultural Investment in Australia

## Uneven Geographies of Agri-Food Globalization

Michaela Boehme

Routledge
Taylor & Francis Group
LONDON AND NEW YORK
earthscan
from Routledge

First published 2025
by Routledge
4 Park Square, Milton Park, Abingdon, Oxon OX14 4RN

and by Routledge
605 Third Avenue, New York, NY 10158

*Routledge is an imprint of the Taylor & Francis Group, an informa business*



*British Library Cataloguing-in-Publication Data*
A catalogue record for this book is available from the British Library

ISBN: 978-1-032-75585-4 (hbk)
ISBN: 978-1-032-75586-1 (pbk)
ISBN: 978-1-003-47466-1 (ebk)

DOI: 10.4324/9781003474661

Typeset in Sabon
by codeMantra

# Contents

# Figures

# Tables

# Abbreviations

| | |
|---|---|
| ABARES | Australian Bureau of Agricultural and Resource Economics and Sciences |
| ABC | Agricultural Bank of China |
| ACBC | Australia China Business Council |
| ANZ | Australia and New Zealand Bank |
| AoA | Agreement on Agriculture |
| ATO | Australian Taxation Office |
| AUSTRADE | Australian Trade and Investment Commission |
| BOC | Bank of China |
| BRI | Belt and Road Initiative |
| CAAS | Chinese Academy of Agricultural Sciences |
| CCB | China Construction Bank |
| CCIEE | China Center for International Economic Exchanges |
| CCPIT | China Council for the Promotion of International Trade |
| CHAFTA | China-Australia Free Trade Agreement |
| CPC | Communist Party of China |
| EABER | East Asian Bureau of Economic Research |
| FAIF | farmland and agricultural investment fund |
| FIRB | Foreign Investment Review Board |
| GP | general partner |
| ICBC | Industrial and Commercial Bank of China |
| IFC | International Finance Corporation |
| IPO | initial public offering |
| LP | limited partner |
| MARA | Ministry of Agriculture and Rural Affairs |
| NDRC | National Development and Reform Commission |
| NGO | non-governmental organization |
| NSW | New South Wales |
| POE | privately-owned enterprise |
| SOB | state-owned bank |
| SOE | state-owned enterprise |
| SWF | sovereign wealth fund |
| TRQ | tariff rate quota |
| USDA | United States Department of Agriculture |
| WTO | World Trade Organization |

# Acknowledgments

Writing this book has been a long and winding journey that has taken me to many places around the world—from Germany to Australia, China, and back again. I am grateful to the many people I met along the way and who generously shared their time and thoughts with me. It is these individuals who have made this book possible by offering me insights into their worlds, beliefs, and struggles. The critical angle developed in this book is not a critique of the people whose accounts have co-produced the story I tell here but of the broader structures, institutions, and power relations within which China's global agri-food integration is unfolding.

Completing this journey would not have been possible without the significant help, guidance, and support from a large number of people. First and foremost, I would like to thank Sarah Ruth Sippel from the University of Münster for her intellectual, moral, and practical support throughout all phases of the project. Sarah taught me how to approach the uncertainties and vagaries of empirical research with commitment, perseverance, and intellectual honesty. I am deeply indebted to her support. Eva Sternfeld from the Sino-German Agricultural Centre has also been a great source of support, particularly in the later stages of this book project. Her China expertise, networks, and wisdom have been invaluable to me.

Martina Keilbach and my fellow PhD students at the Graduate School for Global and Area Studies in Leipzig have offered a supportive environment to try out arguments and hone academic skills. In particular, I would like to thank my colleagues Cynthia Gharios and Felicitas Sommer, who have provided constructive criticism on various parts of the book. Special thanks to CHEN Ling, CHEN Yi, and WANG Xue at Leipzig University for helping me to navigate the mysteries of doing research on and in China.

I am also grateful to have had the chance to meet many people of the Australasian Agri-Food Research Network at various conferences and workshops throughout the course of my research. Their passion for all things related to food, agriculture, and the rural sector has been hugely inspiring. Particular thanks go to Geoffrey Lawrence, Kia Smith, and Alexandra Langford from the University of Queensland for including me in their research group on the financialization of Australian agriculture and for generously sharing their thoughts and ideas; to Nicolette Larder and Neil Argent from the University of New England for offering me an opportunity to present parts of my research; and to Angga Dwiartama from the Institute of Technology in Bandung, Katharine Legun from University of Otago, Jérémie Forney from the University of Neuchâtel, and Ramalis Sobandi from Tunas Nusa Foundation for hosting a memorable postgraduate workshop in Bandung.

In China, numerous people were extremely helpful in facilitating my research, especially SHENG Yu and HUANG Jikun from the China Center for Agricultural Policy (CCAP) at Peking University. I thank them for providing me with a base for doing field work in China—across all disciplinary, methodological, and cultural differences. Special thanks to Andreas Gruschke at Sichuan University, HAN Jianlin from the China Office at the International Livestock Research Institute (ILRI), and XU Yong from the Foreign Economic Cooperation Center (FECC) at the Ministry of Agriculture and Rural Affairs for helping me to set up interviews with experts from the academy and government. I would also like to thank Mateusz Filipski from the International Food Policy Research Institute (IFPRI), who kindly leveraged his professional network to help me build connections in China.

Furthermore, I am indebted to the Collaborative Research Center SFB 1199 "Processes of Spatialization under the Global Condition" at Leipzig University, which has provided the financial support and infrastructural support that have made this project possible. Many individuals at the SFB 1199 have accompanied me along the different phases of this journey.

A special thanks goes to all family and friends for supporting me throughout the ups and downs of this journey. Finally, I wish to thank David Walker for accompanying me throughout my thoughts and providing the occasional sanity check. I am grateful for his unwavering optimism and encouragement without which this book would not have been completed.

# Maps

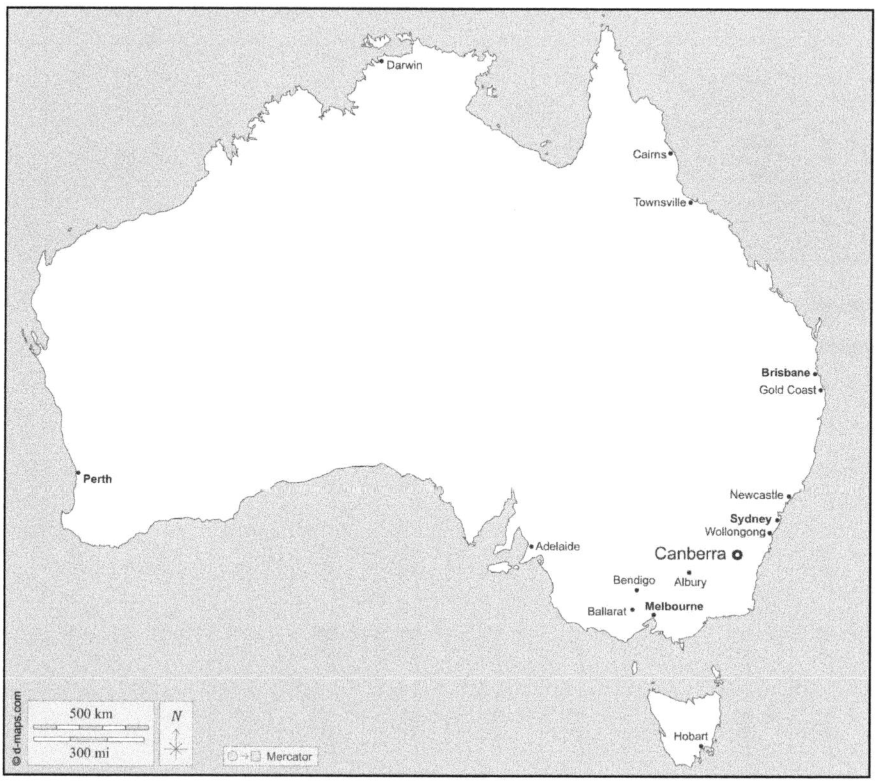


*Figure 0.1* Map of Australia.

*Source:* d-maps.com.

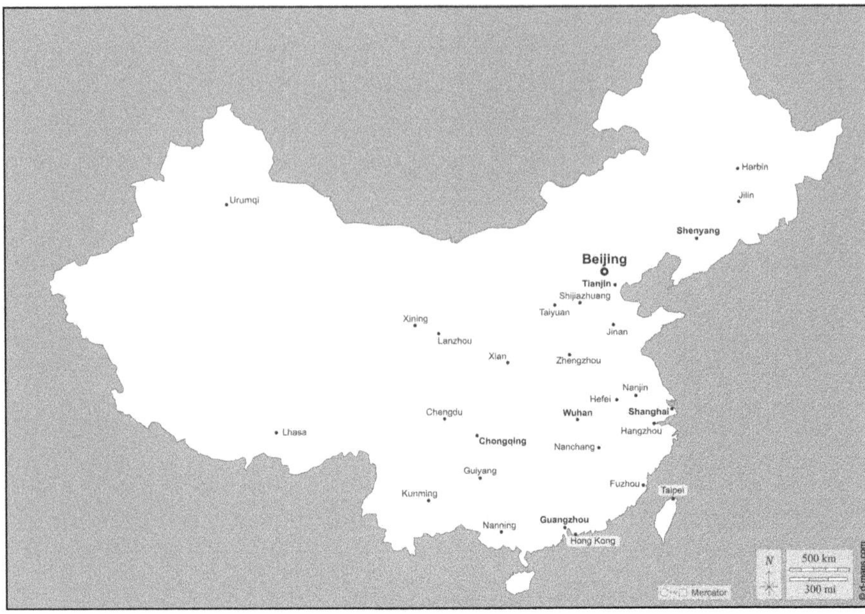


*Figure 0.2* Map of China.

*Source:* d-maps.com.

# Introduction

# 1 China's rise as a global investor in food and farming

In early 2018, I am attending a photo exhibition in the city of Oldenburg in northern Germany. What is on display there are the pictures that won the 2018 World Press Photo contest. One series of photographs particularly captures my imagination. It is a series by American photographer Georg Steinmetz on the Chinese food industry that shows the scale and scope of what it means to produce food for 1.4 billion people.[1] Steinmetz's camera captures an automated chicken farm near Beijing, where 3 million hens produce 2.4 million eggs a day, while robots equipped with German technology remove dead birds. Visitors marvel at a picture capturing the unloading of a soybean cargo at a state-run processing facility just above the mouth of the Yangtze River. The picture provides a vivid impression of what it looks like to move over 100 million tons of soybeans each year, most of which are grown in the fields of the American Midwest and Central-Western Brazil, to convert into cooking oil and fodder for Chinese farm animals. Yet another shot shows a massive, industrial-scale dairy operation that relies on tens of thousands of Holstein cows imported from Australia, semen for artificial insemination from Canada, and alfalfa feed imported from the United States, as the accompanying text explains to the baffled visitor. Each of the large format photographs imprints on the mind of the visitor the story of 1.4 billion "booming Chinese appetites" and their transformative impact as China's quest for food is reshaping its agriculture—and the world's.

* * *

China's growing demand for food is a captivating subject that has inspired hopes and fears among experts and China watchers around the world ever since, in 1995, American environmental activist Lester Brown raised the question of "who will feed China" in a short booklet of the same name (Brown 1995). In Brown's vision of a Chinese Malthusian tragedy, growing food supply problems brought about by billions of Chinese consumers rapidly moving up the food chain would lead to global food shortages and a world food crisis. Evidently, not everyone has shared the resource pessimism encapsulated in Brown's view. For free-trade advocates, China's changing consumption

DOI: 10.4324/9781003474661-2

habits and growing imports have been reasons for optimism and profits. Yet, others have marveled at China's growing domestic production capacity, underpinned by a mixture of technological innovation and supportive policies, which has enabled the country to, by and large, feed itself despite the rapidly growing demand for more diversified food products.

When the global food price crisis hit in 2007/2008, anxieties about China's impact on global food security returned in a new guise: large-scale land acquisitions by Chinese investors in countries around the globe. As particularly poorer countries struggled with rising food prices and shortages in global food markets, China was singled out as a frontrunner in a new, global land rush. This image was fed by sensationalist media headlines suggesting that the Chinese were buying up millions of hectares of farmland in Africa, Latin America, and elsewhere in the global South. What was driving these activities? Did they signal a tipping point in China's ability to feed itself, forcing the government to outsource domestic food production by controlling farmland in other countries? And what would that mean for global food security and the rules and mechanisms shaping the global agri-food system?

This book tries to answer these questions in the context of Australia. With its vast expanses of fertile land, diverse climates, and modern farming technology, the continent down under has drawn some of the largest sums of Chinese agri-food capital globally. According to an annual survey among Chinese companies compiled by the Chinese Ministry of Agriculture and Rural Affairs (MARA), at the end of 2016, Australia was the third largest recipient of accumulated agricultural investment from China, following Singapore[2] and Israel (MARA 2017). That same year, the Oceanian region (Australia and New Zealand combined) had also received the second largest inflow of agricultural investment after Asia (see Figure 1.1)—a finding that goes against the grain of media headlines emphasizing China's agricultural engagement in Africa and Latin America. While these numbers include not only farm purchases but also acquisitions of agri-food processing, warehousing, and logistics assets, there is no doubt that farmland has become an increasingly attractive investment for buyers from China. Since 2016, *Australia's Register of Foreign Ownership of Agricultural Land* has provided an annual overview of the amount of Australian farmland owned by foreign entities. In its 2018 edition, the register listed China as the second largest source of foreign investment. With over 9 million hectares, entities from China owned about 2.3 percent of Australia's total farmland area, a number only surpassed by the United Kingdom, which, at that time, was listed as beneficially owning 2.6 percent of Australian agricultural land (ATO 2018). By 2022, China had moved to become the largest foreign landowner in Australia, even as the total area of Chinese-owned land holdings had seen a slight decline (ATO 2022).

These direct investment flows are underpinned by a strong trade relationship. In 2010–2011, China overtook Japan as Australia's top agricultural export market. Around 25 percent or 11.8 billion AUD of Australian agricultural exports were destined for China in 2017–2018, with wool, barley, and beef being the top export commodities (Fell 2019). In the 2010s, China also became a major export destination for Australian dairy products and wines. Not surprisingly, Chinese agri-investments are closely correlated with trade patterns, concentrating on the production of food products such as beef and dairy, for which demand in the Chinese market is growing (see Figure 1.2). A bilateral trade agreement entering into force in 2015 further enhanced Australia's attractiveness as an investment destination for Chinese agri-food capital.

The pace of acquisitions has subsided as diplomatic tensions between the two countries flared up at the end of the decade. Mutual accusations of undue interference into each other's political affairs have not only curtailed agri-food trade flows but also reduced Chinese interest in Australia as an investment destination. Since 2019, no major investment deals in the agricultural sector have been recorded, and some early high-profile investors have begun to offload farmland properties or downsize operations. But while the peak of China's agri-investment in Australia appears to have passed, its effects linger. Today, there is not only a well-established group of Chinese agri-food companies operating in Australia but also an ongoing debate about how to accommodate China's demand for natural resources in a way that benefits Australia's "national interest."

## The argument

This book unpacks the aspirations and fears that have informed understandings of "who will feed China" and interrogates how these have become entangled with Chinese investments in Australian food and farming. Two opposing perspectives have shaped the debate about China's role as a major agri-investor in Australia. Supporters have emphasized the "natural complementarity" between a resource-rich Australian agri-food sector and growing "Chinese appetites." Chinese agri-food capital is seen as a driver of growth and profits as it helps expand Australian export capacity to meet the growing Chinese demand. In contrast to this "dining boom" narrative, critics worry that Australia risks "selling out the farm" to Chinese investors. Framed as a state-led quest for overseas natural resources to feed populations at home, China's agricultural investment conjures up fears about a loss of control and sovereignty over Australian farmland ownership and agricultural production on the continent.

Although both views arrive at very different interpretations concerning the potentialities, impacts, and consequences of China's overseas agricultural investment, they share a fundamental commonality. Implicitly, they both render Chinese investment an aggregate, abstract, and black-boxed "force," unilaterally transforming Australian agricultural landscapes—whether through "win-win" cooperation or loss of control. By framing investments from China as internally homogenous and fundamentally guided by the Chinese state, both alarmist and optimistic accounts gloss over the significant internal diversity characterizing Chinese agri-investments and the multiple, contested, and, at times, contradictory forms of state, corporate, and transnational elite relations that determine if, where, and how investment projects materialize in Australian ruralities.

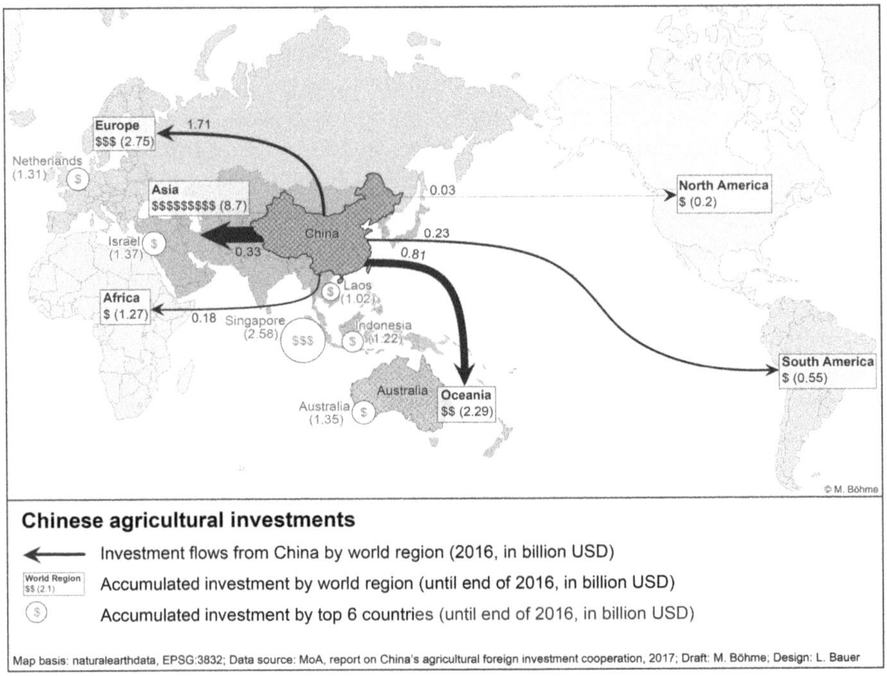


*Figure 1.1* China's agricultural investment flows by world region and top six recipient countries.

*Source:* The author.

In this book, I challenge the unilateral and monolithic framing that shapes common understandings of China's overseas investment in food and farming. Rather than debating the assumed opportunities and risks that Chinese agri-food capital represents to Australia, I ask how investments are produced and negotiated on the ground by a multiplicity of actors operating on multiple scales—from rural farming contexts to transnational business elites and finance networks. What matters to me is how diverse actors, interests, logics, and practices align or come into conflict with one another within the specific historical and geographical context of China-Australia agri-food relations. This means that the question I pose is not whether China's rise as an overseas agriculture investor is good or bad for Australia but *for whom* it is beneficial, how investment projects are negotiated on the ground, and who is marginalized by them. This is then a story about a multiplicity of individual investment projects, from powerful Chinese state companies to globalizing agribusiness corporations and astute private entrepreneurs. It is a story about the ways in which the interests of transnational agribusiness elites align around Chinese investment flows, often at the expense of marginalized groups and spaces in both national contexts. It is also a tale of the diverse logics of accumulation

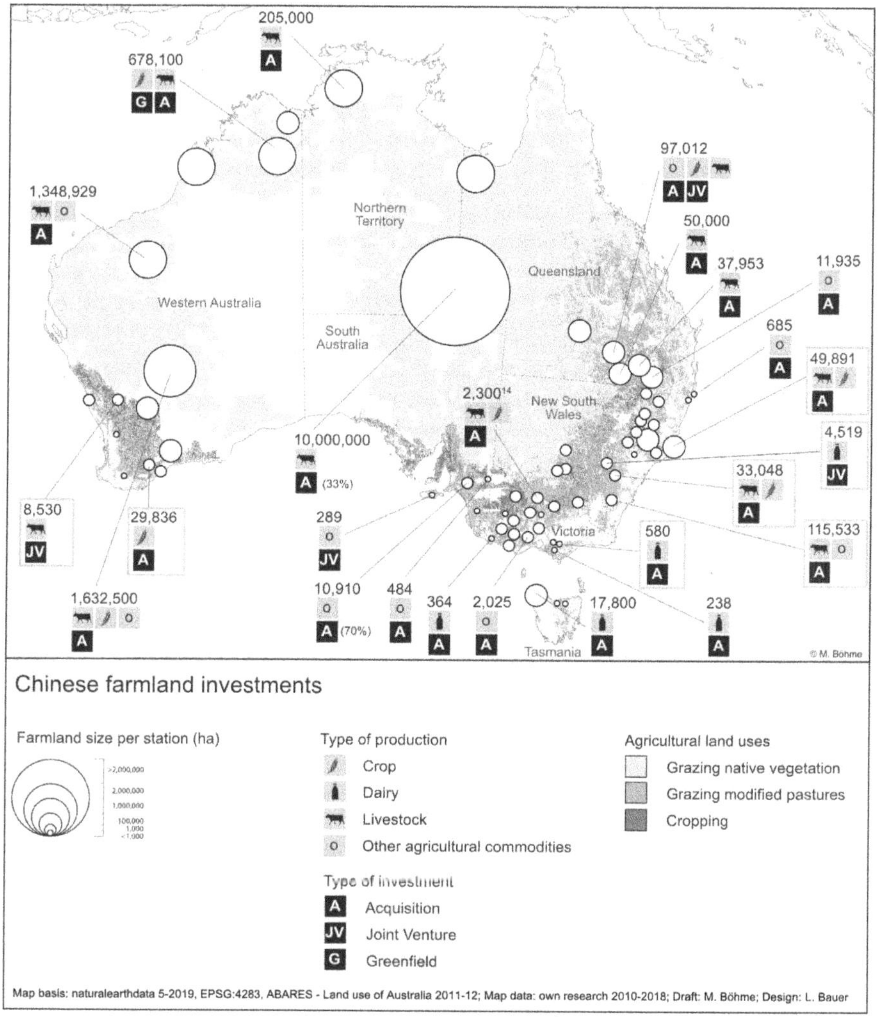


*Figure 1.2* Chinese investments in Australian farmland as of December 2019.
*Source:* The author.

by which agri-investments create profits from "nature" and the new market connections and commodity chains that investment projects enable (or fail to do so). And it is an account of the dialectic relationship between flows and control that shapes how state actors govern access to natural resources.

By putting its concreteness and contestedness into focus, I demonstrate that China's agricultural "going out" is not singular and uniform but diverse and multiple. My account reveals that Chinese investment in overseas food and farming is most productively understood as being constituted by networks of powerful political and economic elites cutting *across* national boundaries rather than as a national, state-led project governed by a single and coherent logic. Although mine is not primarily a story of bottom-up reactions to Chinese agri-investments by farmers and local communities, my findings suggest that China's global agri-food integration produces uneven geographies of "winners" and "losers" that are by no means contiguous with national territory. As a transnational alliance of agri-food corporations, local elites, and financial institutions constructs and profits from a new Chinese "dining boom," it simultaneously deepens the socially unjust and ecologically unsustainable relations that characterize how food is produced, circulated, and consumed in a global context. In contrast to conventional wisdom, I argue that China's "booming appetite" is not the natural outcome of shifting consumer tastes nor does it signal an impending food security crisis. Instead, Chinese demand for overseas farmland and agricultural resources is the product of an agrarian-capitalist dynamic that has placed China at the center of a new food import complex, which, in turn, exacerbates economic, social, and environmental problems for the many while creating profits for the few. As this book will show, China's global agri-food integration deepens a set of agri-food relations that ultimately benefits transnational elites in pursuit of power, profits, and market share—irrespective of nationality—while simultaneously deepening many of the contradictions and inequities inherent in the global agri-food system.

## China, Australia, and the global land rush

In the late 2010s, a remarkable new trend began to attract worldwide attention: large-scale transnational investments in farmland. Private corporations, investment firms, and even national governments were reported to buy or lease large amounts of farmland overseas. Motivations for these land deals were varied, ranging from food security concerns to profit-making. The trend was embedded in a broader context of crisis. In 2008, global food prices began to increase steeply, leading to unrest in many parts of the world. In Mexico, protesters gathered to demonstrate against the soaring costs of maize tortillas, a local staple, while bread shortages became the focus of a wave of anger among Egyptians struggling to meet their daily food needs. The rise in food prices coincided with the worst financial shock since the Great Depression. As the 2007/2008 financial crisis sent stocks into free fall and the failure of major financial institutions was looming, farmland turned from an overlooked to a sought-after object of investment (Fairbairn 2020). Large tracts of overseas farmland could not only serve as sites of food production in the event of further price hikes, thus allowing their owners greater control over future food supplies, but they also promised stable returns at a time when financial markets offered few opportunities to investors.

The new-found investor interest in farmland was met with much criticism from activists, scholars, and journalists alike. Dubbing the phenomenon "land grabbing," many expressed concerns that a sudden demand for land among governments and corporations with big check-books would risk displacing peasant and indigenous communities from lands they have traditionally depended on for their food and livelihoods, particularly in the global South, where the land rights of rural populations are often poorly protected (Hall 2013; McMichael 2012). Meanwhile, in richer countries with private landownership structures, a sudden influx of foreign capital was feared to drive up land prices, thus pushing smaller farmers out of the market and adding to the inequalities that characterize many rural communities (Larder et al. 2018; Sippel et al. 2016). There were also ecological concerns. Large-scale land acquisitions in the global South are often associated with deforestation and the loss of biodiversity as monocultures expand. The accelerated loss of Brazilian rain forest to make room for large-scale soybean plantations as the country is emerging as one of the leading exporters of this important cash crop is a case in point (Wilkinson et al. 2015). Even in rich, developed countries with sound regulations and law enforcement, farmland investments can become drivers of environmental deterioration as has been shown in the case of New Zealand, where the investment-fueled expansion of dairy farming has caused severe damage to the quality and availability of the country's freshwater resources (Ouma 2020).

The amount of land being snapped up by investors is hard to calculate, but an early report by the Food and Agriculture Organization (FAO) of the United Nations put the number at 50–80 million hectares in the first decade of the new millennium (Toulmin et al. 2011). China was quickly identified as a key actor in this global land rush. GRAIN, a Europe-based non-governmental organization (NGO), published a report in 2008 that portrayed China as a global leader in seeking farmland abroad to ensure food security at home (GRAIN 2008). The notion of a capital-rich but resource-poor China racing to secure food overseas was soon picked up by others. Newspapers cited stories of Chinese investors acquiring outrageous amounts of farmland in Africa and elsewhere (The Economist 2009), while independent monitoring initiatives such as Farmlandgrab.org or the Land Matrix amplified their claims by including them in their databases.

Meanwhile, scholars in critical agrarian and food studies pondered the significance of Chinese acquisitions of overseas farmland in a newly emerging "polycentric food regime" (Borras Jr. et al. 2013; Margulis et al. 2013) and their impact on the established rules of global food production and trade. McMichael (2013), for example, interprets China's overseas agricultural investment as a form of "agro-security mercantilism" that allows the Chinese state to circumvent the market rules enshrined in the World Trade Organization (WTO) by securing direct access to land and food resources overseas (p. 52). By mobilizing its state-owned enterprises (SOEs) or sovereign wealth funds (SWFs), so the argument went, the Chinese government was able to access productive land abroad and repatriate the food grown there back to its home market. Early debates thus quickly solidified three claims concerning

China's role in the global land rush: China was acquiring large swaths of farmland with a focus on land-rich regions in the global South, the Chinese state was leading the effort, and the purpose was to outsource food production for China's food security at home.

### *Rethinking patterns of China's overseas agri-investments*

These early certainties no longer hold. As scholars began to move beyond media reports to investigate investment sites on the ground, a new picture of China's role in the global land rush has emerged. Many farmland investments cited in media reports were found to be far smaller than generally believed, had collapsed in the face of regulatory hurdles and practical challenges, or could not be confirmed at all by researchers visiting investment sites. For example, fieldwork by Brautigam and Zhang (2013) revealed that a much-reported 3-million hectare "land grab" by Chinese telecommunications giant ZTE International in the Democratic Republic of the Congo ended up operating on a paltry 256 hectares, while a heavily publicized 800-million dollar land deal between Chinese investors and the government of Mozambique was found to be complete fiction. Likewise, Chinese land deals in Latin America, when investigated on the ground, turned out to be far smaller than sensationalist headlines would suggest (Myers & Guo 2015). Given the stark contrast between media hype and reality, some scholars even argued that Chinese investment was deliberately singled out for concern by U.S.- and European-based agribusinesses wishing to shift attention away from their own role in the global land rush while also meeting with resistance from peasant movements in the global South that had formed to protest rising food prices and agribusiness domination (Oliveira 2018).

Hyperbole concerning China's land rush in the global South coincided with the underreporting of Chinese agri-investments in developed economies. Despite ranking among the top investment destinations for Chinese agri-food capital, Australia, for example, remained conspicuously absent from the initial tone-setting reports of NGOs, activists, and Western media criticizing Chinese land investments in Africa or Latin America. This oversight was built into the very structure of early research on the global land rush. The Land Matrix, for example—a widely used investment database that collects data on land deals—lists developed countries as sources of investment but not as investment destinations, thereby making invisible capital flows that go beyond assumed North-South or South-South investment geographies. Today, it is clear that farms and food companies in developed countries have attracted considerable amounts of Chinese investments (DuBois 2022; Böhme 2021, 2020), yet China's public image as an agri-investor remains closely centered on the global South.

Fieldwork-based research has also challenged the notion that China's role in the global land rush is driven solely by food security concerns. Few of the investigated investment projects turned out to be directly supportive of the country's food security objectives, whereas the need for making profits was generally the key driving force (Gooch & Gale 2018). Of those projects focused on growing staple crops, production was mostly bound for local markets rather than for export to China (Zhan et al. 2018; Brautigam & Zhang 2013). A closer look at what exactly the Chinese were doing with the overseas farms they had acquired also provides us with a more nuanced understanding of the actors involved. Rather than state-led endeavors, land deals were overwhelmingly led by private companies that needed to make profits in order to survive (Hofman 2016). While the government would use loans and subsidies to incentivize certain deals, it did not directly control investment decisions, making its role contextual rather than directive in character (Gu et al. 2016).

Finally, the debate about China's role in the global land rush has moved beyond a narrow focus on the acquisition of farmland to encompass investments along the entire agricultural value chain. Indeed, some of the largest deals have involved the acquisition of foreign agri-businesses rather than farms. In 2013, China's largest producer and processor of pork, the Henan-based Shuanghui (subsequently renamed to WH Group), acquired American pork processing giant Smithfield, providing it with access to advanced processing technology and a mechanism for vertical integration with American contract farmers (DuBois 2022). In the largest acquisition ever undertaken by a Chinese company, ChemChina, in 2016, acquired seed and chemical producer Syngenta for 43 billion USD, while state-owned China National Cereals, Oils and Foodstuffs Corporation (COFCO) came to own a global network of grain trading infrastructure and logistics by acquiring agribusiness companies Nidera and Nobel in a succession of investment deals between 2014 and 2016. None of these companies owned any farmland, yet they were attractive investment targets for Chinese companies eager to enhance control over global agri-food markets and counterbalance the influence of the big Western grain-trading companies—the so-called ABCDs: Archer Daniels Midland, Bunge, Cargill, and Louis Dreyfus (Keulertz & Woertz 2016).

Recent scholarship has challenged the notion of a resource-strapped China racing to buy farmland overseas in order to guarantee food security at home. Despite claims made about its distinctive nature, Chinese farmland investment is surprisingly similar to the investment practices and goals of leading agribusiness companies from the global North (Klinger & Muldavin 2019). There is also little practical evidence to suggest that Chinese investors are using neomercantilist strategies to bypass the global agri-food system (Mefano Fares 2023). Rather than imagining the Chinese state as gobbling up large tracts of farmland overseas to repatriate food, China's role in the global land rush is characterized by a multitude of diverse business entities acquiring profitable agricultural assets—from farms to agri-food companies—to enhance their own economic position in the global agri-food system while benefitting from state incentives at home. Yet, how their strategies play out abroad is contingent upon the regulatory and political context of the host country.

### *Foreign investments and national farmland governance*

Not all farmland is available for investment. Some countries may not allow foreign investors to purchase any farmland at all. Others may only offer land leases, thus making sure that long-term ownership of farmland ultimately remains in the hands of domestic actors. In other cases, land acquisitions might be conditional upon a commitment by the foreign buyer to use the land for predefined purposes and development goals. On the other end of the spectrum, those countries with the most open investment regimes allow both foreign individuals and corporations to acquire farmland—sometimes in unlimited amounts. Levels of openness to transnational farmland acquisitions vary greatly, even among countries with similar economic profiles and development histories. For instance, Canada and Australia, two developed economies and major agricultural exporters, regulate farmland ownership in very different ways. While foreign ownership of farmland is outright prohibited in some Canadian provinces, foreign buyers have generally been welcome by Australian governments to purchase and develop huge land-holdings—even though some acquisitions must undergo a review by the national authorities (Magnan 2015).

The differences in how host countries regulate access to farmland show that states are not passive bystanders in the global land rush. Rather, they play a central role in managing and regulating investment flows into land and agriculture. Even in the case of politically and economically weaker states, host governments become "calculating partners in land deals, negotiating the costs and benefits of the contemporary moment" (Wolford et al. 2013, p. 192). In doing so, they often have to mediate between conflicting interests. As states seek to provide profit opportunities for business entities while engaging with land claims from local communities or answering to international demands for environmental protection, they take on a contradictory role, acting as both enablers and arbiters in the global land rush (Borras et al. 2019, p. 2).

The contestations around who can own farmland and for which purposes are not only linked to land's life-sustaining characteristics but also connected to its cultural significance. Farmland, like few other elements on the surface of the earth, is a symbol of national identity and sovereignty. Australia is a good example. On the continent down under, land and national identity became fused as Europeans settled there throughout the late 18th and 19th centuries. Legally defined as *terra nullius* (unowned land), Australia was conceived of as an empty space that had to be "opened up" and made "productive" by the hard work of the white settler (Sippel 2018). Given the many national myths and identity-giving stories related to farmland, it is not surprising that the global land rush has provoked harsh policy responses in host countries around the world as governments have been scrambling to better control and govern the influx of investment capital. In 2010, as public debate over foreign acquisitions of Brazilian farmland was reaching fever pitch, the government reinstated a law limiting the amount of land that foreigners could own. It also required government approval for land deals above a certain ceiling (Fairbairn 2015; Oliveira 2013). Argentina followed suit under a similar law in 2011, limiting foreign ownership to 1,000 hectares. In 2012, Hungary amended its constitution to ensure that only Hungarian farmers could buy farmland, while Uruguay instituted a ban on foreign governments and their associated entities such as state-owned enterprises and sovereign wealth funds, restricting them from acquiring any farmland in the country (GRAIN 2013). This wave of farmland re-regulation also included Australia, which, in 2015, lowered the threshold at which farmland deals by foreign buyers must be approved by the government and, for the first time in its history, implemented an open register of foreign farmland ownership (Magnan 2018; Sippel 2015).

Concern over a loss of national sovereignty was generally quoted as the main driver behind such efforts to re-regulate investment in farmland. As states reasserted control over farmland resources within their territories, a new wave of resource nationalism appeared to reconfigure the neoliberal mechanisms hitherto dominant in global agri-food trade and investment. For the most part, the re-regulation of farmland ownership was framed in state-centric terms (Fairbairn 2015). Most regulatory responses emerging in the wake of the global land rush were designed to reign in *foreign* ownership of farmland, while other effects of land deals, such as the growing concentration of property and wealth in the hands of large corporations and financial institutions, usually remained uninterrogated. Worse yet, in some places, particular kinds of foreigners, mostly from China or Arab countries, were singled out for concern, giving the debate decidedly xenophobic undertones (Oliveira 2017; Sippel 2015). In Australia, for instance, the land purchases of a Qatari investment fund in the mid-2010s caused heated public debate, whereas much larger investments from the domestic financial sector faced almost no scrutiny (Larder et al. 2015).

The preoccupation with land acquisitions by foreigners has largely failed to address the social and ecological concerns associated with the global land rush. An investment deal that appears to be linked to one specific foreign country—generally the home country the investing entity is registered in—may involve capital from multiple and changing sources, making the category of foreignness a "deeply *inadequate* basis upon which to regulate [land deals]" (Fairbairn 2015, p. 584). This is also true for Chinese investors, who, as this book will show, often acquire Australian farmland in partnership with local entities or backed up by international, mostly Western sources of finance. This means that financial institutions, businesses, and sometimes even governments from the global North are deeply implicated in Chinese overseas agri-investments. Despite their alarmist rhetoric, they frequently share common profit interests (Klinger & Muldavin 2019, p. 11). Yet, in many countries, foreigners—or foreigners with particular nationalities—were singled out for concern, while the investment deals of national investors or entities from "friendly" countries based in the global North continued to expand unheeded.

The myopic focus on land is another blind spot in the way many countries have responded to the growing inflow of investment capital into the agricultural sector (Oliveira 2018). As was highlighted above, some of China's largest agri-investment deals do not involve any farmland at all, yet they arguably have a significant impact on the structures of power and control in the global agri-food system. My research shows that in Australia, throughout the 2010s, Chinese buyers have invested more capital in agricultural processing and logistics assets than in farmland; however, none of these acquisitions ever instigated much public debate. Meanwhile, the bid by a Chinese buyer consortium for one of Australia's most iconic farms, the S Kidman estate, created such a backlash that the deal had to be halted by the national government (Böhme 2020; Sippel 2018). Likewise, in Brazil, another hotbed of debate about Chinese "land grabs," few Chinese investors actually acquired farms, whereas the biggest and most successful deals centered on the acquisition of grain processing and logistics infrastructure (Oliveira 2018).

By responding with a foreign-centered and land-focused logic to a phenomenon that is both transnational and untethered from land, re-regulation in many host countries is unlikely to be effective, as has been convincingly argued by Fairbairn (2015) and other scholars. Indeed, regulatory responses that single out foreign buyers of farmland will do little to address the growing concentration of power and control—not just over land but over food production, prices, and distribution in general—that characterizes the global agri-food system. Moreover, what looks like a break with the neoliberal paradigm of free investment and capital flows is hardly the case. Even as host governments claim to be re-asserting sovereignty over national resources, they often remain dependent on and deeply embedded in transnational capital flows, leading to hybrid forms of resource governance where, as in the case of Australia, land concentration in the hands of wealthy Western individuals and companies continues apace, while capital inflows from Chinese, Arab, and other entities defined as problematic become subject to strict scrutiny (Sippel & Weldon 2020).

### A transnational perspective

This book seeks to shine light on the multiplicity and diversity of the individual investment projects that constitute the fabric of China's land rush in Australia. Unlike much contemporary writing on this subject that frames China as a monolithic actor, I seek to avoid the pitfalls of this "territorial trap" (Agnew 1994) by looking beyond an abstract Chinese state seemingly controlling land deals and investment activities across the globe. Instead, using empirically grounded research methods, I unpack the transnational networks of actors and shared interests through which Chinese agri-food capital is channeled into Australian ruralities. I uncover the personal connections and institutional support structures that make it possible for Chinese buyers with little knowledge about the continent down under to find and acquire farms in Australia. My research highlights the linkages that connect Chinese investors with financiers on Wall Street and ambitious farmer entrepreneurs in the Australian outback. I also make clear that, while Chinese investors must operate within a specific political context at home, the Chinese state does not dictate business decisions and local outcomes abroad. Most importantly, I show how the question of "who will feed China?" has spawned visions of profits and influence that shape the behavior of not just Chinese investors but of different actors across the global agri-food system.

A transnational and grounded perspective on China's land rush in Australia matters, I believe, for both political and intellectual reasons. First, the politics. In a geopolitical climate that increasingly casts China as antagonistic to a Western rules-based order, Chinese investors have become the target of public concern—from their assumed reckless exploitation of the environment to fears about undue political influence and questionable labor practices. Yet, this reflex to single out Chinese investment makes invisible other types of capital and normalizes the practices by which corporate and financial institutions from the global North have long been implicated in the continuing concentration of land and agricultural resources. In Australia, for example, the early 2010s saw farmland investment firms with domestic and international sources of funding, notably from countries such as Denmark, the Netherlands, Canada, Sweden, and the United States, spring up by the dozens, acquiring hundreds of thousands of hectares of farmland to the tune of an estimated 2 billion AUD (Magnan 2015, pp. 6–7). This phenomenon is part of an ongoing process of neoliberal restructuring, in which commercial and financial actors have been crowding out Australian family farms (Pritchard & Tonts 2011), but, unlike investment from China, it has received little public attention.

To be clear, the point here is not to defend land acquisitions by Chinese investors as inherently unproblematic but to avoid reflexively nationalizing the problems associated with concentrated, corporate land ownership as "Chinese." By framing an abstract "China" as the root cause for Australia's rural malaise—from the demise of family farms to the continent's chronic farm income crises—public debate in Australia and elsewhere has not only exacerbated worrisome xenophobic tendencies but also, more concerningly, deflected attention from the real question: how to finance agricultural and rural development in a way that is socially just and environmentally friendly. In other words, the debate we should be having is not about China but about who should own farmland and to which ends? Yet, discourses that represent Chinese land deals as "unnatural" and as warranting particular scrutiny have also resonated with scholars and activist movements critical of the global agri-food system. Here, a transnational perspective that avoids the "territorial trap" becomes all the more important if social activism is not to play into the hands of a neo-Cold War politics that stigmatizes China while obscuring the neoliberal policies and mechanisms at the heart of the social and environmental crises facing the food system today.

To understand the second reason that makes it worth studying Chinese land deals in Australia, we must turn our attention to the ways in which scholars in critical agrarian studies and neighboring fields have dealt with—or rather *not* dealt with—the phenomenon. While scholarly interest in China's role in the global land rush has been high, it has almost exclusively focused on Chinese land deals in the global South. To date, there has been no other study in the critical social sciences investigating what Chinese investors are doing in rural Australia. Why this gap? It exists, I argue, because China's land rush in Australia poses an intellectual challenge to the established analytical categories of the critical geographical imagination. One such set of categories, inspired by world systems and dependency theory, is that of "core" and "periphery." It frames the world as being organized by power relations that extract resources from the underdeveloped peripheries to developed core regions. Given its growing influence on the global scene, China is now often grouped with the traditional core regions of the global North as critical scholars have begun to focus on the mechanisms by which the country transfers surplus value from the world's poorer regions to fuel its own development.

Connected to this binary "core vs. periphery" logic is a normative commitment to questions of justice and equity. In the case of large-scale land acquisitions in the global South, for example, this commitment is often expressed through a conceptual language that frames the host country or particular spaces within as frontiers of accumulation where marginalized groups resist their dispossession by actors representing the interests of capitalist core states. Yet, these categories have limited analytical purchase within the context of Chinese land deals in Australia. Who is extracting and who is marginalized in a land deal that aligns Chinese and Australian business interests in pursuit of profits in China's fast-growing market for high-end dairy and meat products? Where do we locate the "core" and where do we situate the "periphery"? Who extracts what from whom? To be sure, justice and equity are at stake here, too—animals and natural environments overexploited for a growing overseas market, local farmers that can no longer compete with corporate businesses and financialized institutions, rural Chinese households that are largely excluded from the transition to the animal protein-based diets enjoyed by urbanites, all demand a fairer distribution of resources, wealth, and opportunities. Yet, these demands no longer neatly fit into an imaginary that divides the world into national spaces of development and underdevelopment and into core regions and peripheral countries. The story of China's land rush in Australia is therefore also an urgent reminder to take seriously the need for a new critical vocabulary that transcends the "territorial trap," enabling us to interrogate questions of resource distribution and justice in a world where power relations can no longer be understood as a hierarchy of nation-states but, rather as transnational "network[s] of political and economic elites spanning privileged localities across the globe" (Sheppard & Nagar 2004, p. 558). In short, the nation-state as an analytical lens falls short of capturing the dynamics and implications of China's overseas land rush. A transnational perspective, by contrast, not only highlights the global networks of interest and profit that are driving China's overseas agri-food investment but also illuminates the uneven spatial distribution of its ecological and social costs across the global agri-food system.

A couple of notes on scope and terminology before proceeding. First, I should be clear on the object of investigation. My research started from the premise that Chinese investors were acquiring large swaths of farmland in Australia. However, it soon became evident that investors didn't stop at the farmgate. In addition to farmland, Chinese entities have acquired agricultural assets all along the value chain, including Australian food processing companies, agri-trade, or logistics infrastructure. Indeed, my research shows that, in monetary terms, more Chinese capital has been spent on the acquisition of downstream agribusinesses than on the purchase of agricultural land. I also found that some companies pursued investment strategies that simultaneously targeted various stages of the agricultural value chain. Through such strategies, a company would, for instance, come to own both several beef cattle farms and an abattoir. In the remainder of this book, I will use the broader term "agri-investments" whenever referring to investments beyond the farmgate and only speak of "land deals" when an investment project focuses on farmland only.

Second, some readers may find my use of the terms "global South" and "global North" misleading, given that Australia is located to the South of mainland China. These terms only make sense when used as indicators of *situational* location, referring to a country's position within capitalist globalization, rather than as shorthand for *geographical* location (being located in the Northern versus the Southern hemisphere). In this sense, the term "global South" addresses spaces negatively impacted by or far behind in the race of contemporary capitalist globalization, whereas the term "global North" refers to spaces that are on the winning end. Here, "North" and "South" serve as a rubric to theorize contemporary geographies of power. At the same time, it is important to note that I am careful to avoid the methodological nationalism criticized above. Rather than assigning China and Australia opposite positions within a North-South global divide, with China representing the global South and Australia representing the global North, my usage of these terms suggests that spaces of power and privilege as well as spaces of marginalization and exclusion cut through national boundaries, connecting different groups of people *across* China and Australia.

## Methodological reflections

An ethnographic approach is best suited to the kind of grounded analysis of Chinese agri-investments that is the goal of this book.[3] The research for this book, undertaken between February 2017 and December 2018 during four field trips to various research sites in Australia and China, not only draws on

Burawoy's model of a "global ethnography" (Burawoy et al. 2000) but also finds inspiration in more recent ethnographic studies on global market-making (Ouma 2015), transnational commodity chains (Neilson & Pritchard 2009), and China's role as a global investor (Lee 2018; Brautigam 2015). These fascinating accounts notwithstanding, there were few practical guidelines on how to conduct an ethnography of China's agri-investments in Australia. Indeed, working as a Germany-based researcher across multiple continents, time zones, languages, and cultures proved to be a complex endeavor, to say the least. The first challenge I encountered was the question of how to actually conceptualize the "field" in my fieldwork. Ethnographic approaches to global phenomena are often conceived of as multi-sited projects. But what constitutes a "site," and how do "sites" relate to each other to form the "field"? Drawing on understandings akin to the more "orthodox," local version of ethnography, much transnational ethnographic research on China's global integration tends to conceptualize the sites of its research as bounded, place-based entities, albeit situated in multiple locations and at multiple scales. Lee (2018), for example, investigates how Chinese state capital touches down in Zambian copper mines, construction sites, and government ministries, while Brautigam (2015) follows Chinese investment flows to the "friendship farms" and commercial farming projects implemented all across rural Africa. Imagined as spatially stable units of analysis, these places act as focal sites from which China's global integration is studied—in other words, as concrete sites of immersive fieldwork where the researcher interacts with her subjects and observes the practices and interactions through which Chinese investment is grounded in specific places. But while this type of analysis has yielded tremendous insights, its epistemological premise of the site as a bounded, spatially discreet area is not entirely unproblematic. Particularly, such a focus fails to capture how multiple and shifting configurations of places, people, and organizations continuously destabilize the boundaries of the chosen field sites, thus blurring distinctions between what is "inside" and what is "outside" of the field. The field of the global ethnographer is thus constantly moving and shifting and cannot easily be anchored in spatially fixed sites, no matter how multi-sited the ethnography is. This insight is underscored by Tsing (2005), who, in her study of global investment in the Indonesian rainforest, shows how global connections are not so much moored to bounded sites, but rather arise out of encounters and interactions that constantly "reappear in new places with changing events" (p. xi). The stubborn notion of boundedness in global ethnographic research is also roundly critiqued by Cook et al. (2009), who insist that "a valid ethnographic field need not correspond to a spatial entity of any kind, and need not be a holistic entity 'out there' to be discovered" (p. 68). Instead, they propose an approach to global ethnography "in which the field is importantly *un*-sited rather than being merely multisited" (Cook et al. 2009, pp. 64–65). For Cook et al., an un-sited field is thus not made up of bounded, immutable areas on which the ethnographer alone must focus her attention but by "a collection of zero-dimensional points" (p. 63) whose actual arrangement in time and space is determined by the unfolding research process rather than by fixed and spatially defined boundaries.

Taking inspiration from the above interventions, I have conceptualized my research not so much as a multi-sited study of the bounded locations where Chinese capital touches down in Australia but as an un-sited series of *moments*, *events*, and *encounters* that occurred *along* transnational investment chains. Speaking with Cook et al. (2009), I think of these events and encounters not as spatially bounded units—as offices, farms, or food-processing factories—but as dispersed nodes or points within a network of socio-political, natural, and cultural relations co-producing the flows of Chinese capital into Australian ruralities. No matter whether I met with hypermobile state and business actors in between offices, airports, and coffee shops, worked my expanding network to secure a last-minute invitation to an exclusive investment event, or scoured the shelves of supermarkets in Chinese cities to see how investor efforts manifested in the form of imported, premium food brands, mine is an ethnography made up by a series of geographically and temporally dispersed encounters rather than a set of spatially bounded sites lying out there for the researcher to discover, observe, and immerse herself in.

Altogether, I spent eight months "in the field," of which slightly more than half the time was dedicated to research in Australia, with the remainder spent on fieldwork in China. During these months, I conducted some 90 semi-structured interviews with investors, deal brokers, state actors, and experts along the investment chain. The purpose of my inquiries was to trace the practices, processes, and multi-scalar actor networks through which investments materialized (or not) in particular Australian ruralities and to understand the multifaceted and, at times, conflicting goals, visions, and anxieties that informed how state and economic elites in China and Australia reacted to and interacted with transnational flows of investment. This meant selecting interview partners who had themselves acquired Australian farms and businesses (or who were in the process of doing so) as well as interview partners who were involved in facilitating investments or in regulating them. Unlike many other studies, this research offers a "view from the top" rather than a "bottom-up" perspective on transnational agri-investments. Interviews ranged from 30 minutes to two hours and were conducted in places chosen by my interview partners. Given the "corporate" setting in which I met most of my interview partners, these were mostly one-off interviews. In a number of cases, however, I had the chance to conduct follow-up interviews with the same interview partner or to conduct a series of interviews with multiple representatives of the same organization. To contextualize the information obtained through interviews, I participated in a range of trade and investment conferences, visited farms and processing plants, and attended industry events where I spoke informally with individuals from business and government. I combined these approaches with an extensive document analysis of Chinese (and, to a lesser extent, Australian) policy documents in order to reconstruct and trace state discourses about agricultural investment, food security, and trade.

Despite extended fieldwork phases spent in both countries, the "un-sitedness" of my field meant that fieldwork was marked by traveling rather than dwelling. During my fieldwork phases, I picked a well-connected city as my base—Sydney in the case of Australia and Beijing in the case of China—from which I would plan and strategize, organizing meetings, visits, and interviews as I followed crucial events and connections along China's agri-food investment chain, from urban financial and commercial centers in China and Australia to Australia's rural hinterlands and back again. The mobility of the people, capital, ideas, and goods I traced demanded my own mobility. Traveling along the investment flows criss-crossing my un-sited field required not only substantial resources but also a considerable amount of coordination skills. A good deal of work was needed to set up meetings and juggle the conflicting diaries of multiple and fast-moving actors, sometimes only to find that my stretched financial resources would not allow me to join an important but out-of-the-way event to which I had been unexpectedly invited or to find that a key business figure I had traveled hundreds of miles to meet had canceled our meeting at the very last minute.

While as a well-funded academic I was certainly on the winning end of the "power-geometries" (Massey 2004) determining a social group's relationship to transnational mobility, flows, and movement, I was a poor match for the speed and flexibility with which the actors I sought to follow moved through time-space. Yet, there were also moments of immense excitement as the loose ends I had pursued through time and space would coalesce into ever more tangible configurations of the people, practices, and places that make up China's rush for land and agricultural resources. Conceptualizing "the field" of Chinese agri-investment in Australia as an un-sited series of moments, events, and encounters taking place along transnational investment chains thus does not yield an ethnography in the orthodox sense, characterized by the researcher's deep immersion in placed-based field sites and thick descriptions of people's lifeworlds. What makes this study ethnographic is not so much the methods it uses but the approach it follows. Drawing on Tsing (2005), such research "may not be a classical ethnography, but it can be deeply ethnographic in the sense of drawing from the learning experiences of the ethnographer" (p. xi).

A second challenge I encountered during my fieldwork was to gain access to the actors that made up my field. To be sure, questions of access are at the heart of all fieldwork, but here they come in the particular form of "studying up." How to get access to powerful corporations, state actors, and business elites who have no interest, desire, or need to entertain academics from abroad has been a constant challenge throughout my fieldwork. Whether I approached investor companies, deal brokers, state actors on different scales of governance, or Australian agribusiness professionals partnering with Chinese investors, I naturally encountered little enthusiasm for "being studied."

In particular, Chinese investor companies wanted to keep a low profile and shunned the kind of negative publicity their activities had been receiving in Australian public and media debates. Although I always made it clear that I did not wish to expose but understand, there were generally few incentives for my interview partners to engage with my research. To paraphrase Ouma (2015, p. 81), the practical reality of "studying up" often amounted to an exercise in trying to follow actors who did not want to be followed.

I also realized that the barriers to gaining access to "the field" were multi-layered. Just because I had finally managed to penetrate into the offices of a powerful investor company or succeeded in organizing a long-awaited meeting with a key business person, this did not signify I had gained "access." My interview partners might treat our conversation simply as an opportunity to assess whether my research presented a "risk" to their business endeavors or as a platform to polish their public image. This meant that I could not necessarily treat the interviews I conducted as a means of uncovering the "truth." Rather, I conceived of them as *situated* accounts reflective of an actor's particular position, perspective, and agenda. Another consequence I drew from the situatedness of the interviews I conducted was that I sought to triangulate information presented to me as "facts" with different sources such as other interviews, media reports, or government and company documents. Hence, the story presented in this book seeks to straddle the divide between an *ethnographic* sensibility to the situated, embodied perspectives of my interview partners and an almost *journalistic* desire to find out the "real facts" of what the Chinese were actually doing on the cattle stations and in the crop fields of rural Australia.

The power disparities at play within the context of "studying up" raise important ethical and moral questions regarding practices of anonymization and informed consent. While it is fair to assume that the elite actors with whom I interacted for this research presented sanitized accounts of what they were doing in the Australian countryside, some (albeit far from all) explicitly asked me to withhold all information that would allow readers to identify company names and transaction details. The ethical and moral dilemmas faced by the researcher are obvious: How to present information crucial to construct a robust narrative without harming the informant or organization? How to anonymize organizations that, to some extent, act publicly and whose elevated social position makes them subject to public and media debate? How to assume a researcher's responsibility toward facilitating an informed debate about issues that are of wider societal concern without violating the trust vested in her by her interview partners? To be sure, principles of informed consent become more complex and ambiguous in the context of "studying up." As Lee (2018) bluntly puts it in her comparative ethnography of global financial and Chinese capital in the Zambian mining and construction sectors, "[if] I interpreted in the strictest possible terms the practice of informed consent [...] I would never have been able to study these powerful corporations, which did not actually need my protection." (pp. 177–178).

The way in which I negotiated this dilemma will become visible to the reader as the book unfolds. Throughout the text, I anonymized the names of all individuals I personally spoke with. As a general rule, I also withhold the names of the companies and organizations these individuals work for. By contrast, government entities, industry peak bodies, and public research organizations are referred to by their original names. An important exception to this practice is Chapter 4, where I present a typology of Chinese investor entities. Here I draw on "real-life" examples to highlight the characteristics and features of the various types of organizations at the forefront of China's land rush.

## Structure of the book

This book proceeds through four main sections and eight chapters. Following the introductory part, section two maps out the broader processes of agri-food restructuring that have provided the context for Chinese acquisitions of Australian farms and food businesses. **Chapter 2** begins by examining China's food security strategy and the role that overseas farmland investment plays for feeding China. Recounting the momentous changes the country's domestic agriculture sector has undergone since China opened up in 1978, the chapter sketches the visions, hopes, and anxieties that have shaped how food security is understood and acted upon by Chinese policymakers. I show that impressive gains in domestic agricultural output and productivity have, by and large, allowed China to feed itself and that growing food on overseas farmland is *not* an integral part of the strategy with which policymakers seek to respond to growing Chinese appetites. China's food security strategy does, however, have a weak spot, namely, the massive inflow of soybeans, for which the country relies almost entirely on world markets. I argue that China's dependence on soybean imports cannot simply be explained by limited farmland and water resources but requires us to take into consideration how processes of agri-food restructuring have placed China at the center of a global grain-livestock complex. Through its agricultural "going out" strategy, the state hopes to secure a more powerful position in that complex for its key agricultural commodity traders, but the policy has also created space for China's emerging private agribusinesses to pursue their own strategies for profit accumulation overseas, including through the purchase of farmland.

**Chapter 3** zooms in on the Australian context, where growing amounts of Chinese farmland investments caused a heated political debate that resulted in the tightening of foreign farmland ownership in 2015. The new investment rules promised to enhance accountability and transparency around Chinese land deals. Yet, as the chapter shows, the political process by which Australia's investment regime was renegotiated precluded rather than promoted a broad-based debate about farmland ownership. This obfuscation was largely brought about by the state's monopoly of information about the individual Chinese land deals taking place in Australia and fed into a "politics of knowledge" that has allowed Australian politicians to appear "tough on China" while accommodating Australian business interests for more food exports to China. Drawing on my own systematic databank on Chinese agri-investment deals in Australia, I demonstrate that fears about "selling out the farm" to state-controlled actors seeking to repatriate food back to China on non-commercial terms were grossly misleading and concealed the emerging alliance of Chinese investors and Australian agribusiness and financial interests in search of new profits from a Chinese "dining boom." As I argue throughout the book, it is this alliance that has facilitated China's land rush in Australia.

**Chapter 4** takes a closer look at the "flesh-and-blood" actors behind Chinese farmland deals in Australia. Drawing on data from my own investment databank, I identify four key groups of Chinese agri-food investors operating in Australia: agribusinesses owned by the central government, state farms, private agribusiness corporations, and agri-food entrepreneurs. By using paradigmatic cases from my fieldwork, I highlight how the different political-economic positions and development trajectories of these firms within China's domestic agri-food landscape condition their overseas investment goals, interests, and strategies. The chapter argues that paying closer attention to China's rural context and contemporary processes of agrarian change is crucial to developing a more nuanced understanding of the actors involved in China's land rush in Australia—one that goes beyond conceptions of a homogenous, state-controlled "China."

The third section zooms in on the empirical material gathered during the qualitative fieldwork conducted for this project. In three chapters, it follows the actors of this book along the entire investment process—from purchasing a farm or food business, to generating profits from it, to opening new markets for its products. **Chapter 5** begins by showing how Chinese capital is assembled with Australian land through the situated practices and contingent linkages between a multiplicity of actors operating across national borders and at different scales, from the local to the transnational. Rather than presenting Chinese investments as an outside force unilaterally impacting Australian ruralities, the chapter seeks to make visible how these investment projects are co-produced in alliance with other actors. These include Australian government officials seeking to ensure the competitiveness of Australia's farming sector, Australian agri-business stakeholders eager to improve their access to the famed "China market," and private individuals acting as deal brokers and mediators in the pursuit of personal advancement. It is the work, commitment, and risk-taking of these individuals that enable Chinese investment capital to touch down in specific places. The chapter also highlights some of the frictions generated by Chinese agri-investment flows as expectations and interests clash between different groups of actors.

Chinese investment in Australian food and farming is overwhelmingly driven by profit motives, even as many investors frame their endeavors as a contribution to China's food security strategy in an attempt to legitimize their activities at home and garner support from domestic policymakers. **Chapter 6** provides an in-depth analysis of the strategies by which Chinese investors seek to derive profits from their investments. It identifies three modes of profit accumulation: *commodification*, where profits accrue from the production and sale of agri-food commodities; *valorization*, whereby investors command premium prices in the Chinese market by leveraging Australia's image as a clean, green, and safe farming environment; and an incipient mode of *financialization*, which values farmland primarily for its financial rather than its productive qualities. In other words, in a financialized mode of accumulation, profits do not hinge on farmland's ability to produce and valorize commodities, but on the rents, dividends, and capital gains that can be generated from farmland ownership. Drawing on empirical material from my fieldwork, I show that most investment projects combine practices of commodification and valorization as Chinese investors seek to position food from their Australian farms as high-quality, high-priced products in the Chinese market. But the chapter also points to the growing role of financialized logics of accumulation. By uncovering the profit logics at work, I show that Chinese farmland investors do not simply respond to growing demand for high-quality food imports but seek to actively *construct* it by valorizing Australia's natural environment and discursively linking Australian food products to meanings of health, success, and the good life. Seen from this perspective, the inflow of Chinese capital into Australian food and farming is not the causal outcome of a "natural" shift toward the consumption of high-quality and animal-based foods by Chinese eaters. Rather, farmland investment and shifting consumption patterns mutually shape and reinforce each other.

**Chapter 7** turns to the supply chains that connect Chinese-invested farms and food businesses in Australia with consumer markets in China. By following agri-food products through different stages of the supply chain—from production to processing and onward to distribution and consumption—this chapter asks how Chinese agri-investments reconfigure market connections across countries. It shows that many Chinese investors do not stop short at simply purchasing farmland but, instead, seek to build vertically integrated supply chains. What makes supply chains so important is their key role in shaping commodity flows and price margins. Only by controlling the supply chain can Chinese investors ensure that the products grown on Australian farms can reach the right consumers—whether domestically or internationally—and capture the best price. This chapter explores the different strategies with which Chinese investors seek to build supply chains and points out the limits they face. My examples make clear that the supply chains necessary to conquer high-end markets in China and beyond do not simply exist "out there," but need to be assembled by bringing together infrastructures, technological devices, narratives, and regulatory regimes—often in messy and frictional encounters in which success is far from guaranteed. Complex market and geopolitical realities often belie straightforward investment aspirations, highlighting that what investors ultimately need to be successful—market connections—might be even trickier to achieve than access to overseas farmland and food businesses.

The **concluding section** draws together the main arguments of this book and discusses the implications of China's land rush in Australia for food security and the rules shaping the global agri-food system. Unlike common critical understandings of a Chinese "land grab," the transnational perspective employed in this book highlights the role of transnational business and finance elites in co-producing Chinese investments in Australian food and farming—at the expense of environments, family farms, and human health across national borders. Getting the story of China in Australia right is important, I argue, not least because it enables us to chart a new course of engagement with Chinese actors that will help address the real issues at stake in China's global agri-food integration. For all of us committed to a fairer and more ecologically sustainable food system, this will be a crucial task.

## Notes

1 Steinmetz's series was photographed for a cover story titled "Feeding China" in the February 2018 edition of National Geographic (McMillan 2018) and can also be found online: https://www.georgesteinmetz.com/gallery/Feeding-China/G0000I01kXXDzFPU/.

2 Singapore's appearance as top recipient country of Chinese agricultural investment should not be taken at face value. Rather, it is reflective of one of the key issues in collecting overseas investment statistics, namely, the difficulty in distinguishing between final investment destinations and "pass-through" countries that merely serve as a vehicle for channeling overseas investment flows, for example, due to tax benefits or other incentives they offer to investors. In their research on China's flexible overseas food strategy, Zhan et al. (2018, p. 13) confirm that Singapore acts mainly as a "stepping stone" for the expansion of Chinese agribusiness firms into Southeast Asia, given the attractive financing options provided to agri-investors by Singaporean banks.

3 My reflections on methodology are much indebted to Lee's (2018) excellent in-depth and highly personal account of her multi-sited ethnographic fieldwork on Chinese investments in the Zambian mining and construction sectors, which helped me to make sense of and see my own fieldwork experience in an entirely new light.

## References

Agnew, John (1994): The Territorial Trap. The Geographical Assumptions of International Relations Theory. In *Review of International Political Economy* 1 (1), pp. 53–80.

Australian Taxation Office (ATO) (2022): Register of Foreign Ownership of Agricultural Land. Report of Registrations as at 30 June 2022. Available online at https://foreigninvestment.gov.au/sites/foreigninvestment.gov.au/files/2023-09/2022-rfo-agricultural-land.pdf, checked on 12/15/2023.

Australian Taxation Office (ATO) (2018): Register of Foreign Ownership of Agricultural Land. Report of Registrations as at 30 June 2018. Available online at https://firb.gov.au/sites/firb.gov.au/files/2018/12/Register_of_Foreign_Ownership_of_Agr.pdf, checked on 3/18/2019.

Böhme, Michaela (2021): "Milk from the Purest Place on Earth". Examining Chinese Investments in the Australian Dairy Sector. In *Agriculture and Human Values* 38 (1), pp. 327–338.
Böhme, Michaela (2020): Shared Interest or Strategic Threat? A Critical Investigation of Political Debates and Regulatory Responses to Chinese Agricultural Investment in Australia. In *Globalizations* 18 (3), pp. 441–460.
Borras Jr., Saturino M.; Mills, Elyse N.; Seufert, Philip; Backes, Stephan; Fyfe, Daniel; Herre, Roman; Michéle, Laura (2019): Transnational Land Investment Web: Land Grabs, TNCs, and the Challenge of Global Governance. In *Globalizations* 17 (4), pp. 608–628.
Borras Jr., Saturino M.; Franco, Jennifer C.; Wang, Chunyu (2013): The Challenge of Global Governance of Land Grabbing: Changing International Agricultural Context and Competing Political Views and Strategies. In *Globalizations* 10 (1), pp. 161–179.
Brautigam, Deborah (2015): *Will Africa Feed China?* Oxford, New York: Oxford University Press.
Brautigam, Deborah; Zhang, Haisen (2013): Green Dreams: Myth and Reality in China's Agricultural Investment in Africa. In *Third World Quarterly* 34 (9), pp. 1676–1696.
Brown, Lester R. (1995): *Who will Feed China? Wake-Up Call for a Small Planet.* New York: Norton.
Burawoy, Michael; Blum, Joseph A.; George, Sheba; Gille; Zsuzsa; Gowan, Teresa; Haney, Lynne; Klawiter, Maren; Lopez, Steve; O'Riain, Sean (Eds.) (2000): *Global Ethnography. Forces, Connections, and Imaginations in a Postmodern World.* Berkeley, Los Angeles, London: University of California Press.
Cook, Joanna; Laidlaw, James; Mair, Jonathan (2009): What if There is No Elephant? Towards a Conception of an Un-sited Field. In Mark-Anthony Falzon (Ed.): *Multi-Sited Ethnography. Theory, Praxis and Locality in Contemporary Research.* London: Routledge, pp. 47–72.
DuBois, Thomas David (2022): Behind China's Overseas Food Investments. A Tale of Two Dairies. In *Asian Studies Review* 47 (3), pp. 574–595.
Fairbairn, Madelaine (2020): *Fields of Gold. Financing the Global Land Rush.* Ithaca, New York: Cornell University Press.
Fairbairn, Madelaine (2015): Foreignization, Financialization and Land Grab Regulation. In *Journal of Agrarian Change* 15 (4), pp. 581–591.
Fell, James (2019): *The Future of Chinese Agricultural Policy. Opportunities and Challenges for Australian Grains, Beef and Dairy Exports.* Australian Bureau of Agricultural and Resource Economics and Sciences (ABARES). Canberra (ABARES research report 19.2).
Gooch, Elizabeth; Gale, Fred (2018): China's Foreign Agriculture Investments. U.S. Department of Agriculture, Economic Research Service (EIB-192).
GRAIN (2013): Land Ceilings: Reining in Land Grabbers or Dumbing Down the Debate? Available online at https://grain.org/en/article/4655-land-ceilings-reining-in-land-grabbers-or-dumbing-down-the-debate, checked on 7/1/2024.
GRAIN (2008): Seized. The 2008 Landgrab for Food and Financial Security. Barcelona, Spain (GRAIN Briefing). Available online at https://www.grain.org/article/entries/93-seized-the-2008-landgrab-for-food-and-financial-security, checked on 5/14/2017.
Gu, Jing; Zhang, Chuanhong; Vaz, Alcides; Mukwereza, Langton (2016): Chinese State Capitalism? Rethinking the Role of the State and Business in Chinese Development Cooperation in Africa. In *World Development* 81, pp. 24–34.

Hall, Derek (2013): Primitive Accumulation, Accumulation by Dispossession and the Global Land Grab. In *Third World Quarterly* 34 (9), pp. 1582–1604.
Hofman, Irna (2016): Politics or Profits along the "Silk Road": What Drives Chinese Farms in Tajikistan and Helps them Thrive? In *Eurasian Geography and Economics* 57 (3), pp. 457–481.
Keulertz, Martin; Woertz, Eckart (2016): States as Actors in International Agro-Investments. In Christophe Gironde, Christophe Golay, Peter Messerli (Eds.): *Large-Scale Land Acquisitions. Focus on South-East Asia*. Leiden, Boston: Brill Nijhoff (International Development Policy, 6), pp. 30–52.
Klinger, Julie Michelle; Muldavin, Joshua (2019): New Geographies of Development: Grounding China's Global Integration. In *Territory, Politics, Governance* 7 (1), pp. 1–21.
Larder, Nicolette; Sippel, Sarah R.; Argent, Neil (2018): The Redefined Role of Finance in Australian Agriculture. In *Australian Geographer* 49 (3), pp. 397–418.
Larder, Nicolette; Sippel, Sarah R.; Lawrence, Geoffrey (2015): Finance Capital, Food Security Narratives and Australian Agricultural Land. In *Journal of Agrarian Change* 15 (4), pp. 592–603.
Lee, Ching Kwan (2018): *The Specter of Global China. Politics, Labor, and Foreign Investment in Africa*. Chicago, London: The University of Chicago Press.
Magnan, André (2018): Farmland Values. Media and Public Discourses Around Farmland Investment in Canada and Australia. In Hilde Bjørkhaug, André Magnan, Geoffrey Lawrence (Eds.): *The Financialization of Agri-Food Systems. Contested Transformations*. Abingdon, Oxon, New York, NY: Routledge, pp. 108–132.
Magnan, André (2015): The Financialization of Agri-Food in Canada and Australia: Corporate Farmland and Farm Ownership in the Grains and Oilseed Sector. In *Journal of Rural Studies* 41, pp. 1–12.
MARA (2017): *中国对外农业投资合作分析报告 [Analysis Report on China's Agricultural Foreign Investment and Cooperation]*. Beijing: 中国农业出版社 [China Agriculture Press].
Margulis, Matias E.; McKeon, Nora; Borras Jr., Saturino M. (2013): Land Grabbing and Global Governance: Critical Perspectives. In *Globalizations* 10 (1), pp. 1–23.
Massey, Doreen (2004): Geographies of Responsibility. In *Geografiska Annaler* 86B (1), pp. 5–18.
McMichael, Philip (2013): Land Grabbing as Security Mercantilism in International Relations. In *Globalizations* 10 (1), pp. 47–64.
McMichael, Philip (2012): The Land Grab and Corporate Food Regime Restructuring. In *The Journal of Peasant Studies* 39 (3–4), pp. 681–670.
McMillan, Tracie (2018): Feeding China. In *National Geographic Magazine* 233 (2), pp. 82–107.
Mefano Fares, Tomaz (2023): China's Financialized Soybeans. The Fault Lines of Neomercantilism Narratives in International Food Regime Analyses. In *Journal of Agrarian Change* 23, pp. 477–499.
Myers, Margaret; Guo, Jie (2015): China's Agricultural Investment in Latin America: A Critical Assessment. The Dialogue/Leadership for the Americas (China and Latin America Report).
Neilson, Jeff; Pritchard, Bill (2009): *Value Chain Struggles. Institutions and Governance in the Plantation Districts of South India*. Oxford: Wiley-Blackwell.
Oliveira, Gustavo de L. T. (2018): Chinese Land Grabs in Brazil? Sinophobia and Foreign Investments in Brazilian Soybean Agribusiness. In *Globalizations* 15 (1), pp. 114–133.

Oliveira, Gustavo de L. T. (2017): The South-South Question: Transforming Brazil-China Agroindustrial Partnerships. Doctoral thesis. UC Berkeley. Department of Geography. Available online at https://escholarship.org/uc/item/1v44x1qs, checked on 11/6/2019.

Oliveira, Gustavo de L. T. (2013): Land Regularization in Brazil and the Global Land Grab. In Wendy Wolford, Saturnino M. Borras, Ruth Hall, Ian Scoones, Ben White (Eds.): *Governing Global Land Deals. The Role of the State in the Rush for Land.* Chichester, West Sussex: John Wiley & Sons, pp. 71–92.

Ouma, Stefan (2020): *Farming as Financial Asset. Global Finance and the Making of Institutional Landscapes.* Newcastle upon Tyne: Agenda Publishing (Economic Transformations).

Ouma, Stefan (2015): *Assembling Export Markets. The Making and Unmaking of Global Food Connections in West Africa.* Chichester, West Sussex: Wiley-Blackwell.

Pritchard, Bill; Tonts, Matthew (2011): Market Efficiency, Agriculture and Prosperity in Rural Australia. In Matthew Tonts, Muhammed Abu B. Siddique (Eds.): *Globalisation, Agriculture and Development. Perspectives from the Asia-Pacific.* Cheltenham: Edward Elgar, pp. 29–53.

Sheppard, Eric; Nagar, Richa (2004): From East-West to North-South. In *Antipode* 36 (4), pp. 557–563.

Sippel, Sarah R.; Weldon, Tim (2020): Redefining Land's Investability: Towards a Neonationalization of Resources in Australia? In *Territory, Politics, Governance* 9, pp. 306–323.

Sippel, Sarah R. (2018): Financialising Farming as a Moral Imperative? Renegotiating the Legitimacy of Land Investments in Australia. In *Environment and Planning A: Economy and Space* 50 (3), pp. 549–568.

Sippel, Sarah R.; Larder, Nicolette; Lawrence, Geoffrey (2016): Grounding the Financialization of Farmland. Perspectives on Financial Actors as New Land Owners in Rural Australia. In *Agriculture and Human Values* 34, pp. 251–265.

Sippel, Sarah R. (2015): Food Security or Commercial Business? Gulf State Investments in Australian Agriculture. In *The Journal of Peasant Studies* 42 (5), pp. 981–1001.

The Economist (2009): Buying Farmland Abroad: Outsourcing's Third Wave, 5/21/2009. Available online at https://www.economist.com/international/2009/05/21/outsourcings-third-wave, checked on 6/22/2017.

Toulmin, Camilla; Bindraban, Prem; Borras Jr, Saturnino; Mwangi, Esther; Sauer, Sergio (2011): Land Tenure and International Investments in Agriculture. A Report by the High Level Panel of Experts on Food Security and Nutrition. Food and Agriculture Organization of the United Nations. Rome. Available online at https://www.fao.org/fileadmin/user_upload/hlpe/hlpe_documents/HLPE-Land-tenure-and-international-investments-in-agriculture-2011.pdf, checked on 12/30/2016.

Tsing, Anna Lowenhaupt (2005): *Friction. An Ethnography of Global Connection.* Princeton: Princeton University Press.

Wilkinson, John; Wesz Jr., Valdemar João; Lopane, Anna Rosa Maria (2015): Brazil, the Southern Cone, and China: The Agribusiness Connection (BRICS Initiative for Critical Agrarian Studies (BICAS), Working Paper 16).

Wolford, Wendy; Borras Jr., Saturino M.; Hall, Ruth; Scoones, Ian; White, Ben (2013): Governing Global Land Deals: The Role of the State in the Rush for Land. In *Development and Change* 44 (2), pp. 189–210.

Zhan, Shaohua; Zhang, Hongzhou; He, Dongying (2018): China's Flexible Overseas Food Strategy: Food Trade and Agricultural Investment between Southeast Asia and China in 1990–2015. In *Globalizations* 15 (5), pp. 702–721.

# Part 1

# Contexts

# 2 Feeding China

## Between self-sufficiency and global integration

> When there is food in our hands, there won't be panic in our hearts. Safeguarding food security is an everlasting issue for China that cannot be relaxed at any time. Historical experience tells us that once there is a major food shortage, money won't be of any use. To be up to the task of feeding 1.3 billion people, we must rely on ourselves.
>
> (Xi Jinping, speech held at the Shandong Academy of Agricultural Sciences on November 28, 2013, quoted in China Daily 2017)

Feeding China is undoubtedly a top priority for Chinese leaders. Ever since coming to power in 2012, Chinese President Xi Jinping has stressed the need for China to keep a tight grip on its food bowl, as the above quote shows. Yet, ensuring the food security of close to one-fifth of the world's population is a profoundly challenging task. To the interested observer, China's food security presents a complex and often highly contradictory picture. Speculation about an impending Chinese food crisis is difficult to reconcile with international praise by institutions such as the World Bank for China's impressive gains in food production. Massive imports of grain do not seem to chime with the fact that China holds the largest grain reserves in the world. And anxieties about China as a "land grabber" fit awkwardly with the latest string of Chinese mergers and acquisitions targeting agri-food input and processing firms rather than farmland.[1]

To disentangle these issues, this chapter examines the evolving visions, strategies, and anxieties that shape how food security is understood and acted upon by the Chinese state. How has policy thinking about food security evolved over the past decades? Which policy tools have been developed to address food security concerns? And how do overseas land deals fit within current visions of food security? These are pertinent questions that provide a context for understanding the motivations and actions of the Chinese investors, businessmen, and politicians, as well as their Australian partners and counterparts we will encounter in subsequent chapters of this book. These questions are also significant given the astonishing dearth of in-depth analysis in the Anglophone literature on the land rush on how issues of food security are discussed and understood *within* China.[2]

DOI: 10.4324/9781003474661-4

My analysis diagnoses China's emergence at the center of the global soybean-livestock complex (Weis 2013) as the pivotal, yet unacknowledged contradiction that is shaping the country's food security strategy. As I will show, national policy has long been geared toward maintaining high levels of domestic production—a legacy of the U.S.-led embargo against China during the Cold War era. Yet, food imports have been soaring over the past two decades, driven primarily by a need for soybeans. While China imports a wide range of agricultural products, from meat to dairy, fruits, nuts, sugar, or wines, the only agricultural commodity for which the country is truly reliant on international markets is soybean—an oilseed primarily processed into soymeal to be used as *feed*, rather than *food*, in China's burgeoning industrial livestock sector. My analysis suggests that a neo-Malthusian logic that stresses limited domestic resources and rising demand as key drivers of China's growing imports falls short of explaining the pressures facing China's domestic food security. To understand why Chinese imports have been soaring despite a massive and continuous increase in domestic food production, we must take into account the changing political-economic relations that have made China—the place of soybean domestication—reliant on a handful of soybean exporting countries to feed its growing animal population. While China maintains high levels of self-sufficiency across a wide range of crops and food products, I argue that a logic of agricultural modernization has made industrialized livestock production a central part of China's agri-food system, thereby deepening its dependence on imports, particularly soybeans.

In contrast to common perceptions, China has *not* responded to the surge in imports with a policy focused on securing farmland overseas. Instead, China's leaders have been doubling down on boosting domestic food production and diversifying import sources. To be sure, Chinese agricultural investments in other countries have grown rapidly over the past two decades, but they have tended to focus on trading and logistics infrastructure and have mainly taken the form of mergers and acquisitions, rather than the acquisition of farmland for crop production. While some Chinese companies have acquired farmland abroad, the total number of land deals has been modest, with China being far from a leading country in land acquisitions (Zhan 2022, p. 44). In fact, over the past decade, Chinese policymakers have actively discouraged land deals in favor of investments focused on controlling the whole supply chain in an attempt to wrest greater control over global commodity flows from Western grain trading companies. A closer view of the discourses and actors involved in China's overseas agricultural investment also reveals the important role of Chinese agri-food capital and entrepreneurial groups. What draws these actors into the "global scramble for scarce resources" (van der Ploeg & Ye 2016, p. 6) are not so much strategic concerns about China's food security but an interest in "the associated possibilities for the further accumulation of capital" (van der Ploeg & Ye 2016).

To support my argument, I draw on official Chinese policy documents, government reports, and speeches by government officials dealing with China's evolving food security strategy. Many of these documents are available in Chinese language only and have been obtained from online policy repositories, the websites of Chinese government bodies, policy journals published under the aegis of the Communist Party of China (CPC), or simply from the Chinese news media that regularly publish summaries of policy meetings and official pronouncements.

The chapter proceeds in four parts. First, I give a brief overview of the principle of grain self-sufficiency that has shaped traditional understandings of food security in Chinese policy circles. I then present three main trends that help explain why China's imports have drastically risen over the past two decades, despite policymakers' long-standing commitment to food self-sufficiency before; third, I sketch out the recent policy responses to this trend. Finally, I discuss how Chinese policymakers and corporate actors think about the role of overseas agricultural investment in the context of feeding China.

## Securing the rice bowl

For many older Chinese, the everlasting question of whether China can feed itself is not an abstract policy debate but a concrete personal experience. While a walk through any supermarket on the Chinese eastern seaboard would likely leave the observer with an impression of abundance, China's most recent large-scale famine (1959–1962) dates back little more than 50 years. During the Great Leap Forward—a political campaign under Mao Zedong aimed at rapidly industrializing China—misguided policies combined with unfavorable weather conditions, leading to a country-wide famine that claimed the lives of at least 30 million people. While the exact number of deaths is difficult to determine, the "three bitter years" upending the Great Leap Forward are usually recognized as the worst famine in Chinese history (Höllmann 2010) and remain deeply ingrained in the memories not only of ordinary people but also of China's ruling political and economic elites.

In Chinese, the notion of food security is usually referred to as *liangshi anquan* (粮食安全), which literally translates as "grain security." This terminology captures the fact that, traditionally, grains are considered the most important basis of nutrition and vital for people's welfare (Zhang 2019, p. 31). In current policy debates, the exact meaning of "grains" has itself become a political issue, as we shall see later, but a broad definition would include cereals (e.g., rice, wheat, and corn), oilseeds and beans (e.g., soy), as well as tubers (e.g., potatoes). Furthermore, Chinese understandings of food security or *liangshi anquan* traditionally emphasize self-sufficiency (*ziji zizu* 自给自足) or the ability to grow basic foods domestically rather than relying on global trade. The commitment to food self-sufficiency is closely connected to the political legitimacy of the Chinese state. Historically, food shortages signaled that the ruler had lost the "Mandate of Heaven" and was no longer fit to rule. In imperial times, food shortages would regularly lead to rebellions that could topple entire dynasties (Zha & Zhang 2013, p. 461). To this day, as Morton (2012) writes, "the 'fear of a land in perpetual hunger' is deeply ingrained in the cultural mindset" (p. 18), making the question of "feeding China" a key priority for Chinese policymakers.

Against this cultural and historical background, it is hardly surprising that the Chinese government is highly sensitive to international debates questioning China's capacity to feed itself. In the mid-1990s, when an influential U.S. report with the name *Who Will Feed China?* predicted that China's soaring demand for food would trigger a world food crisis (Brown 1995), Chinese policymakers responded to international anxieties by emphasizing China's unwavering commitment to the principle of food self-sufficiency. In a white paper called *The Grain Issue in China*, the State Council laid out a new blueprint for boosting domestic grain production, establishing a 95 percent baseline of grain self-sufficiency:

> The basic principle for solving the problem of grain supply and demand in China is to rely on the domestic resources and basically achieve self-sufficiency in grain. China endeavors to increase its grain production so that its self-sufficiency rate of grain under normal conditions will be above 95 percent and the net import rate five percent, or even less, of the total consumption quantity.
>
> (China State Council 1996)

The definition of "grain" initially included rice, wheat, corn, tubers, coarse grain, and soybeans, but has since undergone significant changes, as we will see later in this chapter. The changing composition of the self-sufficiency basket notwithstanding, by and large, the 95 percent baseline has remained China's official target for grain production until today—with the glaring exception of soybeans.

During the 2007/2008 food price crisis, when many international commentators blamed demand from rising economies such as China or India for contributing to global price hikes, China's rebuttal came in the form of the comprehensive *Medium and Long-Term Planning Outline for National Food Security (2008–2020)* (China Government 2008). In the document, the government reiterated its commitment to a 95 percent self-sufficiency rate for basic staple grains, announced ambitions to achieve 100 percent self-sufficiency for China's most important staple crops, namely, wheat and rice, and established a "red line" of arable land at 120 million hectares to be maintained under all circumstances for the purpose of agricultural cultivation.

To achieve these ambitious targets, Chinese policymakers have relied on a mixture of government intervention in domestic agricultural markets and technological innovation. Driven by an "ideology of technocratic rationality" (Xu et al. 2016, p. 83), planners have set agricultural output targets for different production areas; implemented price support and subsidy programs; established massive buffer stocks through government procurement policies; and invested in the research and development of new technologies, seed varieties, and cultivation methods. The challenge of feeding China's large population is compounded by the fact that land and water are scarce resources, a geographical predicament captured in the popular trope of *ren duo di shao* (人多地少), or "many people, little land." Indeed, as is often emphasized in policy documents and expert reports, China feeds 20 percent of the world's population on only 9 percent of the world's arable land. In the minds of China's officials and agricultural experts, the answer to this unfavorable people-to-land ratio lies in agricultural modernization (*nongye xiandaihua* 农业现代化) or, more specifically, the creation of an agricultural system modeled after the large-scale, industrialized agriculture to be found in developed economies such as the United States. This is perhaps nowhere more visible than in China's pork sector where decades of modernization have transformed traditional forms of small-scale, localized pig farming into a coordinated and concentrated system of industrialized pork production that replicates the general practices and logics of agro-industrial farming developed in the global North (Schneider 2018). The infamous pig high-rises that policymakers have encouraged ever since multiple outbreaks of African Swine Fever (ASF) devastated the domestic hog industry beginning in 2018 are now widely seen as the epitome of the highly rationalized and industrialized farming logic favored by Chinese policymakers. But also in other sectors of agricultural production, processes of concentration, increasing mechanization, and the replacement of labor by capital can be observed.

Guided by principles of efficiency, productivity, and economies of scale, Chinese planners have been working hard to transform a household-based agricultural model perceived as "scattered, small and weak (*san, xiao, ruo* 散，小，弱)" (Zhang & Donaldson 2008, p. 28) into a modern and efficient agro-industrial sector. But even as capitalist and entrepreneurial forms of agriculture are gaining prominence, peasant farming has remained astonishingly resilient, with still over 200 million rural households farming plots with an average size of five mu (one-third of a hectare) (van der Ploeg & Ye 2016). One important corollary of agricultural modernization has been the rapid growth of a robust domestic agribusiness sector dominated by private, state-owned, and mixed-ownership enterprises who, in their quest for markets and profits, have become a key force in shaping both domestic agricultural policies and China's integration into the global agri-food system (Zhan 2019, pp. 83–87, 2017; Schneider 2017). The result of these uneven processes of modernization is a deeply heterogenous agriculture sector, where a fully automated 40,000-head dairy farm backed by international finance capital exists side by side millions of smallholders farming tiny plots of land with only the most basic agricultural machinery.

Critical voices question the ability of China's agro-industrial development model to provide long-term and sustainable answers to China's food security concerns. Interrogating the social, environmental, and political implications of China's trajectory of agro-industrial modernization, these observers have expressed concerns about the social and environmental impacts of the "meatification" of Chinese diets (Schneider 2014; Schneider & Sharma 2014), the subsumption of smallholder farmers by an increasingly powerful agribusiness sector (Zhan 2019, 2017; Schneider 2017), or the growing influence of transnational capital, particularly in China's soybean industry (Yan et al. 2016). There is also concern about the environmental effects of China's agricultural development trajectory. The widespread use of agrochemicals has allowed for quick gains in yields and productivity, but at a high price. Contamination of soils, water pollution from agricultural runoff, and the rapid loss of valuable topsoil are just some of the environmental concerns voiced by critics (Sternfeld 2022). In addition, the effects of climate change are becoming ever more visible, with key agricultural provinces battling a series of climate disasters from drought to flooding (Sternfeld 2022).

On the flip side, there has also been much admiration for the unprecedented growth in production and productivity achieved by China's agricultural sector and the people involved in it. Between 1978 and 2010 alone, per capita grain supply registered annual increases of 409 kg per capita (Morton 2012, pp. 21–22), allowing farmers to, by and large, meet the government's ambitious self-sufficiency goals. In little more than a decade, from 2003 to 2015, grain production grew from less than 500 million tons to more than 600 million tons (Zhan 2017, p. 154), an output increase of almost 20 percent. Some observers have described these output increases as a remarkable shift from food scarcity to food abundance (Zhou 2015, p. 41). In 2001, Zhu Rongyi, former prime minister of China, proudly declared that for "the first time in Chinese history, the CPC succeeded in solving China's food problem, once and for all" (Zhu quoted in Zhang 2019, p. 34). Similarly, a 2004 report on China's food security situation published by the Ministry of Agriculture and Rural Affairs (MARA) stated that China had "managed to feed its people through its own efforts, thus doing the wonder of supporting 21% of the world's population with less than 9% of the world's arable land" (MARA 2004, p. 1). In other words, by relying solely on China's own resources to guarantee the food security of one-fifth of the world's population, Chinese policymakers had achieved nothing short of a miracle. Even international organizations such as the World Bank have praised the Chinese "success [story] of agriculture as an engine of growth [...] and a major force for poverty reduction" (World Bank 2007, p. 26). Moreover, Chinese officials are eager to point out the global dimension of China's domestic achievements, arguing that by successfully feeding its own population, China is making a great contribution to global food security and economic stability. As a recent opinion piece in the *Global Times* informed its international readership:

> China has maintained a self-sufficiency rate of more than 98 percent in rice, wheat and corn production. It is a global responsibility to fight

> hunger and poverty. By producing one-fourth of the global grain output to feed one-fifth of the world's population with only 9 percent of the arable land, China successfully answers the question 'Who will feed China?' which is undoubtedly a great contribution to the world.
>
> (Wang 2017a)

## The limits to food self-sufficiency

Despite these achievements, China's imports have been growing. Research by the United States Department of Agriculture (USDA) shows that China has been a consistent net importer of grains since 2008, including corn, wheat, rice, barley, and sorghum (Gale et al. 2015, p. 7). Yet, these types of crops pale against China's massive imports of soybeans. In 2021, China imported close to 100 million tons of soybean, accounting for over 60 percent of global soybean trade (Sternfeld 2022) and about 80 percent of China's soybean consumption. The mix of agricultural imports is also becoming increasingly diversified, with commodities such as meat, milk, processed foods, sugar, and wine registering a steep rise in import volume (albeit from very low levels). In 2021, imports reached 207 billion USD, accounting for 11 percent of the global agri-food trade (FAOSTAT 2023).

Unraveling China's paradox of simultaneous growth in domestic agricultural output on the one hand and agricultural imports on the other requires us to shift attention from *how much food* the Chinese eat to *what type of food* Chinese consumers demand. At the same time, we must interrogate how shifting agri-food relations both within China and between China and the outside world have reshaped how, where, and by whom food is produced and distributed. Following this line of inquiry, three trends are of relevance here. First, rising living standards—particularly among China's growing urban middle and upper classes—have led to demands for healthier, safer, and more diverse foods. In a recent analysis by Li Wei—Director of the Development Research Center of the State Council—Li describes the phenomenon as follows:

> As incomes increase, as a new generation of consumers is growing up, and as electronic information exchange accelerates, people's food consumption demands have been changing from "eating one's fill" to "eating well, safely, healthily, and happily".
>
> (Li 2017)

Rising incomes alone do not explain the growing focus on safe, healthy foods. This shift must also be understood against the background of environmental degradation and the severe quality and safety issues China's agro-industrial development model has engendered. Rapid agricultural growth has resulted in massive damage to land and water resources, with serious consequences for the safety and quality of food grown in such environments. According to a survey published by the Ministry of Environmental Protection and the Ministry of Land and Resources in 2014, almost one-fifth of China's arable land, about 20 million hectares, is heavily polluted (Takahashi 2016). Overuse of pesticides and chemicals in food production is producing as many food safety concerns among consumers as are widespread adulteration practices during food processing and retailing. Some of the most egregious cases of food adulteration reported in recent years include the use of chemical whiteners to produce steamed buns that look whiter and more attractive to consumers; the injection of meat with water and its treatment with red colorants to improve its visual appearance on the supermarket counter; the recycling of "gutter oil" from sewers and slaughterhouse waste for sale to restaurants and street food stalls; and the use of toxic chemicals such as melamine in infant formula to increase the milk's apparent protein content, producing serious health damage in infants fed on such formula (Zhou 2015, pp. 44–45). To be sure, Chinese policymakers are well aware of these issues and, for some years now, have been stressing the significance of food quality in policy efforts aimed at safeguarding China's food security. Yet, food safety, public health problems, and environmental pollution are increasingly becoming liabilities in China's current agro-industrial growth model. Unsurprisingly then, many Chinese consumers, or at least those that possess the necessary economic means, prefer food products imported from regions associated with high levels of quality and safety, such as Australia, New Zealand, the European Union, or the United States.

Second, in addition to demands for safer foods, imports have been spurred by changing dietary patterns. Following a global trend toward an increasing "Westernization" of diets, Chinese consumers have been moving over the past decades from a diet based on carbohydrate-rich staples (such as cereals, roots, and tubers) to a diet dominated by animal products (meat and dairy), with profound implications for grain import levels. With meat consumption seen as a symbol of the good life, industrial meat production has grown rapidly, triggering massive imports of soybeans used to feed China's growing animal population. Faced with the predicament of feeding both China's population and its animal herd, Chinese leaders opted to prioritize the domestic production of grains destined for human consumption, while leaving the supply of soybean to the international market. Liberalization of the soybean sector did not only see policy support for domestic soybean farmers drop precipitously (Yan et al. 2016) but it also entailed the re-classification of soybean as a *feed crop* rather than a *food crop*—a move that quietly removed soybean from the basket of grains for which the 95 percent self-sufficiency baseline applied. While imports of soybeans were allowed to soar, policymakers continued to promote "grain self-sufficiency" in crops defined as food grains, such as wheat and rice (Schneider 2014, p. 624).

Similar to rising meat consumption, the growing importance of dairy products as part of the daily Chinese diet is increasingly throwing the policy goal of food self-sufficiency into jeopardy. Here, it is worth remembering that, traditionally, China has been what Wiley (2016) calls a "lactophobic" food culture, in which dairy products played a peripheral role at best. However, with the shift toward a more Western-style diet, the Chinese have begun to consume remarkable amounts of milk, yogurts, ice creams, and even cheese—as reflected by the increasing popularity of Western fast food chains such as Pizza Hut and McDonald's (Höllmann 2010, p. 228). Most of the dairy products consumed in China today are produced by a massive domestic industrial dairy complex that has emerged over the past decades. This industrial dairy complex, akin to the meat industry, is heavily dependent on imported feedstuffs, thus spurring a rapid growth of feed grain imports such as soy and alfalfa (Sharma & Zhang 2014; Wiley 2007).

China's food security strategists have paid a hefty political price for their choice to "abandon soybean and protect grains" (*qidou baoliang* 弃豆保粮) (Yan et al. 2016). Not only has China turned from a soybean net exporter up until the mid-1990s into the world's biggest importer of (genetically modified) soy from Brazil and the United States, thus precipitating a rapid decline in domestic soybean production, but global traders now also control most of China's domestic soybean crushing capacity (Schneider 2017; Yan et al. 2016). These restructuring processes have precipitated the rise of a global oilseed-livestock complex, linking China, the United States, and Latin American countries in an intricate set of power relations and which, I argue, is at the heart of China's current self-sufficiency woes. Indirectly, this has also made China the driving force of soybean expansion in Brazil and other Latin American countries. As trees have to make room for soybean plantations, the recycling of soybean grown in the Americas through the bodies of animals in China is widely expected to have long-term impacts on the global environment and will likely accelerate the dynamics of climate change (Zhan 2022, p. 30).

Industrial meat production has not just deepened dependencies on soybean imports but also increased pressure on domestic grain output. While China has achieved large yield increases across all three key cereals wheat, rice, and corn, it is corn production that has contributed the most to China's overall grain output growth. At the beginning of China's reform period in 1978, corn production stood at 56 million tons. By 2020, it had increased to 260 million tons—a more than four-fold increase (Sternfeld 2022). This massive boost in corn production is not due to a sudden infatuation of Chinese consumers with tortillas but, rather, highlights the role of corn as a cost-efficient and versatile feed grain in animal farming operations. Ever higher goals for domestic grain production are thus also closely linked to an industrial meat production model that relies on external feed inputs.

Paradoxically, although growing meat and dairy consumption has been straining China's cherished principle of food self-sufficiency, China's leaders have encouraged this dietary shift. Indeed, boosting domestic production, sale, and consumption of animal-based products has become, "a hallmark of [China's] post-1978 agricultural development model" (Schneider & Sharma

2014, p. 11). This is for two reasons. First, as highly productive sectors, China's meat and dairy industries have been generating handsome profits for the domestic agribusiness firms involved (Schneider & Sharma 2014). By now, a powerful domestic dairy and meat sector has been fostered, with a vested interest in accelerating the "meatification" of Chinese diets. Second, the consumption of ever more diverse and high-quality foods such as meat and dairy is seen as a visible symbol of the CPC's success in feeding its people. Tied to symbolic meanings of modernity, affluence, health, and national as well as individual competitiveness, the increasing availability of animal products on Chinese people's dinner tables is critical for a state whose legitimacy is intimately bound up with its ability to continuously improve living standards through economic growth and development (Lawrence 2019; Wiley 2007).

Finally, understanding the reasons for the steep growth in agricultural imports requires us to shift our focus from domestic dietary patterns to the ways in which the institutions of global agri-food trade, most notably the World Trade Organization (WTO), have constrained domestic policy options in China. When China joined the WTO in 2001, it simultaneously acceded to the Agreement on Agriculture (AoA). Agriculture had been one of the most contentious issues in the negotiations since it forced Chinese officials to lower agricultural tariffs, eliminate import quotas for most agricultural commodities, and limit the scope of its agricultural support programs (Zhan 2017; Gale 2015). With the exception of some key products such as rice, wheat, and corn, over which the Chinese authorities retain import control via the use of so-called tariff rate quotas (TRQs), China imposes an average tariff rate of just 15 percent, turning it into one of the countries with the lowest tariffs for agricultural products (Cheng 2012, p. 5). Low tariffs under China's WTO commitments have facilitated the import of crops that can be produced more efficiently and cheaply overseas. Eager to maintain high levels of domestic production, the Chinese state supports farmers by buying their crops at minimum purchase prices, but this form of support has only increased the price gap between domestically produced grain and grain imports. Taking rice as an example, in 2016, the average price of imported rice was 1,600 RMB per ton, whereas the minimum purchasing price for domestically produced rice stood at 2,300 RMB per ton (Zhang 2019, pp. 182–183), highlighting the declining competitiveness of Chinese farmers on liberalized world markets. With domestically produced grain selling at higher prices than imports, Chinese state buyers are forced to store away large amounts of the grain bought from farmers via the minimum purchase price policy in the massive state reserve system, leading to an occasional and rather paradoxical coexistence of high domestic outputs, high domestic stocks, and high imports—known in Chinese policy circles as the "triple-high problem" (*sangao wenti* 三高问题) (Qiu 2016). According to one Chinese study, in 2014 alone, China imported 50 million tons of "non-essential" grains (Chen 2015, p. 2), which, in the language of Chinese policymakers, refers to grain imports not motivated by production deficits but by gaps between domestic and world market prices.

**State responses to rising imports**

Chinese policymakers may have wished otherwise, yet, throughout the 2000s, the rise in imports became too big to ignore. At the 2013 Central Rural Work Conference, China's leadership acknowledged the new reality by announcing a new dual food security strategy based on "domestic supply with 'moderate imports'" (Zhang 2019, p. 7). Although self-sufficiency was still at the center, the policy introduced two major changes. For one, the definition of "grain" was once again revised, now not only excluding soybean but also loosening the focus on root tubers and coarse grain. Under the new definition, the previous 95 percent self-sufficiency baseline for all types of grains and tubers was replaced by the new principle of "basic self-sufficiency in cereals and absolute security in food grains" (*guwu jiben ziji, kouliang juedui anquan* 谷物基本自给，口粮绝对安全), with "food grains" now interpreted to include only rice and wheat and "basic self-sufficiency" referring to an 80 percent baseline for all other staples (Guo & Myers 2017, pp. 95–96). Second, for all other food products, "moderate imports" now officially formed part of the national food security strategy.

In practical terms, the dual food security strategy has meant that Chinese policymakers have doubled down on domestic grain production while also optimizing imports. Maintaining the farmland area and improving its quality is a major part of the first pillar of the dual strategy. Environmental damage from industrial development and the repurposing of farmland for construction and real estate purposes have seen the farmland area decline by 5 percent between 2013 and 2019 (Dong et al. 2024), raising the alarm among China's top leaders. In response, a "red line" of 120 million hectares of farmland was declared, for which provincial authorities are to take direct responsibility. In addition, a *National High-Standard Farmland Construction Plan (2021–2030)* seeks to drive the consolidation of small plots into larger areas equipped with modern irrigation infrastructure and ready for mechanized production, while a *Black Soil Protection Law* seeks to halt and reverse the loss of valuable black soils in China's Northeast. Since 2021, quantitative targets for annual grain production have also started to take a more prominent role in official policy announcements. Provincial governments all over the country have been tasked with achieving local production quotas that will ensure China produces a minimum of 650 million tons of grain annually—leading to worrying reports about local campaigns removing orchards and fish ponds or rolling back ecological restoration projects to expand grain production (Zuo 2023). The central authorities have also fixated their view on soybeans—the Achilles' heel of China's agri-food imports. A *Soybean Revitalization Plan* released in 2019 aims to increase both the soybean planting area and soybean yields, trying to close the significant yield gap of around 40 percent that separates China from the United States (Zuo 2024). Higher targets for the domestic production of soybeans are also laid out in China's *14th Five-Year Plan on Crop Farming* issued in 2022. The plan targets

*Table 2.1* Key policies aimed at ensuring domestic grain production

| *Aspect* | *Policy document/goal* |
| --- | --- |
| Farmland area and quality | National High-Standard Farmland Construction Plan (2021–2030) |
| | Black Spoil Protection Law (2021) |
| | Farmland "red line" of 120 million ha |
| Grain production | Grain Security Law (2023) |
| | 14th Five-Year Plan on Crop Farming (2021–2025) |
| | Soybean Revitalization Plan (2019) |
| | Minimum grain output target of 650 million tons/ year |
| Seeds and breeding | Revised Seed Law (2021) |
| | Action Plan for Seed Industry Revitalization (2021) |
| Food loss and waste | Anti-Food Waste Law (2021) |
| | Clean Your Plate Campaign (2020) |
| Food quality and integrity | Food Safety Law (2015) |
| | Agricultural Product Quality and Safety Law (2006) |
| Technology and innovation | Bioeconomy Development Plan (2021–2025) |
| Climate change and environment | Methane Action Plan (2023) |
| | Green Agriculture Development Plan (2021–2025) |

*Source:* Author's own research.

the production of about 23 million tons of soybeans by the end of 2025, up 40 percent from 2022 (but still well below current import levels). Fighting food loss and waste and improving seeds for higher yields and resilience are other prongs in China's approach to achieve "absolute security" in key staple grains. With China's first-ever *Grain Security Law* adopted in December 2023, many of these policy goals and implementation mechanisms are now legally enshrined in a comprehensive document, reflecting the continued importance Chinese policymakers attach to maintaining high levels of domestic food production amid rising geopolitical tensions with the West. So far, these efforts appear to have paid off. In 2023, China reported its biggest grain harvest ever—a whopping 695 million tons, outperforming the country's own ambitious grain production target (Qiu 2023). But with climate change and rural demographic decline throwing the countryside into uncharted waters, questions about the environmental and social sustainability of China's agricultural development model loom larger than ever.

Meanwhile, state officials have been working hard to diversify sources of food imports. Ever since adjusting the food security strategy to one based on "domestic supply with moderate imports," there has been a general consensus among Chinese politicians and experts that the pursuit of absolute food self-sufficiency is neither a possible nor a desirable goal. What Chinese policy wants to avoid, however, is over-reliance on any one supplier of key agricultural products. Particularly since the trade war with the United States and increasing geopolitical tensions with Western countries, policymakers have been adamant to identify and address "choke points" in China's food trade relations with other countries. While China remains reliant on large Western food exporters such as the United States, Canada, and Australia for much of its food imports, it has been actively promoting trade relationships with countries in the global South and other emerging economies. For example, Southeast Asian countries now take up a significant share in global fruit and starch exports to China as well as in specialty rice imports (Zhan 2022, p. 22). China has also been looking to Eastern European and Central Asian countries to diversify wheat and corn imports. In 2012, it signed a loan-for-crops contract with Ukraine worth 3 billion USD that made the Eastern European country into China's largest supplier of corn, accounting for over 60 percent of corn imports. Ukraine's rise came at the expense of the United States, which used to be China's biggest corn supplier before 2014 (Zhang 2019, p. 186), but to the chagrin of Chinese officials, this success story abruptly ended when war broke out between Ukraine and Russia in 2022. Supported by the expansion of overland logistics infrastructure built as part of China's Belt and Road Initiative (BRI), Eastern European and Central Asian countries such as Russia or Kazakhstan have also emerged as major exporters of wheat as well as other agricultural goods that benefit from the growing number of continental railway links connecting China to Europe (Zhang 2019, p. 191). Even in the soybean trade, China has started emancipating itself from Western dominance. When the trade war with the United States started in 2018, China reduced soybean imports from the United States by 50 percent in the course of one year, replacing the shortfalls with imports from Brazil and Argentina (Zhan 2022, pp. 20–21). Trade figures speak to the success of China's diversification strategy. Between 2000 and 2020, food exports from the five major Western exporters to China—the United States, Canada, the EU, Australia, and New Zealand grew from 5.6 billion USD to 52 billion USD, but at the same time, their share in global food exports to China decreased significantly from 61 percent to 32 percent, highlighting the growing role Southern countries play in Chinese food imports (Zhan 2022, p. 23). Yet, in many aspects, China has been unable to break the dominance of Western institutions and businesses shaping the global agri-food markets on which China relies for its imports—an issue overseas agricultural investment is meant to address.

## The place of overseas agricultural investment in China's food security strategy

By the mid-2000s, the recognition that China was now firmly placed at the center of global food trade raised debates about whether Chinese firms should not just buy agricultural commodities from abroad but also invest in the supply chains that controlled the flow of these commodities on world markets. Agricultural "going out" (*nongye "zouchuqu"* 农业"走出去"), as the policy is referred to in the official language, encourages Chinese firms to "actively use international agricultural markets and agricultural resources" (China Government 2014) by not just buying from world markets but also investing in food and farming assets abroad. The policy was first launched in 1999 as China was negotiating its accession to the WTO (Zhan 2022, p. 31), but it would take well into the following decade before first details emerged on how the state was planning to turn rhetoric into practice. In 2006, following a preliminary plan jointly issued by the Ministries of Commerce, Finance, and Agriculture, debates picked up speed as officials were beginning to work out the details of a coherent policy support framework that would combine incentive schemes, investment guidance catalogs, and support from China's policy banks (Brautigam 2015, pp. 58–64). Also emerging from such discussions was a set of multiple goals to be pursued by the policy. These goals did include access to natural resources but also highlighted the quest for advanced agricultural technology, new export markets for Chinese firms, and the need to foster the international competitiveness of Chinese agribusinesses as China was seeking to challenge the dominance of Western-based agribusinesses in global food markets (Wang 2017b).

Despite several support measures, Chinese companies, initially, showed little enthusiasm to invest in agriculture overseas. Risks appeared too high, rewards seemed uncertain, and support was considered insufficient (Brautigam 2015, pp. 64–65). Yet, as policy debates within China continued on how the state could better support the expansion of its agribusinesses abroad, alarm bells began to ring in Western media houses. The point of contention revolved around a purported plan by the Ministry of Agriculture and Rural Affairs (MARA) to set up overseas production bases, particularly for the planting of soybeans, thereby relieving pressure on domestic farming resources and reducing soybean imports (Myers & Guo 2015, p. 8). These concerns coincided with skyrocketing global food prices during the 2007/2008 food crisis and warnings about an impending land grab in poorer countries of the global South.

No such plan by MARA was ever publicly released, yet China was brandished as a "land grabber"—a reputation that has stayed with the country until today, despite much subsequent research pointing out the misleading character of this label (see Chapter 1). Naturally, it is impossible to know whether such ideas were ever seriously discussed within the several ministries in charge of promoting agricultural "going out"; however, public announcements point to a rather different set of concerns that seem to have guided formulations of the policy. In 2008, the National Development and Reform Commission (NDRC), which at that time was in charge of developing a long-term framework for Chinese food security, made no mention of using overseas farmland in its *National Framework for Food Security (2008–2020)*, instead emphasizing trade and the need to build stable partnerships with China's key soybean suppliers Brazil and the United States (Brautigam 2015, p. 70). At a subsequent press conference, an NDRC spokesperson, when asked about plans to set up large-scale overseas farms to grow food for China, set the record straight by saying:

> We want to have a stable and reliable system to be able to import a broad range of foods, including soybeans and edible oils. [...] International cooperation, logistics, and so on particularly for soybean procurement—*this* is what we are very concerned about.
>
> (conference readout quoted in Brautigam 2015, pp. 70–71)

There is good reason to believe that a focus on international trade rather than overseas production was in fact the key factor shaping China's agricultural "going out" policy, and soybeans were at the center. As we have seen already, Chinese soybean imports exploded when the country opened up its soybean sector to foreign imports in the wake of its accession to the WTO. Almost instantly, a small number of agricultural commodity trading companies from the United States and Europe began to dominate the trade. Collectively known by their acronym ABCD (denoting the company initials of Archer Daniel Midlands, Bunge, Cargill, and Louis Dreyfus), these companies have controlled the global grain market for over a century through ownership of key logistics infrastructure (e.g., grain elevators in deepwater ports) and extensive trading networks that allow them to source most of the world's grain destined for export and sell it to buyers on global markets (Murphy et al. 2012). Chinese companies had sought to bypass the ABCD oligopoly since the early 2000s, trying to set up direct trade relations with China's biggest soybean supplier, Brazil, but a series of mishaps led to spectacular failure, driving multiple Chinese traders into bankruptcy and leading to a takeover of Chinese soybean processing and trading operations by the ABCD themselves (Oliveira 2018). By 2008, foreign firms had thus ended up controlling 80 percent of soybean crushing and 60 percent of soy oil refining capacity in China, meaning that "the same transnational corporations controlling soybean exports from the U.S. and Brazil also became the major importers controlling the flow of soy to China" (Oliveira 2018, p. 127).

It is therefore no coincidence that agricultural "going out" really began to pick up speed around 2008, with the global financial crisis, food price hikes, and overall economic slowdown impressing the urgency upon Chinese policymakers to wrest back control over the flow and price of soybean and other important agricultural commodities that were being imported to China in growing volumes. Bypassing the oligopoly of the large Western grain traders would, as Chinese experts agreed upon, hinge more on the ownership of trade logistics and infrastructure than on owning farmland. After all, as the experience with the Brazilian soybean sector had taught the Chinese, even the largest growers were reliant on the infrastructure and contracts provided by grain trading companies if they wanted to send their crops to China.

As Cheng Guoqiang, senior academic advisor at the highly influential Development Research Center of the State Council, put it:

> [...] no matter how much money you spend, merely leasing overseas land and hiring farm labor does not give you pricing power. In the end, your import price will still be decided by the four major grain traders [—the ABCD].
>
> (Cheng 2014)

Hence, China's agribusiness firms should "'go out' to be 'grain traders' and not 'farmers'," Cheng insisted (2014). In a similar vein, a study by MARA researchers published in the business magazine *Caijing* highlighted food processing, logistics, and transportation as core targets of overseas agricultural investment (Jiao 2013). The focus on trade and value chains, of course, has not meant that no Chinese firms have acquired farmland abroad—after all, the Chinese state, though powerful, is in no position to dictate the business plans of the myriad of bigger and smaller firms that had by then began to warm to the idea of mobilizing some of their capital for agricultural ventures abroad. Here, the point is not to say that there has not been investment in overseas farmland by Chinese capital but that farmland investment was not the focus of the policy.

The preoccupation with the global grain trade system has also meant that Chinese policymakers see the country's state-controlled trading companies as forerunners of China's agricultural "going out." The China National Cereals, Oils and Foodstuffs Company (COFCO) is a case in point. Through a series of government-backed strategic investments in agricultural assets and acquisitions of smaller grain trading companies, COFCO has emerged as the world's fourth largest agricultural commodity trading company and a serious competitor to the ABCD oligopoly—turning this formerly sleepy state behemoth into a modern, international cooperation not so different from the Western trading companies it is competing with (see also Chapter 4). But while key support might be focused on the large state firms considered to have the most potential to compete internationally, the policy has left much room for private forms of corporate capital to participate in China's agricultural "going out." According to a report compiled by MARA, in 2016, state-owned enterprises only accounted for 5.6 percent of investors, while privately owned enterprises made up the rest. Some of these belong to China's so-called dragon head firms (*longtou qiye* 龙头企业) that are seen by the Chinese state as leading the modernization and industrialization of agriculture at home, while others yet are from entirely different sectors with no background in agriculture. These firms are driven primarily by the quest for profits, even as they may pay lip service to strategic goals around food security and food trade dominance. Some of them like the New Hope Group have become international agribusiness corporations in their own right. Through their overseas investments, the most successful of these firms now manage their own global supply chains and operate subsidiaries in multiple countries, sometimes with outright ownership of farmland and other times focusing more on downstream links in the value chain, such as processing and marketing (see Chapter 4).

As the Chinese state is allying with corporate capital in pursuit of its domestic and global food security goals, the rise of modern Chinese agribusinesses such as the New Hope Group is not only transforming the global food system but also altering agri-food relations at home. Corporate interests increasingly dominate supply chains, squeezing profit margins for smaller farmers who must rely on an ever smaller number of firms for farm inputs and access to consumer markets (Zhan 2022, p. 52) or who are being subsumed by corporatized farm entities as wage labor (Yan et al. 2015). Hence, China's agricultural "going out" policy has not only resulted in the re-ordering of global food relations, with multifaceted effects on farmers and natural environments elsewhere but also deepened capitalist dynamics in China's own agricultural sector, aligning the country more closely with the Western paradigm of corporatized and industrialized agriculture while marginalizing the forms of Chinese peasant agriculture that have been so integral to China's food security over the past five decades (van der Ploeg & Ye 2016).

*****

As we have seen, China's food security strategy is based on maintaining high levels of self-sufficiency for key staple crops but accommodates moderate imports of agricultural products deemed non-essential. The determination with which Chinese officials have pushed for maintaining domestic production levels has resulted in impressive gains in agricultural output and productivity. These results have *not* been achieved on the back of using overseas farmland, but are overwhelmingly due to China's persistent policy support for agriculture at home and the millions of Chinese farmers who, together, produce amazing amounts of grain on plots far smaller than the global average and with limited support from mechanization. Today, Chinese leaders could give a proud retort to Lester Brown's question of "Who will feed China?," stressing that, indeed, China is feeding itself—with the exception of soybean.

The vexed issue of China's dependence on soybean imports, however, remains unresolved and, in fact, has only worsened over the years, despite all efforts to increase domestic production and diversify into other types of animal feed. This conundrum will likely remain unsolvable unless policymakers begin to ask painful questions about the model of industrial livestock farming the country has embraced since the beginning of the reform period. The model's reliance on external feed and other inputs (rather than the recycling of household waste as in backyard farming still practiced well into the 2000s) and its demand for large amounts of corporate capital make it highly sensitive to swings in global commodity prices and financial markets. Chinese agriculture officials may wish to see more soybean produced domestically, but neither China's limited farmland area nor the relatively lower competitiveness of its farmers compared to the world's top soybean producers will turn this wish into reality in the foreseeable future. And the overleveraged, corporate entities on which policymakers are banking to fuel the meatification of Chinese diets may further add to volatility and wastefulness in the system as they need to respond to shareholder demands, service company debt, and pursue short-term profit motives.

One attempt by the Chinese state to address the soybean conundrum has been to encourage its own companies to invest in global commodity supply chains and gain more dominant positions in global agri-food markets. Despite high-profile failures and some companies incurring huge losses, from the perspective of Chinese policymakers, the agricultural "going out" policy is likely seen as a success story, helping expand the presence of Chinese agribusinesses overseas. Whether it is COFCO's emergence as a major grain trader taking away market share from the ABCD or the acquisition of Swiss seed and fertilizer group Syngenta by ChemChina, Chinese companies have come to control key links in global agri-food value chains. The policy has also opened the door for many private Chinese agribusinesses to seek fortune and profit in overseas market—and Australia has been one of their favored destinations. There, however, China's reputation as a "land grabber" with a big appetite for food did not make for an unconditional welcome. To the Australian context, we must now turn.

## Notes

1 Among others, these include the $43 billion takeover of Swiss seed and fertilizer group Syngenta by Chinese chemical company ChemChina in 2017 (China's largest foreign takeover to date), COFCO's acquisition of grain traders Noble and Nidera in 2014, and Shuanghui International's acquisition of US pork producer Smithfield Foods in 2013.

2 There are exceptions to this general observation. Zhan (2022), for example, brings an insightful analysis of China's domestic agri-food dynamics into the land rush literature.

## References

Brautigam, Deborah (2015): *Will Africa Feed China?* Oxford, New York: Oxford University Press.

Brown, Lester R. (1995): *Who will Feed China? Wake-Up Call for a Small Planet.* New York: Norton.

Chen, Wei (2015): 中国农业对外直接投资研究 [*Research on China's Agricultural Foreign Direct Investment*]. Beijing: 中国农业出版社 [China Agriculture Press].

Cheng, Guoqiang (2014): 中国农业"走出去"要做"粮商"不做"农民" [China's Agriculture Should "Go Out" to Be "Grain Traders" and Not to Be "Farmers"]. In 农经 [*Agriculture Economics*] 1 (274), p. 10.

Cheng, Guoqiang (2012): 中国农业对外开放：影响、启示与战略选择 [China's Agricultural Opening to the Outside World: Impact, Learnings, and Strategic Choices]. In 中国农村经济 [*Chinese Rural Economy*] 3, pp. 4–13.

China Daily (2017): 习近平的"三农"情怀和战略智慧 [Xi Jinping's Sentiments and Strategic Wisdom on the "Three Rural Issues"] In 中文网 *[Zhongwen Wang]* 2/6/2017. Available online at https://china.chinadaily.com.cn/2017-02/06/content_28117863.htm, checked on 4/26/2024.

China Government (2014): 关于全面深化农村改革加快推进农业现代化的若干意见 [Several Opinions on Comprehensively Deepening Rural Reform and Accelerating Agricultural Modernization]. Available online at http://www.moa.gov.cn/ztzl/yhwj2015/wjhg_1/201502/t20150202_4378630.htm, checked on 8/9/2019.

China Government (2008): 国家粮食安全中长期规划纲要(2008—2020年) [Medium and Long-Term Plan for National Food Security (2008–2020)]. Available online at www.gov.cn/jrzg/2008-11/13/content_1148414.htm, checked on 10/10/2017.

China State Council (1996): The Grain Issue in China. Available online at http://www.china.org.cn/e-white/grainissue/index.htm, checked on 10/8/2017.

Dong, Kevin; Prytherch, Mallie; McElwee, Lily; Kim, Patricia; Blanchette, Jude (2024): China's Food Security. Key Challenges and Emerging Policy Responses. In *Center for Strategic & International Studies* (CSIS Briefs). Available online at https://www.csis.org/analysis/chinas-food-security-key-challenges-and-emerging-policy-responses, checked on 3/31/2024.

FAOSTAT (2023): Food and Agriculture Data. Food and Agriculture Organization of the United Nations. Available online at https://www.fao.org/faostat/en/#home, checked on 12/12/2023.

Gale, Fred; Hansen, James; Jewison, Michael (2015): China's Growing Demand for Agricultural Imports. In *EIB-136. U.S. Department of Agriculture, Economic Research Service*. Available online at https://www.ers.usda.gov/publications/pub-details/?pubid=43940, checked on 4/10/2017.

Guo, Jie; Myers, Margaret (2017): Chinese Agricultural Investments in Latin America. Less There Than Meets the Eye? In Margaret Myers, Carol Wise (Eds.): *The Political Economy of China – Latin America Relations in the New Millennium*. Brave New World. New York, London: Routledge Taylor & Francis Group, pp. 92–114.

Höllmann, Thomas O. (2010): *Schlafender Lotus – trunkenes Huhn. Kulturgeschichte der chinesischen Küche*. München: Beck.

Jiao, Jian (2013): 中国米袋子系在别人腰间：大豆及三大主粮依赖进口 [China's Rice Bag Is Tied Around the Waist of Others: Soybeans and the Three Main Staple Grains Rely on Imports]. In 财经 [*Caijing*], 9/12/2013. Available online at http://finance.ifeng.com/a/20131209/11235014_0.shtml, checked on 8/14/2019.

Lawrence, Felicity (2019): Can the World Quench China's Bottomless Thirst for Milk? In *The Guardian*, 3/29/2019. Available online at https://www.theguardian.com/environment/2019/mar/29/can-the-world-quench-chinas-bottomless-thirst-for-milk, checked on 5/3/2019.

Li, Wei (2017): 李伟：以更高标准保障中国粮食与食品安全 [Li Wei: Using Higher Standards to Safeguard China's Food Security and Food Safety]. In 中国经济时报 [*China Economic Times*], 11/20/2017. Available online at http://d.drcnet.com.cn/eDRCnet.common.web/DocSummary.aspx?chnid=1002&leafid=1&docid=4904529&uid=02&version=integrated, checked on 4/25/2019.

MARA (2004): *Report on the State of China's Food Security*. Beijing: MARA.

Morton, Katherine (2012): *Learning by Doing: China's Role in the Global Governance of Food Security*. Indiana University. Indiana (RCCPB Working Paper 30).

Murphy, Sophia; Burch, David; Clapp, Jennifer (2012): *Cereal Secrets. The World's Largest Grain Traders and Global Agriculture*. Oxfam: Oxfam Research Reports. Available online at https://www.oxfam.org/sites/www.oxfam.org/files/file_attachments/rr-cereal-secrets-grain-traders-agriculture-30082012-en_4.pdf, checked on 5/8/2017.

Myers, Margaret; Guo, Jie (2015): China's Agricultural Investment in Latin America: A Critical Assessment. The Dialogue/Leadership for the Americas (China and Latin America Report).

Oliveira, Gustavo de L. T. (2018): The Battle of the Beans: How Direct Brazil-China Soybean Trade Was Stillborn in 2004. In *Journal of Latin American Geography* 17 (2), pp. 113–139. DOI: 10.1353/lag.2018.0024.

Qiu, Haifeng (2023): 2023年全国粮食总产量13908.2亿斤 [Total National Grain Output in 2023 at 695 Million Tons]. In *People's Daily*, 12/12/2023. Available online at http://paper.people.com.cn/rmrbhwb/html/2023-12/12/content_26031458.htm, checked on 12/12/2023.

Qiu, Haifeng (2016): 中国粮食"三高"矛盾如何解决 [How to Solve the Contradiction of China's "Triple-High" Phenomenon in Grain Production]. In 人民日报 [*People's Daily*], 11/15/2016. Available online at http://paper.people.com.cn/rmrbhwb/html/2016-11/15/content_1727580.htm, checked on 8/5/2019.

Schneider, Mindi (2018): Reforming the Humble Pig. Pigs, Pork and Contemporary China. In Roel Sterckx, Martina Siebert, Dagmar Schäfer (Eds.): *Animals through Chinese History. Earliest Times to 1911*. Cambridge (UK), New York: Cambridge University Press, pp. 233–243.

Schneider, Mindi (2017): Dragon Head Enterprises and the State of Agribusiness in China. In *Journal of Agrarian Change* 17 (1), pp. 3–21. DOI: 10.1111/joac.12151.

Schneider, Mindi (2014): Developing the Meat Grab. In *The Journal of Peasant Studies* 41 (4), pp. 613–633.

Schneider, Mindi; Sharma, Shefali (2014): China's Pork Miracle? Agribusiness and Development in China's Pork Industry. In *Institute for Agriculture and Trade Policy* (Global Meat Complex: The China Series). Available online at https://www.iatp.org/documents/chinas-pork-miracle-agribusiness-and-development-chinas-pork-industry, checked on 11/14/2017.

Sharma, Shefali; Zhang, Rou (2014): China's Dairy Dilemma. The Evolution and Future Trends of China's Dairy Industry. In *Institute for Agriculture and Trade Policy* (Global Meat Complex: The China Series). Available online at https://www.iatp.org/sites/default/files/2017-05/2017_05_03_DairyReport_f_web.pdf, checked on 5/22/2018.

Sternfeld, Eva (2022): Ernährungssicherung in China. In *Federal Agency for Civic Education*. Available online at https://www.bpb.de/themen/asien/china/513234/ernaehrungssicherung-in-china/, checked on 4/3/2024.

Takahashi, Goro (2016): Damage and Heavy Metal Pollution in China's Farmland: Reality and Solutions. In *Journal of Contemporary Asian Studies* 5 (1), pp. 11–25.

van der Ploeg, Jan Douwe; Ye, Jingzhong (2016): The Conundrum of Chinese Agriculture. In van der Ploeg, Jan Douwe, Jingzhong Ye (Eds.): *China's Peasant Agriculture and Rural Society. Changing Paradigms of Farming*. New York: Routledge, pp. 1–24.

Wang, Jiamei (2017a): Success in Maintaining Food Security in China Contributes to Global Economic Stability. In *Global Times*, 10/17/2017. Available online at https://www.globaltimes.cn/page/201710/1070771.shtml, checked on 05/02/2024.

Wang, Qi (2017b): 我国对外农业投资的目标与任务 [The Goals and Tasks of China's Foreign Agricultural Investment]. In 经济纵横 [*Economic Perspectives*] 2, pp. 93–98.

Weis, Tony (2013): *The Ecological Hoofprint. The Global Burden of Industrial Livestock*. London: Zed Books [e-book version].

Wiley, Andrea S. (2016): *Re-Imagining Milk. Cultural and Biological Perspectives*. New York: Routledge.

Wiley, Andrea S. (2007): Transforming Milk in a Global Economy. In *American Anthropologist* 109 (4), pp. 666–677.

World Bank (2007): *World Development Report 2008*. Washington, DC: Agriculture for Development.

Yan, Hairong; Chen, Yiyuan; Ku, Hok Bun (2016): China's Soybean Crisis: The Logic of Modernization and its Discontents. In *The Journal of Peasant Studies* 43 (2), pp. 373–395.

Yan, Hairong; Chen, Yiyuan (2015): Agrarian Capitalization without Capitalism? Capitalist Dynamics from Above and Below in China. In *Journal of Agrarian Change* 15 (3), pp. 366–391.

Xu, Xiuli; Li, Xiaoyun; Qi, Gubo; Tang, Lixia; Mukwereza, Langton (2016): Science, Technology, and the Politics of Knowledge: The Case of China's Agricultural Technology Demonstration Centers in Africa. In *World Development* 81, pp. 82–91.

Zha, Daojiong; Zhang, Hongzhou (2013): Food in China's International Relations. In *The Pacific Review* 26 (5), pp. 455–479.

Zhan, Shaohua (2022): *China and Global Food Security*. Cambridge: Cambridge University Press.

Zhan, Shaohua (2019): *The Land Question in China. Agrarian Capitalism, Industrious Revolution, and East Asian Development*. Abingdon, Oxon, New York: Routledge

Zhan, Shaohua (2017): Riding on Self-Sufficiency: Grain Policy and the Rise of Agrarian Capital in China. In *Journal of Rural Studies* 54, pp. 151–161.

Zhang, Hongzhou (2019): *Securing the 'Rice Bowl'. China and Global Food Security*. Singapore: Palgrave Macmillan.

Zhang, Qian Forrest; Donaldson, John A. (2008): The Rise of Agrarian Capitalism with Chinese Characteristics. Agricultural Modernization, Agribusiness and Collective Land Rights. In *The China Journal* 60, pp. 25–47.

Zhou, Zhang-Yue (2015): Food Security in China: Past, Present and the Future. In Udaya Sekhar Nagothu (Ed.): *Food Security and Development. Country Case Studies*. Abingdon, UK: Routledge, pp. 35–56.

Zuo, Mandy (2024): China Food Security: Inflated Crop Yields Threaten 'Rigour, Authority' of Scientific Research. In *South China Morning Post*, 2/22/2024. Available online at https://www.scmp.com/economy/economic-indicators/article/3252701/china-food-security-inflated-crop-yields-threaten-rigour-authority-scientific-research, checked on 4/4/2024.

Zuo, Mandy (2023): How China's Farmland-Reclamation Campaign is Driving Aggressive Crop Expansions and Land-Use Crackdowns. In *South China Morning Post*, 5/10/2023. Available online at https://www.scmp.com/economy/china-economy/article/3219939/how-chinas-farmland-reclamation-campaign-driving-aggressive-crop-expansions-and-land-use-crackdowns, checked on 7/4/2024.

# 3 Renegotiating Chinese farmland investments in Australia

> As the mining boom recedes into a distant memory, a new opportunity for Australia is fast emerging. Welcome to the dining boom – where milk, beef, wheat and wine are our new iron ore.
>
> (PwC office in Sydney, Agribusiness & Food Showroom)[1]

> [...] a new wave of foreign investment in Australian agriculture is starting to emerge. Rather than being underpinned by genuine commercial forces where profits are the driver, food security has emerged as a new factor for investment. With state owned enterprises entering the market, it is becoming blurred as to whether all of this investment is still interested in the profitability of the venture, or rather in ensuring that a consistent stream of food can be delivered to its people.
>
> (Submission by the National Farmers' Federation to the Economic Legislation Committee, 2011)

Australia is a key exporter of agricultural commodities to China. While selling food to Chinese consumers has been largely uncontroversial, the question of whether to sell farmland to Chinese companies has been a different story altogether. When the first tantalizing news stories about Chinese investors snatching up Australian farms began to appear in the early 2010s, the public was electrified and a heated debate ensued in the country's media and political circles. Some voices framed Chinese interest in Australian farmland as a tremendous opportunity. As China's trade patterns with Australia were shifting from a focus on natural resources to a focus on consumer items, including high-quality food products, Chinese investment would be crucial to boost Australian food exports to these new markets, the argument went, with business groups like PwC boldly predicting a new "dining boom." Others were less optimistic. Framing growing Chinese interest in Australian farms as a state-driven strategy to ensure food security, critics like the National Farmers' Federation worried that too much land in the hands of Chinese investors would lead to a loss of control and sovereignty over Australia's food production. If the trend was allowed to continue unchecked, these pundits argued, it would not only undermine profits for Australian food producers but potentially even put at risk the country's own food security.

DOI: 10.4324/9781003474661-5

The debate remained largely confined to Australia's national media and political circles, leaving little impact on global discussions, which still centered on China's land rush in developing and poorer countries of the global South. In Australia, however, the question of how to respond to growing Chinese interest in Australian farmland ended with a small sensation. In 2015, following two independent senate inquiries, the government tightened the rules for foreign investment in agricultural land. This was the first time the government had attempted a full-on overhaul of the investment regime since the 1970s. A new law was passed that promised more government scrutiny over the kinds of land deals foreign investors from China and elsewhere could undertake in Australia. By significantly lowering the investment review threshold, the new legal framework subjected a great share of land deals previously below the radar of Australia's government to assessment by the authorities. Land deals that were deemed to be against Australia's national interest could now be identified more easily and stopped, sponsors of the bill hoped. The new law also promised to address the paucity of public information about foreign investment in farmland by establishing Australia's first national register of farmland investment.

But was farmland a big target of Chinese investment? If so, why? And who exactly were the Chinese buyers? Curiously, the new investment rules have neither improved transparency about foreign landownership nor quelled public contestation about its perceived benefits and risks. Rather than enabling an informed debate about who should own Australian farmland and to which ends, the re-regulation increased the state's discretionary power over determining which land deals to accept and which ones to reject, all the while leaving the public in the dark about the entities actually investing in Australian farmland and the ways in which these investments altered relationships with Australian agribusiness interests. As has been shown by Sippel and Weldon (2020), for Australian politicians, the new rules serve as a convenient tool to appease public concern over foreign, and particularly Chinese farmland ownership, while remaining responsive to business demands. This is problematic, for the new investment rules obscure rather than expose the complex interests and power relations that make Australian farmland a desirable target for Chinese investors.

Drawing on policy documents, official reports, and stakeholder interviews, this chapter reviews the re-regulation of Australian farmland ownership against the continent's layered histories of colonialism and productivism, as well as the recurring controversies over foreign investment that have shaped public perceptions and national politics around farmland. I proceed in three steps. I begin by providing a short historical overview of farmland ownership in Australia. I then discuss publicly available data about Chinese land deals and compare these to my own investment database, compiled from a systematic review of media reports, corporate and financial documents, as well as personal interviews, raising critical questions about how a lack of transparency has been shaping policy responses in Australia. The final section examines the re-regulation of farmland ownership in Australia following a public backlash against Chinese investment and examines the effects of the regulatory overhaul on the inflow of Chinese capital into the Australian agriculture sector.

## Land relations: colonial histories, closer settlement, and the neoliberal turn

To understand why Chinese investment in Australian farmland became such a point of contention in Australian politics, we must first know more about the history and meanings of farmland ownership on the continent down under. Australian land relations are inextricably linked with the country's past as a settler colony. Before the arrival of the First Fleet in 1788, indigenous nations possessed the entire continent of Australia. Following its takeover as a penal colony by the British, Aboriginal land was quickly appropriated by white settlers on the premise that it belonged to no one ("*terra nullius*"). As a legal doctrine, *terra nullius* legitimized "the annexation of 'uninhabited lands' by settlement as an acknowledged means, alongside conquest and secession, for the proper conduct of colonization by 'civilized' nations" (Whatmore 2002, pp. 63–64). Deeply engrained racial stereotypes on the part of the colonizers meant that the overwhelming majority conveniently overlooked any signs of indigenous land use and management. Australian land was thought of as unclaimed and Aboriginal people as non-productive, despite an abundance of evidence that there existed an intricate system of Aboriginal land tenure and management practices that were not only far-reaching in scale but also well attuned to the natural environment, creating livelihoods far less exposed to the vagaries of nature than the European farming practices to be installed by the newcomers (Gammage 2013). Narratives about the supposed absence of productive land use by Aboriginal people were central to legitimizing the white "land grab." A piece in the *Sydney Herald* declared about First Nations people that "[t]hey bestowed no labour upon the land and that-and that only-it is which gives a right of property to it." (Gammage 2013, pp. 308–309).

The dispossession of indigenous nations and the overturn of their land tenure and management practices went hand in hand with the expansion of settlement by well-placed and ambitious Europeans looking for a path to fortune in Britain's remote penal colony. Radiating outwards from the first colony established by the British at Sydney Cove in 1788, occupation quickly spread along the coastal areas, with further colonies being set up in what is now Hobart (1804), Brisbane (1824), Perth (1829), Adelaide (1836), and Melbourne (1837). The quest for land rapidly expanded the settler frontier from the central cities to the hinterland. Occupation spread from each new base at varying speeds as settlers rushed to occupy Aboriginal land for grazing and farming activities, punctuated by occasional "frenzied rushes" (BITRE 2014, p. 36) for gold and other minerals. Competition for land was high, and occupation by "squatters" closely followed the explorers' trail (BITRE 2014).

Many were driven by world demand for merino wool, a key raw material powering the industrial revolution in the British empire. In what amounted to an illegal occupation of "Crown" land (given that Aboriginal rights were not recognized), aggressive pastoralists swept across the continent in pursuit of individual fortune and wealth from the raising of sheep and other livestock—initially without the blessing of colonial administrations and often seeing their economic ambitions clash with first peoples and their perceptions of the land (Weaver 1996). As the pastoralists consolidated their possessions and pressed for legal transfer of title, squatting was gradually legalized by the colonial authorities. By the mid-1800s, pastoral squatters were among the wealthiest people in the colony, controlling large leases of pastoral land, and came to be described as the "squattocracy."

The wool economy set up by the pastoralists became the basic industry on which other activities would build. The sheep and cattle stations themselves turned into regional centers, and improved transportation links between them made it easier for goods, services, and workers to travel between them. By the mid-1800s, the Australian colonies had become the dominant suppliers to England, and wool was their most important export commodity, dominating agricultural export patterns throughout much of the 19th and even 20th centuries (Lawrence et al. 2019). Indeed, such was the importance of wool as a source of prosperity for the large landowners that Australia was seen by many to be "riding on the sheep's back." But the establishment of pastoral activities as the backbone of colonial economic activity did have a flaw, as it left large land holdings concentrated in the hands of a small number of people.

As pressures mounted to provide more land access to "free settlers," squatters saw their grip on territory challenged by movements campaigning to "unlock the land" and offering new work and investment opportunities to people with farming ambitions (Connors 1970, p. 73). From the 1860s onward, colonial governments pushed to reform the land tenure system by cutting up sheep runs into farming blocks available for sale to settlers. In the colony of New South Wales, the Robertson Acts were directed at opening up the land for selection or homesteading and similar acts followed in the other colonies of Australia (Connors 1970).

Proponents championed the closer settlement movement not only for the impetus it provided to Australia's rural economy but also as an instrument to acquire a "virtuous and industrious rural population" (Connors 1970, p. 74). At its core was the family farm as a productive force and stabilizing political influence. Linked to the belief that Australian wealth depended on a healthy farming sector made up by a large number of fairly equally sized family farms, an ideology labeled "countrymindedness" emerged between 1890 and 1920 that fused depictions of Australia's emerging national identity with images of Australian rurality. The countryman and his struggles in making the natural environment amenable to settlement and productive for agricultural purposes came to embody Australia's national character—and the countryside the true voice of the nation (Lockie 2000).

The closer settlement schemes led to the redistribution of land from earlier land grants and squatters to family farms. Although their appeal to egalitarianism overlooked indigenous people, women, and non-British ethnic groups (Lockie 2000, p. 18), these schemes were significant in breaking up many of the large grazing properties and allowed the emergence of thousands of new farms across Australia (BITRE 2014, p. 37). Egalitarian land ownership patterns were further deepened by the soldier settlement policies following the two world wars. The schemes provided financial incentives to former servicemen to take over farm spaces and were complemented by national irrigation projects, such as in the southern Murray-Darling basin. The economic outcomes of the policy were mixed. In fact, many of the newly minted farmers lacked an aptitude for farm life, were unable to weather the impact of prolonged periods of drought, or simply did not possess the resources necessary for farm investment. Combined with the downturn in world commodity prices that set in after the First World War, closer settlement resulted in hardship for many (Connors 1970, p. 77). Yet, the schemes left the newly federated nation-state with a legacy of fairly equally-sized land holdings in the hands of its former white settlers, with large grazing estates from the time of the squatters now only remaining in the far Western and Northern-Central parts of the continent.

Following the Second World War, a period of protectionism further entrenched a legacy of family-based land ownership arrangements. To support producers, Australian governments created a number of protective institutional structures. State intervention was extensive and included measures as diverse as the setup of import restrictions and tariffs to protect domestic production; the provision of cheap credit to farmers by state-guided agricultural development banks; tax breaks to reduce the costs of input and capital expenditure required to expand farming output; investments into rural infrastructure for the transportation and storage of bulk commodities; and statutory marketing boards that negotiated farm gate prices on behalf of Australian growers in domestic and international markets (Argent 2011). While agriculture remained strongly export-oriented, an apparatus of institutional support structures shielded it from the vicissitudes of global markets, ensuring the expansion and stability of the sector.

By the late 1970s, the situation had changed dramatically. A global economic crisis, oil price shocks, and the collapse of the Bretton Woods system of fixed exchange gave rise to a new ideology that celebrated market efficiency and competition rather than Keynesian state involvement as the key drivers of agricultural development (Pritchard & Tonts 2011). Over a period of more than two decades, Australian governments largely dismantled the institutional structures that had supported the farming sector thus far, arguing that it was the very system of government intervention and support prevailing until then that had distorted market forces and stifled innovation in the sector. Hence, the 1980s and 1990s saw a great reversal of previous agricultural support policies as politicians began to implement a comprehensive program of domestic agricultural deregulation that culminated in the removal of virtually all government support for Australian agriculture while increasing the farm sector's exposure to (global) market forces (Lawrence et al. 2019).

The dismantling of state support and declining terms of trade have taken a heavy toll on the institutional legacies characterizing Australian farm ownership and production patterns. For decades, pressures to "get big or get out" have been forcing the least competitive farmers out of the sector. According to the Australian Productivity Commission, between 1982 and 2002, the total number of Australian farms declined by around a quarter from approximately 178,000 to 132,000, while average farm size increased from 2,720 to 3,340 hectares, an increase of 23 percent (2005, p. 31). Among the remaining farmers, socio-economic differences in terms of output and efficiency are widening, with the top 20 percent of Australia's broadacre farms accounting for around 64 percent of production. Linked to the shift toward larger farm sizes, there have also been striking differences in the rates of return on capital. While cash incomes for the smallest 25 percent of broadacre farms have been consistently negative, the 25 percent largest broadacre farms obtained an average annual rate of return on capital of 7 percent if the effects of capital appreciation are included (Pritchard et al. 2012, p. 28).

The restructuring of Australia's agricultural sector has also had important consequences for the structure and availability of farm finance. While up to the late 1970s, the lion's share of farm credit was publicly facilitated or sourced from policy banks, corporate and financial-sector interests have emerged as new sources of agricultural funding, with many of them concerned more about creating value for their shareholders than to provide long-term support to the farming sector (Larder et al. 2018, p. 7). Much, albeit not all, of this funding has come from abroad, generally linked to countries figuring prominently among Australian export markets. Before the 1970s, the United States was both a major export market and a big investor. Between the 1970s and 1990s, this position shifted to Japan and Korea, while the first two decades of the new millennium were dominated by China (and other Asian countries) as well as the Middle East (Keogh & Tomlinson 2014). Others that have filled the financing gap left by the retreat of the state were overseas pension funds such as the U.S.-based Teacher Insurance and Annuity Association (TIAA) or the Canadian Public Sector Pension Investment Board, who, between 2007 and 2017, invested in excess of 1 billion AUD in Australian agricultural assets (Anthony 2017). While few Australian commentators question the reliance of the agriculture sector on market-based finance, the lack of interest by domestic superannuation funds and institutional investors has been the cause of some criticism, with experts warning against putting the future of Australian agriculture "solely in the hands of disengaged foreign agri-giants who have no stake in developing Australia's bush communities" (Anthony 2017, p. 6).

What has the neoliberal turn meant for land ownership in Australia? A 2012 report by University of Sydney researchers identified a dual pattern of fragmentation and aggregation (Pritchard et al. 2012). While farmland near cities is being broken up into smaller "lifestyle" plots, agricultural land in more remote areas is being consolidated into large holdings by big corporate players. These trends have reconfigured relationships between farmland ownership and management. Today, the traditional model of family-owned and operated farms is giving way to more complex legal arrangements, including partnerships and trusts, where hired farm managers run agricultural businesses on behalf of corporate owners. Corporate ownership has also driven the geographical diversification of agricultural holdings across several properties in different regions. Deregulation of the sector has meant that, today, Australian farmers are among the world's least subsidized, with many of them relying on inflows of capital investment to fund economic growth. The role of corporate and financial capital, both domestic and foreign, and the corporatization of farming have not been welcomed by everyone. Already today, increasing farmland prices have put agriculture out of reach for many younger Australians. Smaller family-operated farms also find it increasingly difficult to compete with corporate farming businesses, which enjoy the advantages of higher capitalization rates and geographically diversified property portfolios allowing them to better withstand the climate extremes that, more than ever, challenge agricultural producers. It is against this background that we must now examine Chinese farmland ownership in Australia.

## Chinese investments and shifting land ownership patterns in Australia

Despite sustained public interest in the matter, little information about investment from China in Australian farmland is openly available, making a detailed mapping of Chinese farmland ownership a notoriously difficult task. Each of Australia's six states and two territories collects information on land ownership in state-based land titles databases, but different data structures make it challenging to share and compare data across jurisdictions. Not only is the data inconsistent and often of low quality but it also comes with a hefty price tag. State governments charge hundreds to thousands of dollars for each dataset, and some of the data are released in proprietary formats, requiring expensive software for analysis (Nicholas et al. 2021). As a result, information about who owns Australia's farmland has remained largely out of reach for individual citizens and researchers, and even the national government has been struggling to marshal data from land titles databases for generating insights into nationwide patterns of land ownership change (Pritchard et al. 2012).

With information about individual land ownership buried in a messy system of incompatible data frameworks and millions of land titles, the only option remaining is to resort to aggregate statistics about Chinese investment in Australian farmland. One institution that provides such statistics is the Australian Taxation Office (ATO). Since the revision of Australia's foreign investment regime in 2015, the ATO is in charge of compiling the *Register of Foreign Ownership of Agricultural Land*. Published annually, this report lists shares of foreign land ownership across different states and territories and by types of land use. For 2022, the *Register* listed China as the largest agricultural landholder, owning 2.0 percent of Australian farmland, followed by the United Kingdom with 1.9 percent, Canada with 0.7 percent, and the United States and Netherlands with 0.6 percent each (ATO 2022). The report showed that Chinese investors owned 7.7 million hectares of leasehold, a land title connected to pastoral activities, as well as 830,000 hectares of freehold used for cropping.

The data made available by the *Register* hide as much as they reveal. The most crucial weakness lies in their central analytical category—that of "foreignness." According to the methodology applied by the *Register*, a land deal is either classified as foreign—if a non-Australian entity holds an interest of at least 20 percent—or as domestic, in case non-Australian ownership is below that threshold. Representing information about land ownership as a foreign-domestic dichotomy may appear straightforward, but, in fact, it flattens complex investment landscapes characterized by fluid webs of ownership—an observation that also holds true in many other places affected by the global land rush (see Fairbairn 2015 for the case of Brazil). Indeed, many of the Chinese companies I have come across during my research had multiple ownership structures that could not be easily linked to any one national territory. Rather than constituting a unitary Chinese entity, these companies were made up of a dizzying network of subsidiaries and holding companies, making it extremely challenging to pin down ultimate ownership. Yet others were listed on international stock exchanges or operated through private equity funds. In the case of New Hope Group, for example, one of China's largest agribusiness corporations in Australia, investments were co-financed via the group's own private equity arm, involving such high-profile international investors as Singapore's sovereign wealth fund Temasek, the International Finance Corporation (IFC)—a member of the World Bank Group, or U.S.-based agribusiness firm Archer Daniels Midland (ADM) (see Chapter 4). To identify New Hope Group's investments in Australian agriculture as "Chinese" is not wrong, but it obscures the cosmopolitan and, indeed, also Western origins of the capital supporting the company's overseas expansion. International capital support for China's agricultural expansion overseas also suggests that there is an alignment of elite interests across national borders. As Klinger and Muldavin (2019) aptly point out:

> [d]espite alarmist rhetoric that periodically issues from the capitals of Europe and North America, the governments and financial institutions of these places are financing China's overseas activities and therefore have a tangible stake in China's banks and firms making a return on their investments.
>
> (p. 11)

Another shortcoming of the *Register* is its hectare-centric focus. By measuring foreign ownership based on land area, the report overemphasizes size over productivity (Smith et al. 2022). Much of the remoter parts of Australia are made up of low-value grazing land—it's "a big, brown place," as one of the Australian investment managers of a Chinese company put it in an interview with me (February 2017, Sydney). These properties are often unirrigated and remote with limited carrying capacities that allow for only the most extensive forms of animal husbandry. Grazing properties are many times larger than most cropping or horticulture farms, yet they produce far less value by hectare. Nonetheless, public scrutiny seems to concentrate mostly on the size of the properties changing hands, while investments in small but high-value farms have remained very much below the radar. But one could even go further. Agriculture and investment do not stop at the farm gate. Even more value is produced further downstream in the supply chain when agricultural commodities are turned into food brands through processing, labeling, and marketing. Yet, the *Register*, whose express purpose is to provide information on foreign land ownership, does not trace investment beyond the farm. To be sure, farmland is of high symbolic value and much more intertwined with Australian national identity than a food business or processing plant, yet the myopic focus on farmland has obscured the fact that Chinese investors have spent more money on buying Australian agribusinesses than on acquiring farmland.

Curiously then, the *Register*, while hailed as a key component in the revision of Australia's foreign investment regime, has not brought much clarity to the debate about foreign influence in Australia's food and farming sector. If anything, it has further entrenched a public framing of Chinese investment as land-focused, state-driven, and directed toward ensuring food security. At the same time, it has obscured the transnational capital interests that have propelled the expansion of Chinese companies in Australia.

My data tell a different story. Covering the period 2011 through 2019, I have produced the most comprehensive mapping of Chinese purchases of Australian farmland that, to my knowledge, exists to date. The information I collected is based on a systematic review of media reports, corporate and financial documents, as well as personal interviews. For every land deal, my dataset included information on land area, land use, location, and investment value—where available. On the investor side, I traced the ultimate owner of the acquiring entity and categorized it by investor type, distinguishing between privately and government-owned companies as well as joint ventures between one or several private Chinese and Australian companies. I used a similar data structure to gather information on Chinese investments in Australian food and agri-businesses. Table A.1 (see Appendix) presents a simplified overview of all land deals that I could confirm during this research project, while Figure 1.2 (see introduction) maps out the geographical distribution of the deals. Table A.2 in the Appendix displays equivalent information on all Chinese investments in Australian agribusiness, while Table A.3 lists investment deals that were announced but ultimately aborted.

My mapping has not only served as an entry point through which to identify individual actors but also added nuance to the official knowledge about China's land rush as represented in Australia's farmland register.[2] First, my data show that most Chinese land deals focus on the production of beef and dairy. Close to two-thirds of all investments are concentrated in the beef cattle and dairy sector, whereas investment in food crops and horticulture accounts for only 20 percent (see Figure 3.1). As we have seen in the previous chapter, there has been growing interest of China's urban and more affluent consumers in "high-quality" animal proteins from lean meats and dairy, promising handsome profits for companies able to control imports to China, but it is important to remember that these "lifestyle" foods are not at the center of China's food security strategy. Second, private investors and joint ventures with Australian companies clearly dominate the investment landscape. Only 3 percent of land deals I could confirm for this research were linked to state-owned companies (see Figure 3.2), but this relationship

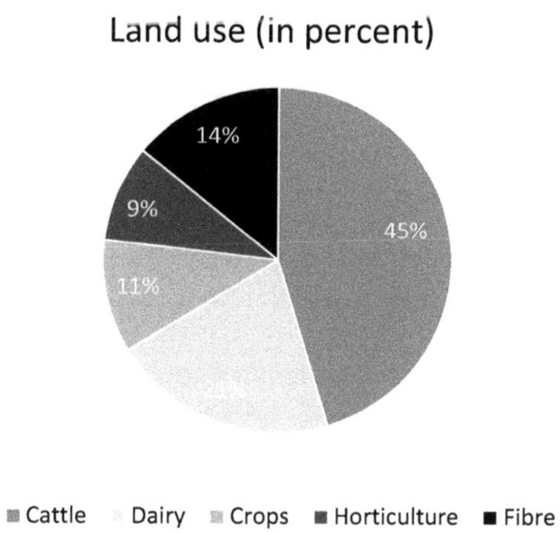


*Figure 3.1* Land use of Chinese-owned Australian farmland by investment value, 2011–2019.

*Source:* Author's database.

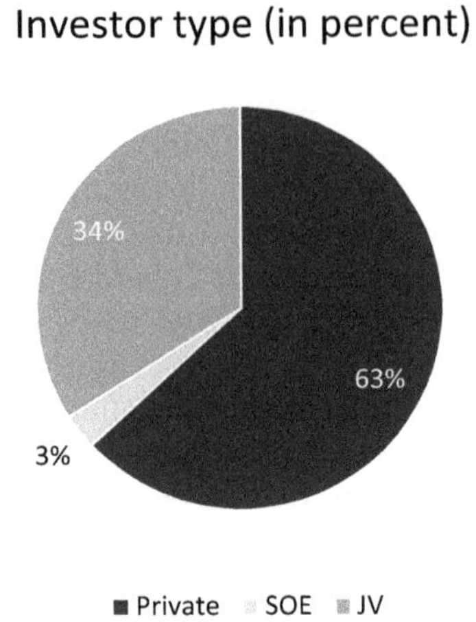


*Figure 3.2* Investor type acquiring Australian farmland by investment value, 2011–2019.

*Source:* Author's database.

reverses when looking at investments in food processing and mergers and acquisitions of agribusiness companies. In the latter case, an astonishing 82 percent of all deals are linked to Chinese SOEs. This suggests that the Chinese state is decidedly *not* interested in burdening itself with the risks and uncertainties of operating farms in Australia and, instead, is steering its companies toward investments that promise control over supply chains and trade. This is also supported when, third, examining the amount spent on buying farms versus acquiring agribusinesses. As my data reveal, over 1 billion AUD more were spent on the acquisition of dairy processing companies, abattoirs, and meat packaging plants than on buying Australian farmland (see Figure 3.3), with the Chinese state in the lead. This calls into question the usefulness of farmland as a category through which to make sense of China's agri-food ambitions on the global stage. Fourth, my data on investor type also call into question the often-assumed leading role of sovereign wealth funds in China's global land rush. Contrary to common assumptions, I could not confirm a single land deal by a Chinese sovereign wealth fund, although, to be fair, the Chinese Investment Corporation (CIC), the country's leading sovereign wealth fund, did make several statements announcing its interest in Australian agriculture in the early 2010s. China's sovereign wealth funds have been indirectly involved in China's agricultural expansion, e.g., by providing financing for China's agribusiness expansion in the grain trade via state-owned agribusiness behemoth COFCO, but overall, the role and impact of these state-owned financial entities appear to be grossly overstated (Sippel et al. 2018). Finally, my databank also makes clear that the total number of Chinese entities buying Australian farmland is surprisingly small, with no more

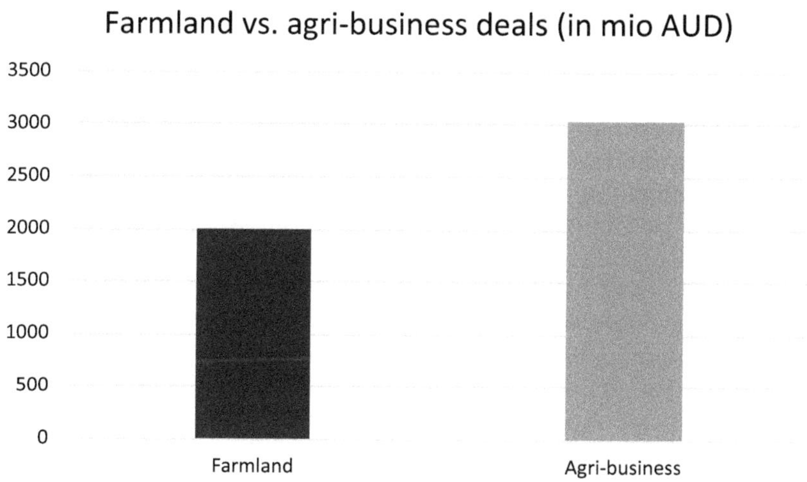


*Figure 3.3* Value of Chinese investments in Australian farmland versus agribusiness, 2011–2019.

*Source:* Author's database.

than two dozen firms involved. Of those that do invest, however, many acquire more than just one property. Owning a geographically diversified farm portfolio is a key strategy in mitigating the risks from climate change and drought, other research on the land rush in Australia and also my interviews confirmed—and one that Chinese investors share with big corporate farms and institutional investors (see Smith et al. 2022).

In many countries around the world, "legal requirements of 'financial secrecy'" (Oliveira 2018, p. 115) that protect investor interests have created significant knowledge gaps about the nature of China's land rush—and Australia is no exception. In the absence of transparent information about who is investing, in what sectors, and for which purpose, speculation about a state-led campaign to ensure China's food security has taken the place of informed debate. The revision of Australia's foreign investment regime was meant to address the lack of knowledge around Chinese ownership of Australian farmland, but while the new rules make more deals subject to a non-public review process by the state, the Australian public knows little more than before about the Chinese entities buying farmland and even less about the entanglements of Australian and international interests in these deals. As the next section will show, the state's monopoly on information has given rise to a "politics of knowledge" (Sippel & Weldon 2020) centered on the question whether Chinese investment is good or bad for Australia. This framing has diverted public attention from the deeper consolidation processes that have been reshaping land access, farm size, and profit opportunities in Australia's agricultural sector.

## Land politics: re-regulating foreign ownership of Australian farmland

On a hot February day in 2017, a distinguished group of Chinese and Australian agribusiness managers, food investors, farmland brokers, and government officials gathered in an office building in Melbourne's central business district for a summit on "Chinese Investment in the Australian Agribusiness Sector." Organized by the Australia China Business Council (ACBC)—an Australian industry peak body dedicated to promoting business and trade between Australia and China—the summit promised to give attendants greater insights into the issues and pathways to successful Chinese investment in the Australian food and farming sector. Among the speakers present at the event was the Australian manager of a large and well-known Chinese agribusiness firm with significant investments in the Australian agri-food sector. "What's really driving all of this is the Asian middle class," the manager described the company's investment rationale to his keenly listening audience. With a focus on "high-quality animal protein" and Australia's "clean, green, and safe" image, the manager was confident his company's investments would have the potential to "unlock the consumption patterns" of increasingly urban and wealthy consumers in China and the Asian region. And this, he emphasized, meant profits not only for Chinese investors but also for Australia's farm sector.[3]

The message the manager left his audience with is in many ways emblematic of the "dining boom" narrative which, in the early 2010s, gained hold among Australian industry leaders and policymakers. The hope was for Australia to capitalize on growing Chinese demand for safe, high-quality food by boosting production and improving market access, similar to the ways in which the continent had responded to Chinese demand for natural resources during the "mining boom" of the 2000s. Chinese investment was seen as part of the equation and a necessary catalyst to grow Australian exports to the burgeoning Chinese middle class. But the activities of Chinese investors proved to be surprisingly controversial and, very much from the get-go, provoked calls for a stricter regulation of farmland access.

In Australia, foreign land ownership is regulated by the *Foreign Acquisitions and Takeovers Act* from 1975. The *Act* is generally permissive of farmland purchases by foreigners with two exceptions: acquisitions by foreign entities and individuals above a designated monetary threshold must undergo review by the government as well as all land acquisitions by foreign governments, regardless of their investment value. The review is conducted by the Foreign Investment Review Board (FIRB), a non-statutory body that advises the Australian treasurer and government on foreign investment matters. If deemed against the national interest, the land deal under review can be canceled by the treasurer.

As China's land rush began to make headlines in the Australian media, around 2010, a coalition of critical politicians from across Australia's political spectrum began to advocate for a revision of Australia's foreign investment framework.[4] One key argument was that the monetary threshold triggering a review by the government was exceedingly high. With a volume set at 231 million AUD, few land deals would be large enough to rise to the attention of the regulators, critics argued. In this view, bringing down the threshold and thus subjecting more investments to an assessment by the government was essential if Australia were to retain control over foreign farmland ownership. To increase transparency around foreign investor interest in Australian farmland, critics also demanded to publish all foreign investment proposals in a public database—a suggestion that would have revolutionized Australian business disclosure policies. Finally, early proponents of a revision of Australia's foreign investment framework called for stricter guidelines determining what is and what isn't in Australia's national interest. Until then, the FIRB and the Australian treasurer had enjoyed a significant amount of discretion in determining which land deals to approve and which ones to block, with little accountability to the Australian public. Indeed, while few foreign farmland purchases had triggered the national interest test in the years prior, given the high monetary threshold, fewer even had been rejected by the state.

Debates around the re-regulation of Australia's foreign investment regime had been catalyzed by a number of highly publicized land deals involving foreign entities. One of the earliest, Hassad Australia, was from Qatar rather than China, but its status as the overseas investment arm of Qatar's sovereign wealth fund resonated with the same concerns about a state-driven food security strategy that had already informed global debates about China's role in the land rush. Established in 2009, Hassad Australia quickly assembled a portfolio of 13 farms with a total farmland area of 250,000 hectares—20 times the arable land area of Qatar (Sippel 2015, p. 986). The company focused on wool, grain, and sheep production, with an export target of 100,000 lambs annually to Qatar. Although the company was primarily run by Australians, presenting a familiar face and management style to the wider public, its outspoken goal to "grow food and ship it to Qatar" (Sippel 2015, p. 991), ensuring food security in a country highly dependent on food imports, sounded the alarm among many pundits critical of Australia's laissez-faire attitude toward foreign land deals. In a senate hearing on foreign farmland ownership, Australia's National Farmers' Federation warned that in the wake of the global food price crisis, foreign governments were emerging as new farmland investors, seeking food security rather than commercial profits (Economic Legislation Committee 2011, p. 45), the corollary being a shrinking market for Australian farmers. The discursive link between national governments, food security, and farmland investment had been firmly established, and Chinese companies were soon to be seen by almost everyone as a prime example.

The concerns about China were curious, given the absence of any early Chinese investments even remotely resembling Hassad's, and probably owed more to Chinese-Australian histories in the mining sector, where SOEs have dominated, than to what was going on in Australian farming. Yet, such concerns struck a chord with both the Australian public and some politicians, as several senate committees began to look into the issue of re-regulating foreign farmland ownership. One early Chinese investment case that attracted particular attention was that of Cubbie Station. Located in Queensland and spanning close to 100,000 hectares, Cubbie Station was one of Australia's largest irrigated farming properties. A Chinese-Australian consortium had won the highly controversial bid, receiving approval by then-treasurer Wayne Swan in 2012, but the public and critical politicians were up in arms over the sale of such a large area of high-value, irrigated farmland to a Chinese-controlled consortium. Although the Chinese partner in the joint venture, Shandong Ruyi, had been privatized in 2001 as part of China's market reforms and was now traded publicly on the Shenzhen stock exchange, a senate committee investigation appeared particularly concerned about the potential non-commercial nature of the deal. The fear was that, beholden to the Chinese government, the new Cubbie owners would sell to China at a discount, thereby undercutting market prices and harming other Australian producers. Moreover, if Chinese investors traded their products with Chinese entities at below market rate, they would artificially lower their profits and, hence, avoid paying a fair tax share to the Australian government. Made to appear before the committee, Shandong Ruyi's Australian partner Lempriere emphasized that "[...] we have every incentive to maximize the profitability of this business within Australia [and no interest in selling] for anything less than the full price" (RRATRC 2013, p. 61), but these pronouncements did little to change the widely shared Australian perception that, in one form or another, the Chinese state coordinates and controls the activities of all Chinese companies. As a manager of the National Farmers' Federation put it in an interview with me: "I suppose to an extent, all large companies in China have some sort of connection to the Chinese Communist Party, whether that's formal or otherwise" (interview March 2017, Canberra). The senate committee, too, expressed reservation over the way in which the deal had been assessed by the FIRB and the treasurer, calling for a more transparent approval procedure (RRATRC 2013, pp. 59–64).

The case of Cubbie Station as an early catalyst in the debate about re-regulating Australian farmland ownership is not only curious for the absence of a state-owned entity in the deal but also for the type of commodity produced on the farm—cotton. As a non-edible fiber, cotton would clearly not be the first investment choice of a foreign government concerned about national food security. Yet, China had become widely identified as one of those countries whose government was seeking to ensure food security at home by buying farmland abroad. Public opinion polls regularly saw China rank in the top when it came to concerns over strategic food security investments at the expense of Australia's commercial interest, with 57 percent of Australians saying that the Australian government was allowing too much investment from China (Sanyal 2014, p. 19).

Despite criticism that Australia risked "selling out the farm" to foreign interests, the government's overall position on foreign purchases of Australian farmland remained largely positive. As a country with a small population and limited financial resources, foreign investment had long been seen as a cornerstone of national development by generations of government coalitions across the political spectrum. Exporting around 60 percent of its agricultural output (Lawrence et al. 2013), Australian agriculture is highly dependent on overseas markets, and nobody doubted that growing demand from China would present the next growth opportunity. According to projections from the Australian Bureau of Agriculture and Resource Economics (ABARES), by 2050, the value of Chinese beef imports alone would increase by a breathtaking 985 percent to 8.3 billion USD (Hamshere et al. 2014, pp. 21–22), with Australia seen to be ideally positioned to capitalize on this appetite for more Western-style diets. And while there were misgivings about "strategic" investment by foreign governments, there was an overwhelming consensus among Australia's political and business elites that the country required substantial amounts of commercial foreign capital, including from China, if it were to remain competitive in the race for China's lucrative markets. So, when a Liberal-National coalition government under Prime Minister Tony Abbott finally set out to revise Australia's foreign investment regime, it had to strike a balance between tackling concerns around foreign governments pursuing food security while maintaining Australia's reputation as being "open for business." The result has been a new legal framework that has given the Australian government greater regulatory flexibility in managing foreign land deals but has utterly ignored the deeper questions around land consolidation, commodification, and corporate control that have gone hand in hand with the deregulation of Australia's farming sector.

### *Aligning elite interests through regulatory flexibility*

In place since 2015, Australia's new foreign investment rules introduced two main changes. First, as recommended by the various senate committees reviewing the country's foreign investment regime, the threshold triggering an investment review was lowered from previously 231 million AUD to a cumulative value of 15 million AUD. As my database shows, of the individual land deals for which the transaction value is publicly known, more than half would have been subject to government approval under the new rules, and even more when taking into account cumulative investments by one and the same entity. Under the old rules, only four out of 53 deals would have been above the designated monetary threshold. The second change concerned the creation of a public land register tracking foreign ownership of Australian farmland. However, unlike earlier proponents might have hoped, the register did not list individual deals, instead providing aggregate statistics only, the shortcomings of which I have discussed above. What is most interesting about the revision of Australia's foreign investment regime, however, is not what the new rules addressed but what they did *not* address: the national interest (Sippel & Weldon 2020). Earlier discussions had made clear that critics saw a key problem in the fact that there was no legal definition stipulating what actually *was* Australia's national interest when it came to foreign farmland ownership, leaving that decision entirely to the FIRB and the Australian treasurer to be decided on a case-by-case basis. Yet, with the national interest being left undefined under the new rules, lower screening thresholds have arguably done little to increase government accountability on foreign farmland investment, instead giving regulators more discretionary power over which deals to approve and which ones to reject.

Not regulating the national interest has not only enhanced the Australian government's discretionary power to accept or reject foreign land deals but also diverted attention from a wider debate over the types of land ownership that would be in the interest of Australians. To be clear, the agricultural sector surely needs capital. Investment in resource-saving technologies, sustainable farming practices, and people is indispensable if agriculture is to meet the challenges of today and the future—from mitigating climate change to sustaining rural livelihoods and communities. But not every land deal is environmentally sustainable and socially responsible. Investment may also be driven by speculation about profits from rising farmland values or follow strategic exit plans, seeking to reap high returns from fluctuations in commodity prices—with little benefit for rural communities and the environment. Foreign land deals do not have to fall into the latter category, but the lack of a clear definition specifying what beneficial investment should look like introduces much room for backroom dealing and favoritism, ultimately benefitting the privileged few over the wider group of farmers and rural communities. As one farm group representative responded when asked about whether farmers felt that the national interest test had encouraged productive investment:

> I can't say that's felt by a lot of farmers across the board because they're just seeing land purchased, and it's not being any more productive than it previously was. [...] Investment should be about increasing productivity, increasing efficiency, ensuring that good infrastructure is there to help the supply chain. These are the things, to me, that good investment looks like. If investment is to continue doing the same and not making improvement, then it's questionable what the reason is why they're investing.
>
> (interview March 2017, Melbourne)

A debate around what constitutes Australia's national interest when it comes to farmland ownership and investment could have also helped to break open the domestic-foreign dichotomy that has shaped public perceptions. For instance, speculation in rising land values is likely going to have negative impacts on rural communities regardless of whether a farm has been acquired by a Chinese company, a U.S.-based pension fund, or a domestic farmland investment vehicle. Conversely, long-term and patient capital targeting sustainable productivity growth or providing additional sources of funding to farmers can be expected to bring social and environmental benefits, again independent of its national origin. Yet, the politics of land ownership remains focused on investor nationality rather than investment type.

How has the reregulation of foreign investment in Australia reshaped investment landscapes on the ground? At first glance, the new investment regime seems to have had a limited impact on investment flows from China. Since the new rules came into effect, the government has approved numerous large-scale land deals, including a 678,100-hectare greenfield project by Chinese investment group Kimberley Agricultural Investment in the Ord irrigation area in northern Western Australia and a string of grazing property purchases by Zhejiang Rifa Group and Harmony Agriculture & Food Company (see appendix). In fact, to date, only one Chinese land deal has been rejected by the Australian government, involving the sale of beef company S Kidman & Co., Australia's largest private land owner, to a private consortium of Chinese investors. There is also little evidence that tightened screening rules have deterred Chinese investors, at least not in a systematic fashion. To be fair, Chinese land deals in Australia plummeted after 2019 and, as of this writing, have not recovered, but the decline of investment is linked to a broader set of macro-economic factors, including stricter controls on outward flows of capital imposed by Chinese regulators in 2016, limited exchanges during the COVID-19 pandemic, and a tense geopolitical climate between China and the West. There is equally little evidence that the new screening rules, when introduced, hardened Australian regulators' traditionally welcoming stance toward Chinese investment. "Regulations have changed," an investment officer working for the Australian Trade and Investment Commission (Austrade) told me back in 2017, "but the outcome hasn't" (interview March 2017, Canberra).

But while the tightened screening rules for foreign investment rarely resulted in the outright rejection of investment proposals, the government's increased control over the conditions and terms upon which Chinese investors can gain access to Australian agricultural land has played out in more subtle ways. Given that there is no legal definition of the conditions under which to approve or to block an investment proposal, the entirely discretionary nature of the investment screening process vests the government with substantial power to make investment approval conditional on case-by-case commitments from the investor, for example, in terms of deal structure, job creation targets, or plans for further capital investment. Attaching additional conditions to investment approval, it turns out, presents a politically expedient and highly flexible bargaining tool with which to control the terms upon which Chinese investors can purchase Australian agricultural land and businesses.

Here again, the case of S Kidman & Co. provides an instructive example. The initial investment proposal for the S Kidman cattle business came from a

Chinese-owned investor consortium made up by two Chinese real estate and investment firms—Shanghai CRED and Shanghai Pengxin. The Australian government, however, considered the sale of S Kidman to Chinese interests problematic, particularly given S Kidman's significance as one of Australia's largest private landholder and an icon of rural Australia. Following a protracted screening process, the government eventually rejected the Chinese investment proposal, citing the lack of adequate Australian participation as the main factor for its decision (The Treasurer 2016a). What this suggested was that government approval of a foreign investment proposal for the S Kidman portfolio would only be forthcoming if Australian ownership in the investor consortium was substantially increased. In December 2016, an entirely restructured investment group eventually obtained approval to acquire the S Kidman portfolio. The new bidding venture was led by Australian-owned mining and agribusiness group Hancock Prospecting, while Shanghai CRED acted as Hancock's minority partner, contributing 33 percent of the total equity. Shanghai Pengxin, the second Chinese party originally involved in the acquisition of S Kidman, was outmaneuvered altogether and eventually redirected its investment activities to New Zealand and Brazil. To the government, the S Kidman sale presented a successful case of how regulatory flexibility could be harnessed to reconcile the ambivalent attitudes shaping Australia's investment relationship with China. As the government explained in a statement following investment approval, the partnership structure between Hancock Prospecting and Shanghai CRED would ensure that S Kidman remained under Australian control, while providing much needed foreign capital to increase production (The Treasurer 2016b).

Partnerships between Australian agribusiness and Chinese investors are now widely seen as the government's favored blueprint for managing future Chinese investment in Australian food and farmland (Ferguson 2018, p. 15) and have started to shape the ways in which Chinese investors approach investment opportunities in Australian food and farming. While Australia's new investment regime in no way legally restricts Chinese investors from obtaining full ownership of Australian farms, a growing number of Chinese investment proposals have been structured as partnerships with Australian agribusiness interests. "Cooperation [with Australian partners] makes life easier for Chinese investors as they are less likely to be viewed as foreign entities that undermine Australia's national interest," explained a Chinese trade and investment official regarding the new calculus with which Chinese investors are responding to the heightened ambiguity surrounding Australia's foreign investment framework (interview June 2018, Beijing). Recent high-profile investments that have been structured as equity partnerships between Chinese investors and Australian companies include, for instance, Australia Fresh Milk Holdings, an Australia-China investor consortium bringing together Chinese capital with some of Australia's largest dairy companies or, in the processing sector, the joint venture between Australia's Burra Foods and Mengniu Dairy.

*****

Australian regulators have considered the new investment rules a success. "We're kind of aligning our interests here," one investment advisor from the government told me when I asked about how the rules were viewed by Chinese companies and the Australian institutions in charge of foreign investment (interview March 2017, Canberra). But what exactly is being aligned here and in whose interest? Is it enough if Australian agribusinesses are allowed to get in on the deals and share the profits? How much emphasis should there be on creating benefits for rural communities? Is the expansion of dairy factory farms through joint ventures such as Australia Fresh Milk Holdings the right choice for Australia given the ever more visible impacts of climate change and animal welfare concerns? What benefits does foreign farmland investment provide to Australian farms too small to produce for export markets? And what about aspiring farmers who are priced out of the sector by rising land and asset prices? Questions like these cannot be addressed in a fair and comprehensive manner in the case-by-case assessments of investment proposals undertaken by the FIRB and the treasurer. Nor are the decisions on approved deals shared with the Australian public for a periodic review. Australia's new farmland investment regime is therefore above all a missed opportunity for a broad-based social debate posing fundamental questions about the kind of farming sector Australians want and the role that the state as well as corporate and financial capital should play in it. Australian politics did not allow for such a debate. Instead, Australian politicians opted for a populist approach that appeals to anti-Chinese sentiment while catering to the interests of lobby groups and the business community. The utter lack of transparency and accountability in the review process has not helped either. To this date, the Australian public does not have a full overview of who the Chinese are that invest in Australian farmland and what they really want. The next chapter addresses this question.

## Notes

1 Field diary, 2017.

2 My data, like all data, should not be taken to represent an unbiased "reality" of Chinese land deals in Australia as it has been shaped by the particular data gathering methods available to me at the time of this research. Most crucially, using a systematic review of media reports as my starting point to identify Chinese investments and actors involved in the deals has, to a certain extent, reproduced the problematic hectare-centric focus characterizing much of the literature on China's role in the land rush. Even as I sought to triangulate information from media reports through follow-up interviews and company research, this approach has meant that smaller-scale investments in vineyards and horticulture production are likely underrepresented in my database.

3 Reconstructed from field diary notes, 2017.

4 Sippel and Weldon (2020) provide a detailed overview and critical discussion of the revision process.

## References

Anthony, Steven (2017): *Driving Super Fund Investment in Agriculture*. Discussion Paper. Industry Super Australia.

Argent, Neil (2011): Australian Agriculture in the Global Mosaic. In Matthew Tonts, Muhammed Abu B. Siddique (Eds.): *Globalisation, Agriculture and Development. Perspectives from the Asia-Pacific*. Cheltenham: Edward Elgar, pp. 7–28.

Australian Taxation Office (ATO) (2022): Register of Foreign Ownership of Agricultural Land. Report of Registrations as at 30 June 2022. Available online at https://foreigninvestment.gov.au/sites/foreigninvestment.gov.au/files/2023-09/2022-rfo-agricultural-land.pdf, checked on 12/15/2023.

Bureau of Infrastructure, Transport and Regional Economics (BITRE) (2014): The Evolution of Australian Towns. Report 136. Canberra, ACT.

Connors, Tom (1970): Closer Settlement Schemes. In *The Australian Quarterly* 42 (1), pp. 72–85.

Economic Legislation Committee (2011): Foreign Acquisitions Amendment (Agricultural Land) Bill 2010. Canberra, ACT. Available online at https://www.aph.gov.au/Parliamentary_Business/Committees/Senate/Economics/Completed_inquiries/2010-13/foreignacquisitionfarmland2011/report/index, checked on 5/17/2019.

Fairbairn, Madelaine (2015): Foreignization, Financialization and Land Grab Regulation. In *Journal of Agrarian Change* 15 (4), pp. 581–591.

Ferguson, Doug (2018): *Advancing Australian Agriculture in Partnership with Asia*. KPMG (ABARES Outlook Conference, 6 March 2018).

Gammage, Bill (2013): *The Biggest Estate on Earth. How Aborigines Made Australia*. Sydney, Melbourne, Auckland, London: Allen & Unwin.

Hamshere, Patrick; Yu, Sheng; Moir, Brian; Syed, Faraz; Gunning-Trant, Caroline (2014): What China Wants. Analysis of China's Food Demand to 2050. Canberra (ABARES conference paper 14.3).

Keogh, Mick; Tomlinson, Adam (2014): Australia Has an Open Door for Foreign Investment, but Voters Hold the Keys. In *Australian Farm Institute's Quarterly Newsletter*, 11, p. 1.

Klinger, Julie Michelle; Muldavin, Joshua (2019): New Geographies of Development: Grounding China's Global Integration. In *Territory, Politics, Governance* 7 (1), pp. 1–21. DOI: 10.1080/21622671.2018.1559.

Larder, Nicolette; Sippel, Sarah R.; Argent, Neil (2018): The Redefined Role of Finance in Australian Agriculture. In *Australian Geographer* 49 (3), pp. 397–418. DOI: 10.1080/00049182.2017.1388555.

Lawrence, Geoffrey; Sippel, Sarah R.; Larder, Nicolette (2019): State-Led and Finance-Backed Farming Endeavours: Changing Contours of Investment in Australian Agriculture. In Hilde Bjørkhaug, Philip McMichael, Bruce Muirhead (Eds.): *Finance or Food? The Role of Cultures, Values, and Ethics in Land Use Negotiations*. Toronto: University of Toronto Press, pp. 125–152.

Lawrence, Geoffrey; Richards, Carol; Lyons, Kristen (2013): Food Security in Australia in an Era of Neoliberalism, Productivism and Climate Change. In *Journal of Rural Studies* 29, pp. 30–39.

Lockie, Stewart (2000): Crisis and Conflict: Shifting Discourses of Rural and Regional Australia. In Bill Pritchard, Phil McManus (Eds.): *Land of Discontent. The Dynamics of Change in Rural and Regional Australia*. Sydney: University of New South Wales Press, pp. 14–32.

Nicholas, Josh; Wahlquist, Calla; Ball, Andy; Evershed, Nick (2021): The Modern Outback. Who Owns Australia? In *The Guardian*, 5/17/2021. Available online at https://www.theguardian.com/australia-news/ng-interactive/2021/may/17/who-owns-australia, checked on 3/26/2024.

Oliveira, Gustavo de L. T. (2018): Chinese Land Grabs in Brazil? Sinophobia and Foreign Investments in Brazilian Soybean Agribusiness. In *Globalizations* 15 (1), pp. 114–133.

Pritchard, Bill; Neave, Melissa; Hickey, Deanne; Troy, Laurence (2012): *Rural Land in Australia. A Framework for the Measurement and Analysis of Nationwide Patterns of Ownership Change, Aggregation and Fragmentation.* Barton, ACT: RIRDC.

Pritchard, Bill; Tonts, Matthew (2011): Market Efficiency, Agriculture and Prosperity in Rural Australia. In Matthew Tonts, Muhammed Abu B. Siddique (Eds.): *Globalisation, Agriculture and Development. Perspectives from the Asia-Pacific.* Cheltenham: Edward Elgar, pp. 29–53.

Productivity Commission (2005): *Trends in Australian Agriculture. Australian Government.* Canberra (Research Paper).

Rural and Regional Affairs and Transport References Committee (2013): *Foreign Investment and the National Interest.* Canberra: The Senate. Available online at https://www.aph.gov.au/Parliamentary_Business/Committees/Senate/Rural_and_Regional_Affairs_and_Transport/Completed_inquiries/2012-13/firb2011/report/index, checked on 7/2/2016.

Sanyal, Kali (2014): *Foreign Investment in Australian Agriculture.* Parliament of Australia (Parliamentary Library Research Paper, 2013–14). Available online at https://www.aph.gov.au/About_Parliament/Parliamentary_Departments/Parliamentary_Library/pubs/rp/rp1314/ForeignInvest, checked on 7/11/2016.

Sippel, Sarah R.; Weldon, Tim (2020): Redefining Land's Investability: Towards a Neonationalization of Resources in Australia? In *Territory, Politics, Governance.* DOI: 10.1080/21622671.2019.1703797.

Sippel, Sarah R.; Böhme, Michaela; Gharios, Cynthia (2018): Strategic Financialization? The Emergence of Sovereign Wealth Funds in the Global Food System. In Hilde Bjørkhaug, André Magnan, Geoffrey Lawrence (Eds.): *The Financialization of Agri-Food Systems. Contested Transformations.* Abingdon, Oxon, New York, NY: Routledge, pp. 62–84.

Sippel, Sarah R. (2015): Food Security or Commercial Business? Gulf State Investments in Australian Agriculture. In *The Journal of Peasant Studies* 42 (5), pp. 981–1001. DOI: 10.1080/03066150.2014.990448.

Smith, Kia; Langford, Alexandra; Lawrence, Geoffrey (2022): Tracking Farmland Investment in Australia. Institutional Finance and the Politics of Data Mapping. In *Journal of Agrarian Change* 23, pp. 518–546.

Weaver, John C. (1996): Beyond the Fatal Shore: Pastoral Squatting and the Occupation of Australia, 1826 to 1852. In *The American Historical Review* 101 (4), pp. 981–1007.

Whatmore, Sarah (2002): *Hybrid Geographies. Natures, Cultures, Spaces.* London, Thousand Oaks, California: Sage.

The Treasurer (2016a): *Preliminary Decision of Foreign Investment Application for Purchase of S. Kidman & Co Limited.* Available online at http://ministers.treasury.gov.au/ministers/scott-morrison-2015/media-releases/preliminary-decision-foreign-investment-application, checked on 3/25/2019.

The Treasurer (2016b): *Approval of S. Kidman & Co. Limited Sale to Increase Australian Ownership.* Available online at https://ministers.treasury.gov.au/ministers/scott-morrison-2015/media-releases/approval-s-kidman-co-limited-sale-increase-australian, checked on 3/25/2019.

# 4 Who are the Chinese purchasing Australian farmland?

> Australia has a vast landmass, good grasslands and sunshine. It is our hope to bring Australia's beef and mutton into the market of China. We should say these investments are beneficial to Australia and China.[1]
>
> (Liu Yonghao, chairman of New Hope Group)

Liu Yonghao is no timid man. The founder and chairman of Chinese agribusiness giant New Hope Group has invested big time in Australian food and agriculture, and he likes to tell others about it, as the above quote illustrates. His company does not only run a large-scale beef operation but has also co-invested in an intensive cow farm together with key players from Australia's dairy industry. Unlike many of his peers, Liu Yonghao's approach to investment has been widely welcomed in Australia, and he regularly appears on public programs or takes interviews from the press. The Sichuan-born septuagenarian may be one of the few faces that come to the mind of the average Australian when being asked about who the Chinese are that are buying Australian farmland.

With a few exceptions, surprisingly little is known about the people and businesses behind Chinese land deals—despite the huge attention the topic has garnered among Australians. Complex business structures and unfamiliar Chinese names mean there is often not even consensus on how to call the Chinese companies involved in a given deal, leading at times to double-counting of one and the same transaction—but attributed to two or three differently named instances of the same investor. Most investor companies and their representatives in Australia have also liked to keep a low profile, not seeking to draw too much attention to their farming activities in a public climate where Chinese land deals have become a hugely political and emotional issue for many Australians.

Drawing on data from my investment databank and from stakeholder interviews, this chapter presents four Chinese investor archetypes I could identify in my fieldwork: state-owned agribusiness enterprises (SOEs), state farms, private agribusiness corporations, and agri-food entrepreneurs (see Table 4.1). They differ from each other not only in terms of ownership and capital structure but also in relation to their role and development trajectory

DOI: 10.4324/9781003474661-6

*Table 4.1* Typology of Chinese agri-food investors in Australia

| *Type* | *Agribusiness SOE* | *State farm* | *Private agribusiness corporation* | *Agri-food entrepreneur* |
|---|---|---|---|---|
| **Ownership structure** | – Majority or wholly-owned by the central government | – Mostly owned by provincial or local-level governments<br>– Some state farms are under direct ownership and control of MARA | – (Partially) listed on China's stock exchanges but effectively operating as family businesses<br>– Often with deep links to local or even central governments | – (Partially) listed on China's stock exchanges but effectively operating as family businesses<br>– Benefitted from different degrees of state support in building their core business |
| **Role in the Chinese agri-food sector** | – Diversified agribusiness conglomerates<br>– Monopoly positions in China's grain trade; no direct involvement in farming | – Production of key crops such as corn, wheat, soy, sugar, rubber but also animal protein<br>– Downstream integration into food processing | – Diversified and vertically integrated agribusiness conglomerates<br>– Focus on feed, processing, or retail in sectors such as pork, beef, poultry, and dairy | – Newcomers to the agri-food sector who made their fortunes with other businesses<br>– Some enter the sector in China and then expand overseas; others enter the sector through overseas agri-investment and export back to China |
| **Overseas investment strategy** | – Investment in trade infrastructure, logistics, processing | – Involved in purchasing or leasing of overseas farmland | – Diversified overseas investment strategies, incl. land purchases and acquisitions of food processing companies or brands | – Diversified overseas investment strategies, mostly focused on farmland with some cases of investment in agribusiness further downstream the value chain (processors, feedlots, abattoirs) |
| **Sources of capital for overseas expansion** | – Preferential access to state funding<br>– Attract co-investment from international sources of institutional investment | – Preferential access to state funding | – Mostly internal cash resources and commercial loans from Chinese and international banks<br>– The largest private agribusinesses are able to attract international capital by setting up/ cooperating with investment funds | – Overseas expansion largely funded through internal cash resources and commercial loans from Chinese and international banks |
| **Number of investors** | 2 (+ subsidiaries operating independently) | 1 | 8 | 12 |

*Source:* Elaborated by the author based on fieldwork in Australia and China throughout 2017 and 2018.

in China's domestic agriculture sector. As I will detail in this chapter, it is these differences that make for radically different approaches when these companies and their executives venture overseas to invest in food and farming. For each of the four investor archetypes, I present one real-life case study from my field research, describing the background and history of the company in case, its relationship to the Chinese state, and the push and pull factors driving its investments in Australia. Much attention in the Anglophone literature on China's land rush has been placed on the role of SOEs and, to a lesser extent, private agribusiness corporations, but there has been little information about the peculiar type of the Chinese state farm—a business entity which, despite ownership by the state, has little in common with the more well-known agribusiness SOEs that have received much attention from scholars and the media alike. Likewise, agri-food entrepreneurs have not been previously identified as key actors in China's agricultural "going out," yet, in Australia, it is them rather than the state-owned agribusiness behemoths who are the driving force behind the purchase of farmland.

The four case studies presented in this chapter show that classifying Chinese businesses by ownership along a state-private dichotomy is not sufficient to understand what is driving Chinese companies to invest in Australia and which strategies these investors are employing. It is also insufficient to understand why some investors fail so spectacularly while others succeed. Lee (2018) eloquently makes this point in her work on Chinese investments in Zambia when she warns of the "false homogenization" (p. 4) implied by the label "Chinese" investment. "Instead of the appearance of ownership and nationality, it is the interest of capital that is of the essence," she notes (Lee 2018).

As with any typology, these categories are not absolute and immutable but, in practice, often fluid and blurred. Yet, they offer a useful entry point into making sense of the variations of Chinese agri-investment in Australia beyond the simple state-private dichotomy offered by much early analysis on the land rush.

## Agribusiness SOEs

Well-known examples of Chinese agribusiness SOEs are the China National Cereals, Oils and Foodstuffs Corporation (COFCO), China National Agricultural Development Group Corporation (CNADGC), or ChemChina. These companies do not only play a key role in China's domestic agri-food industry but are also the most visible group of actors engaged in China's agricultural "going out" strategy. Under direct supervision of the central government through the State-Owned Assets Supervision and Administration Commission (SASAC), central agribusiness SOEs are charged with the procurement, processing, trade, and storage of grain supplies and key foodstuffs and are leading entities in the development of agricultural inputs and technologies the government considers crucial to safeguarding China's food production capacity. Agribusiness SOEs are also the biggest importers of agricultural commodities to China and are preferentially allocated import rights for those key grains (e.g., rice, wheat, corn) over which the Chinese government retains control via tariff rate quotas (TRQ). For instance, in 2018, around 90 percent of the 9-million-ton tariff rate quota for wheat was allocated to one state-owned agribusiness company alone, COFCO, while hundreds of private companies competed for the remaining quota (Zhang 2019, p. 254).

Agribusiness SOEs are also at the forefront of China's agricultural "going out" policy. Since the policy's formal inception in 2006, these companies have been leading China's overseas agricultural investment in terms of investment volume and deal size. A report by the Ministry of Agriculture and Rural Affairs (MARA) on China's overseas agricultural investment corporation found that while central agribusiness SOEs accounted for only 5.6 percent of Chinese companies investing in overseas agricultural assets in 2015, they were responsible for 40.1 percent of all funds invested in that year (MARA 2016, p. 57). Indeed, central agribusiness SOEs lead the list of foreign investment deals across all sectors of the Chinese economy, with ChemChina's acquisition of Swiss biotechnology and agrochemical giant Syngenta in February 2016 for 44 billion USD representing the largest foreign takeover ever undertaken by a Chinese corporation.

Given the magnitude of these deals, it is not surprising that many of them are premised on high levels of political and financial support. Contrary to conventional wisdom, however, the story of Chinese state-owned agribusinesses' expansion overseas does not play out around the acquisition of large swaths of farmland for agricultural production but centers on mergers and acquisitions (M&As) of major transnational agribusiness companies operating upstream and downstream of farming itself as well as of infrastructure and logistics assets throughout the world's key agricultural export regions. As we have seen in Chapter 2, the growing significance of agri-food imports and trade in China's domestic food economy has impressed on Chinese policymakers the need to wrest greater control over the flows and profits of global agri-food trade. By acquiring agricultural multinationals and trade and logistics infrastructure across the world, China's emerging global agribusiness giants have transformed themselves from formerly passive buyers into formidable competitors, vying with the mostly North Atlantic-based agri-food multinationals such as the ABCDs for market share and pricing power in international grain markets (Zhang 2019; Belesky & Lawrence 2018). In the words of Keulertz and Woertz (2016), "China is preparing to compete with the Cargills and Nestlés of this world rather than just gobbling up farmland in the upstream sector" (p. 42). As one of China's most high-profile central agribusiness SOEs, COFCO's overseas expansion strategy, including its activities in Australia, are emblematic of the central government's attempt to groom a group of internationally competitive agribusiness giants.

*Profile: COFCO*

Founded in 1949, the China National Cereals, Oils and Foodstuffs Corporation—in short COFCO (*Zhongliang Jituan* 中粮集团)—is China's largest food and agribusiness company, as well as the country's monopoly importer and exporter of key agricultural commodities. Since its inception as the first state-owned agribusiness and grain trader of the newly founded People's Republic of China, COFCO has transformed itself from a single grain and oil trading company into China's largest food processing company, integrating a large network of subsidiaries that operate in all main categories of Chinese daily consumption, including grains, sugar, cotton, edible oil and oilseed crushing, meat and dairy products, tea, and even wine (COFCO 2017). As the company proudly proclaims on its website, its trade, processing, and production operations feed "nearly a quarter of the world's population" (COFCO 2017).

COFCO's role as a policy company under direct supervision by the central government has not precluded its listing on the stock market. Of COFCO's 18 subsidiaries, 15 are publicly listed on stock exchanges in Hong Kong or mainland China (COFCO 2017). Indeed, motivated by a desire to reform China's ailing state-owned sector, since the mid-2000s, government officials have encouraged stock market listings as a popular avenue for China's SOEs to raise funds from the capital market with which to finance business development and growth while the peculiar shareholding structure common to many SOEs has ensured the continued majority ownership of the state.[2] For COFCO, exposure to domestic and international stock markets has arguably been a key driver in the company's transformation into one of China's key agribusiness SOEs.

Moreover, COFCO has been at the forefront of consolidating China's state-owned agribusiness sector in an effort to reduce domestic competition considered harmful to the government's goal to foster a group of internationally competitive agribusiness giants. Since 2004, COFCO has taken over nine predominantly state-owned domestic agribusiness corporations (Zhang 2019, p. 250). In 2016, COFCO merged with cotton monopoly trader Chinatex (*Zhongfang Jituan* 中纺集团), whose cotton operations in Australia and globally have been integrated into COFCO's trading activities (see Table 4.2). The only privately owned agribusiness transformed into a subsidiary of COFCO so far is Mengniu Dairy (*Mengniu Jituan* 蒙牛集团), China's second largest dairy manufacturing and distribution company. In 2009, Mengniu Dairy sold a 20 percent stake to an investor consortium comprising COFCO and international dairy giants Danone and Arla Foods, following its implication in one of China's most egregious dairy scandals that brought the company to the brink of insolvency.[3] The deal not only made the central government a major shareholder in the previously private agribusiness company but also resulted in significant international ownership. Today, Mengniu has not only rebounded as a major dairy company in China's domestic market

*Table 4.2* COFCO business operations and related agri-investments in Australia

| | COFCO *(since 1949)* | | | |
|---|---|---|---|---|
| *Subsidiaries with operations in Australia* | COFCO International | Mengniu Dairy | Chinatex | COFCO Tunhe Sugar |
| *Key business information* | – Established in 2017 as COFCO's new grain trading platform integrating the assets of Noble Agri and Nidera<br>– Headquartered in Geneva, Switzerland<br>– Public listing planned by the end of 2020 | – Established in 1999 as private company<br>– Headquartered in Hohhot, Inner Mongolia<br>– Since 2004 listed on the Hong Kong stock exchange<br>– Sold 20% stake to COFCO-led investor consortium in 2009; COFCO's stake has further increased to 27.01% in 2019 | – Founded in 1951 as SOE<br>– Headquartered in Beijing<br>– Not publicly listed<br>– Merged with COFCO in 2016 as part of the current policy effort to consolidate SOEs | – Established in 1993 as COFCO subsidiary<br>– Listed on the Shanghai stock exchange<br>– Headquartered in Changji, Xinjiang province |
| *Agri-investments in Australia (2010–2018)* | – Construction of grain terminal at Port Kembla in collaboration with Cargill | – Acquisition of 79% stake in dairy processor Burra Foods<br>– Acquisition of infant formula maker Bellamy's<br>– Attempted Acquisition of formerly Japanese-owned dairy processor Lion Dairy & Drinks | – No recent acquisitions in the time period under investigation for this study (2010–2018)<br>– In 2003, acquisition of 5.000-hectare broadacre farm near Moree, NSW | – Acquisition of sugar processing company Tully Sugar |
| *Major domestic and international shareholders* | – China Investment Corporation (CIC)<br>– Hopu Investment Management<br>– International Finance Corporation (IFC)<br>– Temasek<br>– Standard Chartered | – Danone Group<br>– Arla Foods | – Wholly-owned subsidiary of COFCO | – Majority-owned by COFCO |

*Source:* Chinatex (2010), COFCO (2017), COFCO International (2020), COFCO Sugar (2019), Mengniu (2018, 2019).

but also become a key actor in China's overseas "going out" strategy and one of the largest investors in the Australian dairy sector (see Table 4.2).

More than its expansion and consolidation within China, however, what has put COFCO in the global limelight is the company's rapid transformation into one of the world's leading transnational agri-food trading corporations through its high-profile acquisition of two major international agribusiness companies in 2014: the agribusiness trading arm of Hong Kong-based Noble Group, Noble Agri, and Dutch grain trader Nidera. In fact, responding to central government policy encouraging China's state-owned agribusinesses to enhance access to and control over global value chains, COFCO has been on the lookout for acquisition opportunities since the 2010s (Oliveira 2017, p. 157). "We don't just want to be on the buyer's side, but we also want to be exporters, you know, one of the main exporters in the world," a top executive at COFCO International Australia described the company's ambitious goals to me (interview December 2018, Melbourne). With global footprints in grain trade and a network of well-established trade infrastructure across Brazil, Argentina, Australia, and the Black Sea region, both Noble Agri and Nidera presented ideal targets for COFCO's global expansion strategy. In March 2014, COFCO announced the acquisition of a 51-percent share in both Nidera and Noble Agri, and by the end of 2016, it had acquired the remaining minority stakes in both companies. COFCO then proceeded to integrate Noble's and Nidera's assets, technical expertise, and operational capacities into its own global grain trading platform—COFCO International. Equipped with a supply chain now spanning six continents and storage, processing, and logistics assets strategically located across some of the world's top grain, vegetable oil, and sugar-producing regions, COFCO has transformed itself with astonishing speed into a transnational agribusiness company successfully competing with and, indeed, surpassing some of the established members of the ABCDs (see Table 4.3)—a source of no little pride among COFCO's leadership, as I could gather from my conversation with the COFCO executive (interview December 2018, Melbourne).

COFCO's successful global M&A strategy has also turned it into a major actor in Australia's agribusiness and grain trade. Incorporating grain trading assets and infrastructure formerly owned and operated by Nidera, COFCO has gained access to Australian-grown sorghum, wheat, barley, and chickpeas, supplying these commodities to markets throughout Southeast Asia and the Middle East (COFCO International 2020). To further strengthen its trading capacities, COFCO has also been involved in the construction of a new grain export terminal at Port Kembla in New South Wales in a joint venture with fellow grain trading companies Cargill and Emerald (Locke 2014). Moreover, through its subsidiary COFCO Tunhe Sugar, COFCO secured full ownership of Tully Sugar, one of Australia's largest sugar mills, against stiff competition from ABCD companies Bunge and Louis Dreyfus in a move that has considerably strengthened COFCO's position in the global sugar trade (Yap 2015). As one of the world's major export regions for grains and oilseeds, Australia forms an important part of COFCO's global expansion strategy, according to the COFCO International executive I interviewed (interview December 2018, Melbourne). However, while its Australian footprint has increased rapidly in recent years, the company has steered clear of investments in farmland. "I can tell you that our strategy is not to buy land," the COFCO executive explained to me:

> We will invest in the networks, the logistics to help us accumulate grains from the growers. That's our strategy. But we don't want to go too far downstream to the point where we buy land and produce grains ourselves. [...] We simply have no competitive advantage on that side.
> (interview December 2018, Melbourne)

COFCO's international expansion has been facilitated by China's state-owned financial institutions as well as co-investments involving a select set of global institutional investors. A key actor in this regard is the Chinese sovereign wealth fund China Investment Corporation (CIC). Having acquired a 15 percent share of Noble Group as early as 2009 and thus obtaining a seat on Noble's board of executives, it was the CIC that enabled COFCO's first major takeover of a multinational agribusiness company by providing strategic information about Noble's agri-food business as well as financing to COFCO (Oliveira 2017, p. 320). But COFCO's acquisition of Noble Agri was not only facilitated by China's own sovereign wealth fund but also facilitated by a small group of high-profile institutional investors based outside of China. Under the leadership of Hopu Investment Management, a major Chinese private equity firm spun off in 2007 by top executives of Goldman Sachs in China, COFCO assembled an investor consortium including top institutional players such as World Bank Affiliate International Finance Corporation (IFC), Singapore's sovereign wealth fund Temasek, and Hong Kong-based finance firm Standard Chartered that would act as strategic financial partners in COFCO's global agri-food expansion. As COFCO consolidated its acquisitions of both Noble Agri and Nidera, these financial players have become major shareholders in COFCO's newly established global grain trading platform COFCO International. It seems fair to assume that COFCO International's listing on the Hong Kong stock market—a strategic goal first announced by the COFCO leadership upon COFCO's first acquisition of majority stakes in Noble Agri and Nidera back in 2014—will eventually afford COFCO's financial partners a highly profitable opportunity to exit their investments. The case of COFCO thus not only is emblematic of the interlocking interests between China's state-owned financial institutions and central agribusiness SOEs but also highlights the deep financial ties that exist between China's emerging global agribusiness players and the flows of global capital (see also Klinger & Muldavin 2019; Sippel et al. 2018).

Despite COFCO's prominent role in central government policy, COFCO executives have been eager to depoliticize the company's international

*Table 4.3* COFCO's ranking within the ABCD group by profit, 2018

| # | *Company* | *Profit (USD billion)* | *Revenue (USD billion)* | *Headquartered in* |
|---|---|---|---|---|
| 1 | Cargill | 3.1 | 114.6 | United States |
| 2 | ADM | 1.8 | 64 | United States |
| 3 | Louis Dreyfus | 0.35 | 41 | Netherlands |
| 4 | COFCO | 0.33 | 71 | China |
| 5 | Bunge | 0.26 | 46 | United States |

*Source:* Cargill (2019) and Fortune (2019).

expansion by emphasizing the profit-seeking and commercial objectives pursued by the company. When I asked about the role of government policy in shaping COFCO's operations, the COFCO International executive downplayed any political dimension of COFCO's overseas agri-investment strategy, asserting that COFCO was in no way different from the ABCDs. "We just do business and follow the business rules. Following market supply and demand, that's our policy," he insisted (interview December 2018, Melbourne). Indeed, there seems to be little in the company's governance and operations that set COFCO International apart from its international competitors. Headquartered in Geneva, Switzerland, COFCO International's corporate governance, business operations, and public relations strategy closely resemble those of its private, North Atlantic-based competitors. The company maintains an English-only Internet presence, is deeply integrated into global professional and financial networks, and staffs the upper echelons of its management team with internationally experienced agri-business professionals from competitors such as ADM, Cargill, or Louis Dreyfus. The company's image as a transnational rather than Chinese company combined with its focus on the acquisition of assets situated upstream and downstream of farmland itself have insulated COFCO by and large from the public and media criticism leveled at Chinese investors engaged in high-profile purchases of Australian farmland—an astonishing fact given that the total amount of capital COFCO has invested through its various subsidiaries into Australiana agriculture and agribusiness far outweighs that of any Chinese agri-investment in farmland. "For COFCO in Australia, we don't get negative reactions, we get positive ones," the executive at COFCO International replied to my question (certainly well-aware of the "public relations" character of interviews such as ours). While COFCO has successfully navigated around the pitfalls of overseas farmland investment, the same cannot be said for Chinese state farms.

## State farms

In analyses of Chinese overseas agri-investments, state farms are often lumped together with agribusinesses SOEs, owing to the fact that both are ultimately state-owned entities. However, both types of organizations play fundamentally different roles in China's domestic agri-food landscape and thus pursue distinct overseas investment strategies. In China, state farms are primarily involved in the agricultural production of key crops such as wheat, corn, soybean, sugar, and rubber. Historically responsible for reclaiming and opening up unused "wastelands" in China's border regions, state farms own some of the largest tracts of contiguous land farmed in China today. As a result, state farms are larger and more mechanized than most Chinese farms and are described by policymakers as the "backbone" of China's agricultural development and modernization (Zhang 2019, p. 241).

Given their position as leading farming entities in China, it is not surprising that state farms investing overseas are primarily focused on primary production. When venturing overseas, many of them have focused on acquiring farmland to export their harvests back to China and bypass the grain trading oligopoly of the ABCD. In this sense, state farms come closest to common perceptions of Chinese investment as state-driven and motivated by food security goals. However, these actors have played a much smaller role in China's agricultural "going out" than agribusiness SOEs.

What also sets state farms apart from China's state-owned agribusiness giants is their greater reliance on Chinese management and tight control from the headquarter in managing their overseas agricultural activities. Unlike state-owned agribusinesses such as COFCO, which has successfully recruited transnationally experienced agribusiness professionals to the helm of the company, state farms generally lack internationally trained figures in the upper echelons of their management teams and thus operate in a more "Chinese" manner than some of China's more genuinely transnational agribusiness corporations. This is a key factor explaining their notable lack of success in overseas contexts.

### *Profile: Beidahuang Group*

Beidahuang Group (北大荒集团) from Heilongjiang province is one of China's largest state farms engaged in overseas expansion. In contrast to COFCO, which established itself as a major actor in Australia's agri-food sector through a series of M&As with transnational agribusiness companies, the strategy of state-owned farm Beidahuang Group has been focused on the acquisition of farmland and direct participation in agricultural production. As China's largest agricultural company, Beidahuang is owned by the provincial government of Heilongjiang province and under the direct management of MARA. In Australia, the group operates through its Australian subsidiary Heilongjiang Feng Ao Agriculture & Animal Husbandry Group (HFA), while the management of its farms is undertaken by an Australian-based partner named Vicstock Grain, a farm management company operating in cropping, livestock, and grain trading. Unlike COFCO's new trading platform COFCO International, which has successfully cultivated an image as a genuinely transnational corporation, Beidahuang's overseas practices have remained decidedly "Chinese" in character. At its Australian subsidiary HFA, all management positions are taken up by staff recruited from China, often lacking essential language skills and cultural knowledge about Australia's legal, financial, and commercial environment. While Beidahuang relies on its Australian partner to broker investment opportunities and manage farm operations, it has had a strong preference for staffing top positions with its own farm mangers, mechanics, technicians, and trade experts from its headquarters in Harbin, Heilongjiang province (Thompson 2014).

Beidahuang's reliance on Chinese networks and business connections for its overseas expansion is exemplified by Frank Sheen.[4] Born into an overseas Chinese family of entrepreneurs and traders, Frank had come to Australia some ten years ago and had become involved in the country's agri-food export sector. What qualified Frank for his job was not so much his knowledge about the ins and outs of Australian farming—an area he admitted he knew little about—but his excellent network of personal contacts with the top echelons of the Chinese government and state-owned agribusiness. Of ethnic Han origin and with close links to agricultural commodity trade networks across South East Asia, Frank's family had been able to draw on close connections with top Chinese officials to gain access to the newly opened up Chinese market in the 1980s and establish business relationships with Chinese state-owned agribusiness firms involved in agricultural trade, including Beidahuang. Drawing on his family's trade ties with the Chines state-owned agribusiness sector, Frank began building a successful trading business, managing shipments of agricultural commodities from Australia to buyers in China.

In 2011, Frank teamed up with the Australian farm management and commodities company Vicstock Grain and brokered a deal with Beidahuang that saw the Chinese farming giant acquire three large farms in Western Australia's wheatbelt region in 2012. The farms were to be managed by Vicstock Grain, with Frank taking on top management positions at both Vicstock Grain and Beidahuang's Australian arm HFA. Covering some 35.000 hectares, Beidahuang's Australian farms grow wheat, barley, and canola destined for export back to China. In addition to its own farmland, between 2012 and 2014, Beidahuang leased an additional 60,000 hectares of farmland from neighboring farms, thus increasing its total area under production to an astonishing 100,000 hectares. Speaking to a group of Australian industry professionals at an agribusiness event in 2014, Frank expounded his views on the win-win opportunities Beidahuang's agri-investments presented to both the Chinese farming giant and local Australian growers. To Frank's mind, Australian farmers excelled at growing food but, on the marketing side, were often too dependent on transnational grain traders such as the ABCD. With no direct marketing channels into the most lucrative global markets themselves, Frank saw Australian farmers losing out to the grain traders "who sit in their offices wearing suits while the poor growers, the mum and dad farmers, are working their butts off, and they're not getting anything" (CSRA 2014), he explained to the group of Australian farmers present at the event. By leasing land to Beidahuang or entering into offtake agreements with the Chinese company, farmers would be able to tap into the higher-paying Chinese market, while Beidahuang itself would be able to quickly expand grain supplies from Australia, as Frank laid out the presumed win-win logic of Beidahuang's model. Construction of a grain terminal and storage facilities at Albany port, one of the key Western Australian seaports serving commodity exports from the wheatbelt region, would complete the vision by allowing Beidahuang to establish an integrated supply chain stretching from "farm to table," with the financing expected to be provided by Vicstock Grain and other co-investors Frank was still scouting for at the time of our interview in August 2017.

Beidahuang's plans for its Australian expansion were ambitious and announced with much fanfare, yet the results have been disappointing. The company's focus on farmland ownership, its plans to develop an integrated supply chain allowing them to bypass Australian grain handlers and intermediaries, as well as the often obscure relationships between its Australian partner Vicstock Grain and the government interests behind HFA have turned Beidahuang into a quintessential case of what its critics feared to be "non-commercial" investment for food security purposes. What is more, the lack of local experience concerning Australia's legal and commercial environment has seen the company become embroiled in a number of legal conflicts over lease and sales contracts with neighboring farms. "When we came here, we were stupid. We just wanted to do it big. So, we leased thousands of hectares. But we are not getting the result. We are losing a lot of money," Frank admitted in one of our conversations (interview August 2017, Melbourne). As it turns out, not only have the costs of farming in Australia been much higher than anticipated, but Beidahuang's focus on farmland and cropping has done little in the way of gaining control over the supply chain. Rather than controlling the grain supply chain from "farm to table," Beidahuang sells most of its grain through local grain trader CBH—a situation not all that different from the Australian "mom and dad farmers" Beidahuang had sought to enroll in its scheme during its first years of operation in Australia. Compared to its earlier cropping bonanza of 100,000 hectares, in 2017 Beidahuang farmed a paltry 6,000 hectares, following management decisions to withdraw from its leases and drastically reduce its own cropping area (Hale 2017).

To account for the ways in which state farms such as Beidahuang advance their overseas agricultural interests (and often fail to do so), some historical background is warranted. Chinese state farms originated during the war era of the 1930s and 1940s, which did not just see the Chinese fight Japan's invasion but was also characterized by an almost continuous civil war between Mao's communists and the Nationalist government (*Guomindang* 国民党) of Generalissimo Chiang Kaishek. They were originally tasked with feeding Mao's rebel forces in their war campaigns against the Japanese in Shaanxi province. Following the end of the war and the communist victory over the Guomindang in 1949, the model was adopted all over the country, and especially the country's frontier regions in the Northeast and Northwest, where demobilized soldiers were settled on newly founded state farms to reclaim unused land for agricultural production and enhance the nation's grain output (Brautigam 2015, p. 40). It was at that time that Heilongjiang province became one of the centers of state farm activity. Located in China's far northeast at the border of Soviet Siberia, Heilongjiang boasts rich and fertile black soils, but the many swamps and wetlands that dominated the landscape until then had stifled the development of agriculture in the region. After the founding of the new regime in 1949, over a hundred thousand demobilized soldiers, officers, experts, technical personnel, and, later during the Cultural Revolution, students and urban youths were sent to the Northeast to help establish the Beidahuang state farm system. Clearing forests, draining swamps, and digging irrigation channels, these agricultural pioneers transformed the local landscape from what was considered a largely empty and unproductive space into one of China's most fertile agricultural regions. Indeed, to many Chinese today, the state farm's very name, Beidahuang (北大荒)—the "Great Northern Wilderness"—conjures up images of heroic struggles of man against nature, eventually transforming the wild and harsh environment into China's "Great Northern Granary" or *beidacang* (北大仓), as the region is now often referred to.

These struggles have paved the way for Beidahuang's transformation into China's and, indeed, one of the world's largest farming companies. Today, the group owns nearly 3 million hectares of farmland spread across 113 farms, manages close to 1,000 state-owned companies with operations in the food industry, and produces a total grain output of more than 20 million tons a year, the largest output by any one company in the world (Baike 2019; Chen 2019; Beidahuang Group 2018a, 2018b, 2018c). Indeed, such is the scale of the company's production that its overall agricultural output is said to feed 50 million people per year, a figure that exceeds the entire agricultural export capacity of Australia—currently estimated to feed 40 million people (Lawrence et al. 2013). Beyond cropping, Beidahuang Group also engages in livestock production and forestry and is a key producer not only of grain but also of oilseeds, beets, fruits, meat, milk, and seafood products. Notably, the group is China's only large-scale soybean producer and one of the few domestic soy processing companies to have survived China's accession to the WTO in 2001 and the subsequent opening up of its domestic soybean sector to transnational agribusiness companies. Beidahuang is also involved in transnational soybean trade, and, more recently, it has been granted rights by the Ministry of Commerce to manage the country's rice and corn exports (Zhang 2019, p. 243).

Beidahuang's particular role in China's domestic agri-food system is reflected in the approach the company has taken toward expanding its overseas operations. Since 2007, the company has leased or purchased over 3 million mu of land (about 207,000 hectares) across 13 countries worldwide, establishing 26 overseas subsidiaries (Beidahuang Group 2018a). Framing its overseas activities as an active contribution to the country's "going out" strategy, the company's investment strategy has been predominantly focused on farmland and agricultural production. Much of Beidahuang's direct investment has targeted Russia, given its proximity to Heilongjiang province, where the company leases farmland to grow soybeans for export to its own processing facilities in China. However, the group also made headlines with its failed attempts to develop 200,000 hectares of farmland for rice and corn production in the northern Philippines or its announcement of another, ultimately failed cooperation agreement with the provincial government of Rio Negro in Argentina that would have seen Beidahuang acquire 234,500 hectares of farmland in the province (Oliveira 2017, p. 151). Unsurprisingly, these activities have attracted widespread negative media attention and have shaped the company's overseas image as a quintessential Chinese "land grabber." Yet, many of Beidahuang's investments including in Australia have been spectacularly unsuccessful, often resulting in much smaller areas being put into production than initially announced and limited abilities to control the global flows of agri-food commodities. A major corruption scandal eventually resulting in the removal and incarceration of the company's former chairman Sui Fengfu has certainly not helped Beidahuang improve its reputation as an overseas investor. Given the poor results of Beidahuang's farmland-focused investment strategy, there appears to be some rethinking in the upper echelons of Beidahuang's management. In a 2019 report on the group's business results, the company announced the implementation of a "new strategy focused on grain trade" that would allow Beidahuang to "develop into a new type of grain merchant with international production and operation capabilities" (Beidahuang Group 2019). Some observers have interpreted this rhetoric as an attempt to transform Beidahuang from a farming company into a commodity trader, copying the more successful investment model of COFCO (Zhang 2019)—with limited success, so far.

## Private agribusiness corporations

A third group of investors are private agribusiness corporations. The emergence of this group of companies is directly linked to the liberalization of the agricultural sector beginning in the late 1970s. Several decades of agricultural modernization aimed at scaling up production, opening agriculture to new flows of urban industrial and commercial capital, and introducing commodity and capital relations have resulted in the consolidation of a robust domestic agribusiness sector (Schneider 2017). Today, China's most successful domestic agribusinesses are multimillion-dollar companies that run large-scale, commercialized, and vertically integrated operations in a wide range of agricultural sectors such as pork, dairy, fruits, vegetables, or feed production (Zhang 2019). With many of them designated as the so-called dragon head enterprises (*longtou qiye* 龙头企业), they are important agents in the spread of capitalist and industrialized forms of agricultural production (Zhang & Donaldson 2008) and also actively involved in the country's "going out" strategy. Indeed, as my fieldwork confirms, the goals and aspirations of these firms now often extend far beyond the domestic market.

What sets private agricultural lead firms apart from their state-owned counterparts is the continued control and undisputed authority of the companies' founding figures. Widely celebrated for their entrepreneurial spirit and hard-won success, the self-made billionaires and business tycoons behind China's largest private agribusiness companies—now often in their sixties or older—remain firmly in control of business strategy and investment decisions. Even where they have listed their agribusinesses (or parts thereof) on China's domestic stock markets, most of these businessmen have remained majority shareholders and thus effectively control all major business decisions. Private agricultural lead firms also differ from state-owned agribusinesses in the ways in which relationships with the Chinese state are organized. While many private agribusiness tycoons have forged strong personal ties with policymakers from the local, provincial, or even national level, the state generally does not have formal ownership of these firms. As a result, it seems fair to say that private agribusinesses are less likely to function as vehicles for the implementation of agriculture-related policy goals compared to their state-owned counterparts. Commercial goals rather than policy objectives guide the investment decisions made by these firms. This is not to underestimate the importance of domestic policy. On the contrary, investment regulations, both in the form of restrictions and incentives, are key factors in shaping the business environment in which private agribusinesses operate. Yet, with leading managers or the firms' chairmen ultimately making decisions on where to invest and how, government policy remains "contextual, rather than directive" (Gu et al. 2016, p. 25) for these companies. As one interview partner described it to me: "Our international strategy, our going out approach is constantly evolving alongside three dimensions: government policy, the Chinese market, and the global food economy" (interview April 2017, Beijing). In other words, government policy is a factor to be taken into account, but it is far from the only factor that matters.

### *Profile: New Hope Group*

New Hope Group (*Xin Xiwang Jituan* 新希望集团) is China's quintessential private agricultural lead firm. Celebrated in countless media articles and in personal conversations I conducted during my fieldwork, New Hope Group's success story begins in 1982, shortly after Deng Xiaoping's economic reforms opened up China's agricultural sector for private business. As the story goes, Liu Yonghao, the company's long-time chairman, and his three older brothers seized the opportunity that market reform presented to entrepreneurially-minded Chinese farmers to start what was to become China's largest, privately-owned agribusiness. Raising 1,000 RMB from the sale of their bicycles and watches, the brothers started a quail and chick breeding business in their rural Sichuan. The family operation quickly grew into a million-yuan business, enabling the brothers to expand into the feed industry. By the early 1990s, the business had grown into China's largest animal feed group, and five years onward, when the family operation split into different industry sectors, Liu Yonghao incorporated the agri-food focused branch of the family business as Sichuan New Hope Agribusiness Company, with himself as president and chairman of the board.

The company continued to expand rapidly and now operates integrated value chains in the pig and poultry sectors with operations extending from feed production to animal breeding, slaughtering, processing, and food services. In 1998, New Hope Group was listed on the Shenzhen Stock Exchange, where it now trades as New Hope Liuhe, following its acquisition and integration of leading Chinese poultry producer Shandong Liuhe Group in 2005. Today, New Hope Group produces 20 million tons of animal feed, 1.3 billion chickens, and 8 million pigs annually, placing the company among China's largest agri-food businesses. With recorded profits of 1.7 billion RMB and net assets of 22 billion RMB, New Hope Group has developed into one of China's 500 largest companies (New Hope Liuhe 2019). In addition to its operations in the pig and poultry agro-industrial supply chains, in the early 2000s, New Hope Group entered the dairy sector, where it now operates 11 dairy processing plants and 11 large-scale dairy farms with a combined herd of over 100,000 cows across various provinces in China. The company is involved in production, research, and testing and has developed a number of well-known and high-end dairy brands for fresh milk and yogurt products. In 2019, New Hope Group listed its dairy business on the Shenzhen Stock Exchange and has since further consolidated its position in China's domestic dairy market by acquiring a major share in one of China's largest raw milk producers, China Modern Dairy (King & Wood Mallesons 2019). Of the company's listed businesses, Liu Yonghao and his daughter Liu Chang remain majority shareholders; in fact, with an estimated net worth of 10 billion USD, the Liu family was ranked China's 19th richest family by the 2019 Forbes China Rich List (Forbes 2019). Beyond creating immense amounts of personal wealth, the spectacular success of his business has enabled Liu Yonghao to forge strong connections with China's national-level and provincial-level leadership. According to what one company manager described as the chairman's strategy to "stay close to the government, but stay out of politics" (interview April 2017, Beijing), Liu Yonghao has taken up powerful positions at the intersection of business and politics. He is an active member of the Chinese People's Political Consultative Conference, an advisory body in China's political system, where he lobbies for private entrepreneurship and China's agricultural sector, Vice Chairman of the All-China Federation of Industry and Commerce, and a leading representative of the China Dairy Association and the China Feed Industry Association. As one of the country's key agricultural dragon head enterprises, New Hope Group also receives regular praise from state officials and the media for its leading role in food safety, agricultural innovation, and the promotion of large-scale farming. In exchange for being at the forefront of China's agricultural modernization, the group receives generous state support. In 2018, New Hope Group reported government subsidies on the order of 300 million RMB for its involvement in various agricultural development and modernization programs across the country (New Hope Liuhe 2019).

Beyond its core business in the agri-food industry, New Hope Group has diversified into a range of other industrial sectors such as the chemical industry, real estate, biotech, and finance. Particularly its activities in the finance sector have been instrumental in furthering the group's agro-industrial expansion. In 1995, New Hope Group invested more than 100 million RMB to establish China's first privately-owned commercial bank, China Minsheng Bank, in cooperation with other private entrepreneurs and with backing from the Chinese government. Access to financial capital through its majority shareholding in Minsheng Bank allowed New Hope Group to expand into agro-industrial supply chain finance, providing small-scale loans, insurance, and rural financing services to farming households (Yang et al. 2016). New Hope Group's expansion into the finance sector not only aligns with the group's mandate as a dragon head enterprise to provide small-scale farmers with capital and integrate them into agro-industrial value chains but has also generated handsome profits for the company itself. According to the company's annual report, Minsheng Bank contributed 77.21 percent of the company's net profit in 2018. Furthermore, in 2010, New Hope Group founded its own private equity investment management firm, Hosen Capital, which by now has invested over 300 million USD in food and agri-business related companies that are either directly located in China or involved in China-focused food value chains (Burwood-Taylor 2017). Through its private equity arm, New Hope Group is in a privileged position not only to raise funds for its own overseas expansion but also to benefit from the financialization of agriculture more broadly through the investment returns it receives as Hosen Capital's founding investor.

New Hope Group's international expansion began long before the current wave of Chinese capital into global agri-food supply chains, at a time when overseas agricultural investment "wasn't really a phenomenon," as the company manager I interviewed phrased it (interview April 2017, Beijing). Responding to growing demand for feed from neighboring countries, in 1999, New Hope Group opened its first overseas feed factory in Vietnam. Driven by the success of this venture, New Hope Group quickly expanded into other markets, including the Philippines, Bangladesh, Indonesia, Cambodia, Sri Lanka, Singapore, and Egypt. "It didn't really happen according to a strategic plan," the company manager told me, "but rather by chance. We thought: 'Why don't we do this?' And as it was successful, we expanded step-by-step." (interview April 2017, Beijing). Today, with over 600 subsidiaries in 30 countries and 70,000 employees worldwide, New Hope Group has become one of the most prominent success stories of China's global agricultural integration.

A second phase of the group's internationalization strategy started in 2013 with New Hope Group's expansion into developed markets in the Global North, including the United States, Australia, New Zealand, and France. The group's shift toward developed markets is an important element in its strategy to focus on emerging Chinese demand for high-quality animal proteins and to integrate further into higher value-added stages of the agri-food value chain, including food services and food product design. Guided by its stated goal to become a "worldwide animal protein provider," New Hope Group's recent overseas business includes acquisitions, joint ventures, and partnerships with other investors and governments in the beef, dairy, and seafood sectors. Following the acquisition of a string of abattoirs and beef and seafood processing companies in Australia, the United States, and China, New Hope Group consolidated these assets into a new global food business, Kilcoy Global Foods, which has been operating as a supplier of beef and other high-quality animal protein products to food service providers, retailers, and fast food chains in markets around the world since 2015. Other recent investments include a joint venture in Australian dairy farms with a group of local dairy companies that has seen New Hope Group turn into one of Australia's largest dairy producers, milking around 6,000 cows. To facilitate its entry into developed markets such as Australia, New Hope Group has made partnerships with investors and local agribusinesses the hallmark of its internationalization strategy. Through its private equity arm Hosen Capital, many of the group's recent acquisitions have been co-financed by high-profile institutional investors from around the world, including Singapore's sovereign wealth fund Temasek, the International Finance Corporation (IFC), or US-based agribusiness firm Archer Daniels Midland (ADM).

## Agri-food entrepreneurs

Agri-food entrepreneurs are the largest group of Chinese agri-food investors in Australia (see Table 4.1). Yet, their significance as key actors in China's global agri-food integration has received little attention. Agri-food entrepreneurs share many features with the private agribusinesses presented in the previous section. As self-made business tycoons and archetypical representatives of China's new class of private capitalists, agri-food entrepreneurs have built large and often highly diversified business conglomerates, accumulating huge private fortunes in the process. While these conglomerates (or parts thereof) are frequently listed on China's capital markets, many of them essentially remain family enterprises with a large proportion of the companies' publicly traded shares controlled by the founding family. Patriarchal control remains a common feature of their governance structure as the companies' founders continue to involve themselves actively in the management and future direction of their business empires. What sets agri-food entrepreneurs apart, however, from all other actors we have encountered so far is their astounding lack of background in agricultural production or the Chinese food economy more broadly. Chinese agri-food entrepreneurs investing in Australian food and farming have built their core businesses in a wide range of industries from industrial manufacturing to construction and machinery and, from there, have diversified into many new lines of business. But it was only until very recently that these firms turned to agriculture and food as a promising new arena of corporate profits. Indeed, many of these agri-food entrepreneurs exhibit a stunning lack of experience in agricultural production, whether in China or abroad. It is therefore critical to enquire into the domestic conditions of economic and agricultural transformation that are propelling these companies to venture into the agri-food sector, not just domestically but transcending national borders. Here, the case of Rifa Holding Group from Zhejiang province provides an instructive example.

### *Profile: Rifa Holding Group*

Rifa Holding Group (日发控股集团) has its origins as a state-owned textile machine manufacturing business located in Xinchang county in the east-central part of Zhejiang province. In many ways, the group's transformation into a diversified and internationally competitive business conglomerate is reflective of China's broader development toward a more market-based economy and the policies of marketization and privatization that have accompanied much of China's reform trajectory. Alongside the first attempts by reform-minded officials to restructure China's bloated and inefficient public sector, the ailing company was privatized in 1982 and taken over by its then-director Wu Liangding. The next 20 years would see Wu's rapid transformation from a middling manager of a small state-owned enterprise to one of China's leading private entrepreneurs. To turn around the loss-making company, Wu gradually expanded into the production of aluminum alloy wheels used in car manufacturing. In 1993, he spun off the aluminum alloy wheels business into an independent company and incorporated the venture as Wanfeng Auto Wheel. Today, Wanfeng is a leading manufacturer for the automotive, aerospace, and military industries and among China's top 500 private companies (Sina Finance 2018). In the same year, Wu spun off a second company—Rifa Textile Machinery—from the formerly state-owned textile machine business he had been leading, first as manager and later as its private owner. Under the management of Wu's oldest son Wu Jie, Rifa emerged as a major privately-owned textile and precision machinery manufacturer. Following the listing of the company on the Shenzhen stock exchange in 2010, Wu Jie set about to realize his vision of transforming Rifa into an "agile and international company." He not only rapidly expanded into new, seemingly unrelated lines of business but also began to transnationalize the company's operations by acquiring businesses overseas. In less than a decade after taking the company public, Wu Jie had transformed Rifa from a spinoff of a loss-making, formerly state-owned company into a diversified business conglomerate with operations in textile and precision machinery, agriculture, sports and culture, finance, and general aviation and with subsidiaries in Asia, Europe, Australia, and New Zealand.

When I visited Rifa's headquarters in one of Hangzhou's sparkling new business districts to find out more about the company's newfound passion for agriculture and food, a senior investment manager explained to me that agriculture had become an integral part of the company's growth strategy (interview March 2017, Hangzhou). Following the chairman's decision in 2012 to move into agriculture and food as a key sector for future growth, Rifa had invested in a large-scale sheep breeding farm in the western province of Xinjiang, established a meat processing and trading company there, and developed its own meat brand *Rifa Salutary* under which the company markets and sells its meat products to Chinese consumers. The company's ambitions quickly expanded beyond the domestic market. In 2014, Rifa expanded its fledgling domestic livestock business to Australia, where it began to aggregate smaller beef cattle farms into large-scale operational hubs aimed at producing and exporting beef to the Chinese market. Apparently, the goal was to "build a global agribusiness producing and exporting meat that will be around for 50 years"—a vision in which Rifa was prepared to invest up to 600 million AUD. Hence, at the time of my visit in 2017, the company was not only busy expanding its portfolio in Australia but also eyeing new beef investment opportunities in Kazakhstan and Argentina. What appeared at first sight like a haphazard foray into an industry completely unrelated to Rifa's traditional business as a manufacturing company was in fact, I was told, a "strategic, market-based decision":

> We want to contribute to improving people's lifestyles. The income of Chinese consumers is constantly increasing, you know? People will spend a growing amount of money on food and eating. They will transition from rather low-quality protein consumption to high-quality protein consumption, from a more plant-based diet to a more meat-based diet. Beef and sheep are considered rather high-quality sources of protein. Chinese people like to eat pork, but pork's nutritious value is not as good as that of other types of meat such as beef and sheep. So, that's how we decided to get into the livestock industry.
>
> (interview March 2017, Hangzhou.)

The manager's words demonstrate how assumptions about new dietary habits and changing meanings of food are transforming agriculture from an industry long ignored by China's private entrepreneurs into an exciting new arena for profits. Indeed, in China's domestic economy, "agriculture and food have never been as hot as now," as a mergers and acquisitions manager at a PwC branch in Shanghai summarized the prevailing mood among Chinese investors (interview March 2017, Shanghai). Yet, despite its status as a "hot" new arena for investment, cutthroat competition and monopolistic market structures make it difficult for newcomers to establish themselves as viable players in China's agri-food industry. Choosing the right commodity sector thus becomes a critical first step. With sectors such as cropping, seeds, technology, or feed tightly controlled by established agribusiness corporations, agri-food entrepreneurs tend to engage in niche markets for fruits, vegetables, high-quality meats and dairy, wine, and other premium products where they face less competition from domestic and international agri-food giants. As Rifa's investment manager explained the company's rationale for investing in the beef sector:

> If you are a private company deciding to get into, say, grain production, it will be really, really difficult to get a foot into the industry and control some market share. But the meat market, regardless of whether it's the international or the domestic market, is still fairly fragmented. There is no single big agribusiness corporation that controls the market. So, for a privately-owned company, it's much easier to grow a business in this sector.
>
> (interview March 2017, Hangzhou)

Of course, not all agri-food entrepreneurs share Rifa's assessment of the beef sector as the biggest opportunity for newcomers entering the Chinese food economy. Indeed, I have heard very similar arguments being put forward by agri-food entrepreneurs with investments in Australian dairy production—a sector that Rifa considered too risky given the high costs involved in the import of liquid and particularly fresh milk, as I learned from the manager. While assessments of the risks and opportunities as well as the operational capacities required to establish a market presence in any given commodity sector may vary from company to company, agri-food entrepreneurs consistently described their investment strategies as being driven by the search for those sectors in food and agricultural production with the biggest potential to generate future windfall profits or, in other words, by the search for new sources of accumulation.

Similar strategic considerations also guide agri-food entrepreneurs' focus on particular investment geographies. According to Rifa's investment manager, low production costs, high export capacity, and geographical proximity allowing for the export of chilled meat in addition to frozen beef products all played a role, but in the eyes of Rifa, the biggest geographical advantage consisted in the fact that Australia enjoyed favorable market access for its beef exports to China given its reputation as a "clean and green" environment free from health and food safety issues such as BSE (bovine spongiform encephalitis, commonly known as "mad cow disease")—an advantage which, conveniently, Chinese customers are "prepared to pay for," I was told. With Australia functioning as a source of premium beef imports, Rifa's prospective investments in Argentina and Kazakhstan were intended to supply China's mid and low-end markets respectively, as the manager explained the geography of Rifa's agri-investments.

Australia's reputation as a provider of high-quality, safe foods is widely shared among Chinese agri-investors and, for many, provides a key incentive for investment. Agri-food entrepreneurs I encountered during my research consistently emphasized the significance of Australia's "green and clean" image for their decision to invest in Australian agriculture and food production. The key role these perceptions play in the investment strategies of agri-food entrepreneurs must be understood against a background of repeated food scares and a "crisis of trust" in domestically grown food products that have accompanied the agro-industrial transformation of China's domestic agricultural sector over the past decades. In this context, particularly urban middle-class consumers are increasingly "opting out" of Chinese domestic food production in favor of imported foods from places of production such as Australia associated with higher levels of food quality and safety (Hanser & Li 2015). As another Chinese investment manager described the current sentiment prevailing among the community of Chinese agri-food entrepreneurs investing in Australian food and farming: "The main driver is [...] the rising middle class in China. Everyone is really positive that there will be huge demand for high-quality imported goods from Australia, from New Zealand. So really, that's why everyone is investing here." (interview February 2017, Sydney).

The geography underpinning the investment strategies of agri-food entrepreneurs thus centers predominantly on notions of singularity and quality rather than on perspectives emphasizing agricultural production capacity and output. In other words, it is the perception of Australia as a producer of safe and premium foods rather than images of Australia as a "food bowl" bolstering national food security goals that shape investment rationales of agri-food entrepreneurs. Consequently, agri-food entrepreneurs have been eager to emphasize the profit-seeking and commercial nature of their investments. In fact, private and non-agricultural companies receive little direct incentives from China's agricultural "going out" strategy, multiple investment advisors working for Chinese agri-food entrepreneurs confirmed to me in interviews. "These people invest in Australian agriculture out of their own initiative," one investment advisor told me. "They believe it is going to make money for them. It's a purely commercial motivation for them to select Australia as investment destination and to select agriculture as a sector," she explained (interview March 2017, Sydney). Government policy is only seen as relevant insofar as it affects the regulation of outbound investment flows and agricultural imports. For example, the fact that tariffs for Australian beef imports were on a schedule to be gradually phased out under the 2015 China-Australia Free Trade Agreement had been an important factor informing the company's decision to focus its overseas expansion strategy on Australia, Rifa's investment manager told me. Similarly, the relatively greater ease with which approval can be obtained for overseas investments targeting food and agriculture within a political context of heightened scrutiny over outbound flows of Chinese capital had had some impact on Rifa's diversification strategy (interview March 2017, Hangzhou). However, beyond this "contextual nature" (Gu et al. 2016) of government policy, I have not been able to substantiate evidence of any deeper connection between the investment strategies of agri-food entrepreneurs such as Rifa and the central government's "going out" policy, neither politically, strategically, nor financially.

In sum, the case of Rifa demonstrates how agriculture and food are being transformed into lucrative business opportunities for China's private entrepreneurs, driven by rising incomes and the growing role of personal consumption in the Chinese economy. In this context, investment in foreign farms or food brands, particularly those associated with images of quality and safety, is seen by agri-food entrepreneurs as a key strategy to gain competitive advantages over domestic rivals and establish themselves in niche markets for premium food products. However, the growing interest of agri-food entrepreneurs into agriculture and food is a strategy not only to seek out *new* profit opportunities but also to move away from *old* business models and industrial sectors that are no longer profitable. One investment advisor offered the following insights into the business situation of a large Chinese industrial manufacturer that had recently expanded into Australian beef cattle production:

> They [the Chinese manufacturer] are still making money from the copper business. They are one of the largest players in the world in terms of copper production. But the margins are very low, and they can see the trend. They can see it's not a rising industry, it's a declining industry. Margins are getting worse. So, he [the company patriarch] doesn't see it as a very good business for the next generation. But he sees that [...] Chinese consumers are demanding better and safer food [...]. So, he thinks that's a better business for him to get into.
>
> (interview March 2017, Shanghai)

Seen from this perspective, Australian agriculture does not simply constitute a new *frontier of accumulation* for Chinese agri-food entrepreneurs but a *spatial fix* (Harvey 2006 [1982])—a solution, albeit temporary, to domestic overcapacity and declining profits through the spatial reorganization and expansion of Chinese industrial capital into new geographies and sectors of production (McMichael 2020; Zhan & Huang 2017; Hofman 2016).

*****

In this chapter, I have presented four Chinese investor archetypes that are relevant for understanding China's land rush in Australia. I have argued that making sense of the variety of actors involved in Chinese agri-food investments in Australia requires us to move beyond reductionist conceptualizations of "Chinese investment" as an army of state-owned companies enacting a singular and coherent food security strategy. Such monolithic perspectives have been powerful in erasing the diversity and complexity of Chinese agri-investments on the ground, instead strengthening dominant conceptions of China's overseas agricultural engagement as being homogenous, state-led, strategically oriented toward meeting national food security goals, and thus fundamentally different from other "market-driven" forms of capital investment in the agri-food system. To be sure, Chinese policymakers have formulated a clearer agri-food development agenda than many other governments and established a distinct set of institutions facilitating overseas agri-investments within the context of China's "going out" strategy. However, the ways in which state policy shapes the overseas investment activities of individual actors have been highly uneven and differentiated. By developing a typology that takes into account not only ownership categories but also the legacies and positions of different actors within China's rapidly transforming agri-food economy, my account emphasizes the variations in China's overseas agricultural engagement across five dimensions: first, in terms of the actors involved, from the state-owned agribusiness giants that have captured the imagination of much foreign commentary to the private agents and entrepreneurs operating below the radar of much macro-economic analysis; second, in terms of the investment strategies pursued, from direct investments in farmland to acquisitions of existing agribusinesses and infrastructure further upstream and downstream of farmland itself; third, in terms of the level of state support received, from direct strategic and financial support to a total lack of any privileged connections between investors and the state; fourth, in terms of the arguments advanced to legitimate and rationalize investments, from neo-Malthusian notions of (future) food insecurity to commercial narratives constructing Australian agriculture as a frontier for profits in high-end agri-food value chains; and fifth, in terms of the outcomes achieved, from the creation of globally competitive agri-food corporations to investment failures and political backlash.

Most importantly, the account presented here calls into question assumptions about the "Chinese" nature of such agri-investments. The complex arrangements of capital and interests implicated in large-scale deals such as those of COFCO or New Hope Group demonstrate that the boundaries between state and private, domestic and foreign, as well as financial and commercial capital are far more blurred and unstable than generally assumed. The geography of Chinese agri-investments, then, is much less territorially bounded as the term "Chinese" suggests and is often better thought of in terms of global networks that reflect varying articulations of people, capital, and agri-food commodities *within* and *across* national spaces, as we shall see in the next chapter.

## Notes

1 Quoted in Cranston and Murray (2016).
2 Following Wang (2015), a typical shareholding structure of a publicly listed Chinese SOE is comprised of three major types of shares: state shares, legal person shares, and A-shares, of which only A-shares are publicly tradable whereas state

shares and legal person shares can only be held by government institutions. This shareholding structure ensures that state ownership over the state-owned sector remains largely intact despite the growing number of SOEs listed on the stock market over the past decade and a half (p. 612).

3 The scandal, in which baby milk had been adulterated with the chemical melamine, resulted in the death of six infants and caused illness among several thousand, triggering a severe crisis of trust amongst Chinese consumers. The scandal did not only implicate Mengniu but many other well-known and trusted domestic dairy companies.

4 Based on a series of personal interviews in August 2017, Melbourne and notes from my field diary. I use a pseudonym for the manager's name.

## References

Baike (2019): 黑龙江北大荒农垦集团总公司 [Heilongjiang Beidahuang Land Reclamation Group Corporation]. Available online at https://baike.baidu.com/item/黑龙江北大荒农垦集团总公司, checked on 12/16/2019.

Belesky, Paul; Lawrence, Geoffrey (2018): Chinese State Capitalism and Neomercantilism in the Contemporary Food Regime: Contradictions, Continuity and Change. In *The Journal of Peasant Studies* 46 (6), pp. 1119–1141. DOI: 10.1080/03066150.2018.1450242.

Beidahuang Group (2019): 集团党委会会议报告全文播发 [Full Report of the Meeting of the Group's Party Committee Released]. Available online at https://mp.weixin.qq.com/s/z0JKUGN_mxFVkvfjAhGzcA, checked on 12/17/2019.

Beidahuang Group (2018a): Beidahuang Group. Available online at http://www.chinabdh.com/, checked on 12/17/2019.

Beidahuang Group (2018b): Heilongjiang Beidahuang Agricultural Company Limited. Available online at https://www.hljnknj.com/, checked on 12/17/2019.

Beidahuang Group (2018c): 奋进在重大转型的关键时刻 [Forging Ahead in this Critical Moment of Transformation]. Available online at https://mp.weixin.qq.com/s/EcNBr7nDxiJd073YcpCWlA, checked on 12/17/2019.

Burwood-Taylor, Louisa (2017): China Will Produce 4 of Top 10 Global Food Companies by 2027, Says Leading Food Investor. In *AgFunderNews*, 4/26/2017. Available online at https://agfundernews.com/china-will-produce-4-of-top-10-global-food-companies-by-2027-says-leading-food-investor.html, checked on 5/7/2019.

Brautigam, Deborah (2015): *Will Africa Feed China?* Oxford, New York: Oxford University Press.

Cargill (2019): Five-Year Financial Summary. Available online at https://www.cargill.com/about/financial/five-year-financial-summary, checked on 12/18/2019.

Centre for the Study of Rural Australia (CSRA) (2014): 2014 CSRA Forum. Global Food Issues. Available online at https://www.youtube.com/watch?v=JIO5o3nvl0Y, checked on 1/21/2020.

Chen, Hongshu (2019): 北大荒拓荒、盐碱地改造……"中国碗"装满"中国粮"[Reclaiming The Great Northern Wilderness … Transforming Salinated Land Into a Chinese "Rice Bowl" Filled with "Chinese Grain"]. In *第一财经 [First Financial]*, 11/19/2019.

Chinatex (2010): Chinatex Website. Available online at http://www.chinatex.com/en/cotton.html, checked on 1/4/2020.

COFCO (2017): COFCO Website. Available online at http://www.cofco.com/en/, checked on 1/4/2020.

COFCO International (2020): COFCO International Website. Available online at https://www.cofcointernational.com/, checked on 1/4/2020.

COFCO Sugar (2019): COFCO Sugar Website. Available online at http://www.cofco-tunhe.com/en/index.html, checked on 1/4/2020.

Cranston, Matthew; Murray, Lisa (2016): China's Hunger for Australian Agricultural Land Only the Beginning. In *Australian Financial Review*, 4/26/2016. Available online at https://www.afr.com/property/chinas-hunger-for-australian-agricultural-land-only-the-beginning-20160421-gobh2t, checked on 4/6/2024.

Forbes (2019): China Rich List 2019. Available online at https://www.forbes.com/profile/liu-yonghao/#34da9460222d, checked on 12/2/2019.

Fortune (2019): Fortune 500 Companies. Available online at https://fortune.com/fortune500/, checked on 12/18/2019.

Gu, Jing; Zhang, Chuanhong; Vaz, Alcides; Mukwereza, Langton (2016): Chinese State Capitalism? Rethinking the Role of the State and Business in Chinese Development Cooperation in Africa. In *World Development* 81, pp. 24–34.

Hale, Rueben (2017): Crop Downsizing for Chinese Group. In *The West Australian*, 8/10/2017. Available online at https://www.countryman.com.au/countryman/news/crop-downsizing-for-chinese-group-ng-b88561609z, checked on 1/27/2020.

Hanser, Amy; Li, Jialin Camille (2015): Opting Out? Gated Consumption, Infant Formula and China's Affluent Urban Consumers. In *The China Journal* (74), pp. 110–128.

Harvey, David (2006 [1982]): *The Limits to Capital*. London: Verso.

Hofman, Irna (2016): Politics or Profits along the "Silk Road": What Drives Chinese Farms in Tajikistan and Helps them Thrive? In *Eurasian Geography and Economics* 57 (3), pp. 457–481.

Keulertz, Martin; Woertz, Eckart (2016): States as Actors in International Agro-Investments. In Christophe Gironde, Christophe Golay, Peter Messerli (Eds.): *Large-Scale Land Acquisitions. Focus on South-East Asia*. Leiden, Boston: Brill Nijhoff (International Development Policy, 6), pp. 30–52.

King & Wood Mallesons (2019): KWM Advises on New Hope's RMB710 Million Acquisition of China Modern Dairy Holdings Ltd. Available online at https://www.kwm.com/en/hk/knowledge/news/new-hope-acquisition-of-china-modern-diary-holdings-ltd-20191023, checked on 12/2/2019.

Klinger, Julie Michelle; Muldavin, Joshua (2019): New Geographies of Development: Grounding China's Global Integration. In *Territory, Politics, Governance* 7 (1), pp. 1–21. DOI: 10.1080/21622671.2018.1559.

Lawrence, Geoffrey; Richards, Carol; Lyons, Kristen (2013): Food Security in Australia in an Era of Neoliberalism, Productivism and Climate Change. In *Journal of Rural Studies* 29, pp. 30–39.

Lee, Ching Kwan (2018): *The Specter of Global China. Politics, Labor, and Foreign Investment in Africa*. Chicago, London: The University of Chicago Press.

Locke, Sarina (2014): $75 Million Upgrade at Port Kembla will Double its Grain Export and Make Handling More Efficient by Rail. In *ABC News*, 8/20/2014. Available online at https://www.abc.net.au/news/rural/2014-08-20/nrn-port-kembla-upgrade/5683460, checked on 5/10/2017.

MARA (2016): *中国对外农业投资合作分析报告 [Analysis Report on China's Agricultural Foreign Investment and Cooperation]*. Beijing: 中国农业出版社 [China Agriculture Press].

McMichael, Philip (2020): Does China's 'Going Out' Strategy Prefigure a New Food Regime? In *Journal of Peasant Studies* 47 (1), pp. 116–154. DOI: 10.1080/03066150.2019.1693368.

Mengniu (2019): Mengniu Website. Available online at http://www.mengniu.com.cn/, checked on 1/4/2020.

Mengniu (2018): Annual Report 2018. Available online at https://www.mengniuir.com/en/reports.aspx, checked on 11/27/2019.

New Hope Liuhe (2019): 2018 Annual Report [2018 年年度报告]. Available online at http://www.szse.cn/disclosure/listed/bulletinDetail/index.html?3fdae26f-5756-4aaf-aed3-16b750f1b7d3, checked on 12/3/2019.

Oliveira, Gustavo de L. T. (2017): The South-South Question: Transforming Brazil-China Agroindustrial Partnerships. Doctoral thesis. UC Berkeley. Department of Geography. Available online at https://escholarship.org/uc/item/1v44x1qs, checked on 11/6/2019.

Sina Finance (2018): 2018中国民营企业500强榜单 [List of China's Top 500 Private Enterprises in 2018]. Available online at https://finance.sina.com.cn/zt_d/myqy500/, checked on 12/12/2019.

Schneider, Mindi (2017): Dragon Head Enterprises and the State of Agribusiness in China. In *Journal of Agrarian Change* 17 (1), pp. 3–21. DOI: 10.1111/joac.12151.

Sippel, Sarah R.; Böhme, Michaela; Gharios, Cynthia (2018): Strategic Financialization? The Emergence of Sovereign Wealth Funds in the Global Food System. In Hilde Bjørkhaug, André Magnan, Geoffrey Lawrence (Eds.): *The Financialization of Agri-Food Systems. Contested Transformations*. Abingdon, Oxon, New York, NY: Routledge, pp. 62–84.

Thompson, Brad (2014): Visa Rules a Hurdle for China. In *The West Australian*, 4/10/2014. Available online at https://thewest.com.au/news/wa/visa-rules-a-hurdle-for-china-ng-ya-368982, checked on 1/21/2020.

Wang, Yingyao (2015): The Rise of the 'Shareholding State': Financialization of Economic Management in China. In *Socio-Economic Review* 13 (3), pp. 603–625.

Zhan, Shaohua; Huang, Lingli (2017): Internal Spatial Fix: China's Geographical Solution to Food Supply and its Limits. In *Geoforum* 85, pp. 140–152.

Zhang, Hongzhou (2019): *Securing the 'Rice Bowl'. China and Global Food Security*. Singapore: Palgrave Macmillan.

Zhang, Qian Forrest; Donaldson, John A. (2008): The Rise of Agrarian Capitalism with Chinese Characteristics. Agricultural Modernization, Agribusiness and Collective Land Rights. In *The China Journal* (60), pp. 25–47.

Yang, Xing; Rajaonarison, Haja M.; Hisano, Shuji (2016): Financialization of Agriculture in China: The Role of Private Equity Firms, Agribusiness and Local Governments. Asian Platform for Global Sustainability & Transcultural Studies. Kyoto (AGST Working Paper Series No. 2016-02).

Yap, Chuin-Wei (2015): How China's Cofco Won Tully Sugar. In *The Wall Street Journal*, 3/31/2015. Available online at https://blogs.wsj.com/chinarealtime/2015/03/31/how-chinas-cofco-won-tully-sugar/, checked on 5/10/2017.

# Part 2

# Grounded perspectives

# 5 Grounding

## Placing Chinese agri-food capital in Australian ruralities

On a hot Shanghai summer day, I am sitting on a hotel terrace not far from the Bund where I am speaking to a senior executive of Zhongshan Sunrise,[1] a diversified Chinese business conglomerate in the fabricated metals industry with significant investments in Australian food and farming. With pastoral leases in Western and Northern Australia covering over 1 million hectares of land, the company runs one of the largest Chinese-owned beef cattle operations in Australia. In addition to its three cattle stations, the group also owns two Australian wineries and has built its own Australian wine retail network in China. As an agri-food entrepreneur with no prior background in agriculture and farming, the group's success in building a veritable wine and beef cattle empire in Australia intrigues me. How did the company identify investment opportunities in Australian agriculture—an investment geography and economic sector it knew little about? Was it simply following a "going out" blueprint scripted by national policymakers? What were the processes and practices that actually grounded Zhongshan Sunrise in particular Australian ruralities? "Our investment story began in 2010," the executive explains, "when our chairman participated in an investment delegation to Australia organized by our provincial government [of Zhejiang province]." The delegation's destination was the Western Australian capital of Perth, where a group of officials from the state's Trade and Investment Office was already waiting to welcome the private businessmen from China. In fact, a formal sister state relationship between Western Australia and Zhejiang province established in 1987 had provided a long-standing institutional context for mutual visits by political leaders and business delegations and helped strengthen trade and investment ties between the two regions. The Chinese businessmen were taken to farms and agribusinesses around Perth, shuffled into meeting rooms where Australian trade and investment officials presented the competitive advantages of Australia's agricultural sector and entertained at networking events where they had a chance to mingle with Western Australian agribusiness professionals and local deal brokers. The efforts invested in the business delegation were not in vain. Having left Australia with a promising list of contacts and opportunities, upon his return to China, Zhongshan Sunrise's chairman announced his decision to diversify into the Australian wine sector and, just

DOI: 10.4324/9781003474661-8

a few months later, sealed a deal that saw the Chinese business group acquire an 88 percent equity stake in a boutique Western Australian winery, operating a 250 ha vineyard and its own wine brand. Supported by its local Australian team, Zhongshan Sunrise then set out to expand the winery's sales network from its traditional markets in Europe and North America to China, where an increasingly affluent and aspirational middle class with a newly developed taste for fine wines promised attractive profits. Over the next years, Zhongshan Sunrise's investments in Australian agriculture kept expanding through the same mixture of contingency and business acumen that had characterized the group's initial foray into Australia's wine sector. As Zhongshan Sunrise's familiarity with the sector grew and business contacts deepened, the company began to scour the market for "complimentary" investments in the beef cattle sector. Finally, in 2014, the company's well-connected and highly experienced Australian executive manager brokered Zhongshan's first deal in the beef cattle sector. "Once the initial connection was made, we got more and more deeply involved in the sector," the executive explained the company's fast rise to one of the country's largest beef cattle operators. "It was a process that happened step-by-step. And the more we became connected in the industry, the more opportunities we could identify."

* * *

The Zhongshan Sunrise case is illustrative of the ways in which Chinese investors establish themselves in Australian agriculture. Far from entering Australia as an external force, unilaterally impacting Australian ruralities and agri-food spaces, this chapter shows how Chinese investment is grounded in Australian ruralities through the situated practices and contingent linkages between a multiplicity of actors operating across national borders and at different scales—from the local to the transnational. As recent ethnographic studies have shown, Chinese investments take shape and are assembled through "inherently provisional configurations" between government policies, financial institutions, foreign and domestic investors, and local business interests (Rogers et al. 2015, p. 739; see also Lee 2018; Oliveira 2018; Brautigam 2015). Drawing from and adding to this literature, this chapter provides a grounded perspective on the processes and practices through which Chinese capital is assembled with Australian land and agribusiness. It demonstrates how the individual investment projects that make up the face of China's agri-food expansion in the context of Australia are co-produced in alliance with Australian government actors seeking to achieve policy goals, Australian agri-business stakeholders eager to improve their access to the famed "China market," as well as private individuals acting as deal brokers and mediators in the pursuit of personal gain and power.

Such a perspective is important as it brings to the fore the local and transnational actors inside and outside of China that are frequently obscured by monolithic portrayals of Chinese investment as a state-led national development strategy. To be sure, national investment policies, high-level summits, and bilateral agreements set the context within which investment flows unfold, but individual deals rarely originate at the national scale. Rather it is the work, commitment, and risk-taking of individual deal brokers, investment advisors, and agribusiness professionals that enable investment capital to touch down in specific places and that enforce the terms of its integration (Klinger & Muldavin 2019). Conceptualized as "translocal actors" (Rogers et al. 2015) or "transnational locals" (Klinger & Muldavin 2019), what distinguishes these actors is that they are both locally grounded and transnationally connected. However, a grounded perspective on how Chinese capital articulates with local agri-food spaces also raises questions of agency in terms of host country interests. As scholars have pointed out, portraying China's overseas land rush as a unilateral *force* inexorably advancing on communities abroad glosses over the important role of host country institutions and actors in facilitating and enabling investment (Hofman 2016; Fairbairn 2013). Indeed, despite a tightening of Australia's land investment regime in 2015, political and economic elites have been instrumental in courting and attracting Chinese investors in an attempt to draw capital into Australian ruralities and gain access to market opportunities in China.

Drawing on semi-structured interviews conducted with investors, regulators, and deal brokers in Australia and China, I first outline how political and institutional arrangements at the national scale function to create an environment that facilitates Chinese agri-investments. I then turn to the role of translocal actors in translating investment flows into specific and locally grounded investment projects. The final section highlights some of the frictions generated by Chinese agri-investment flows as expectations and interests clash between different groups of actors.

## Institutional arrangements and state actors

For any Chinese investor with ambitions to establish a presence in Australian agriculture, the journey begins by identifying an appropriate investment opportunity. This can present a significant challenge, given the regulatory, cultural, industry-specific, and managerial challenges involved in the acquisition of agricultural land and businesses in a foreign context. Indeed, in the eyes of Australian agribusiness and investment professionals, many Chinese investors have been strikingly amateurish in their handling of their overseas investments—much in contrast to the mainstream media that tend to cast Chinese investment as a powerful, totalizing force. "They were real babes in the woods. Perhaps they bought things they shouldn't have purchased. They were rushed, they didn't quite understand what they were doing," as one investment advisor described a widely held view among Australian land brokers and experts familiar with the kinds of deals Chinese investors were pursuing (interview March 2017, Canberra).

In the face of these challenges, for many Chinese investors, government agencies in support of China's agricultural "going out" policy (see Chapter 2) present an obvious point of departure. For early stage investors, Chinese government bodies play an important role in providing information, offering trainings, and facilitating introductions to potential Australian sellers and business partners. For instance, the Ministry of Commerce (MOFCOM) regularly publishes foreign investment guides, educating Chinese investors about regulatory regimes, investment policies, and issues pertaining to social and environmental governance of the host country.[2] Similarly, the Chinese Embassy in Australia, in its role as the main conduit between MOFCOM and Australia's Department of Foreign Affairs and Trade, provides advice to Chinese businesses looking to enter the Australian agricultural sector. In 2014, the embassy released one of the most comprehensive Australia-focused investment guide to date—a 450-page Chinese language tome that offers detailed information on issues ranging from possible investment models to in-depth investment analyses of the various sectors constituting Australian agriculture (Ma 2014). Another important entry point for Chinese businesses looking to invest in Australian agriculture is provided by China's state-owned commercial banks (SOBs). Over the course of the last decade, all four major SOBs[3] have established branches in Australia, where they leverage their position at the intersection of finance and agriculture to help their current and prospective Chinese clients explore possible investment deals (VC Group 2016). Investors may also obtain information and advice from industry peak bodies such as the China Council for the Promotion of International Trade (CCPIT), an agency operating under MOFCOM and charged with promoting Chinese investments abroad. From its headquarters in Beijing, CCPIT maintains close contact with its representative offices around the world, gauging the local business climate, carrying out research on trade and investment, and nurturing relationships with host country state and business actors alike. By building transnational relationships, government agencies such as CCPIT act as a springboard for Chinese businesses looking to invest in Australian agriculture. A high-ranking investment official at the Beijing headquarters described the agency's daily work as follows:

> As a trade and investment promotion agency, we set up meetings between investors and sellers, we offer trainings. For example, if you are going to invest in Australia, we train you, we invite people with local expertise such as people from the Chinese embassy in Australia, or organizations that are active in Australia to talk about their experiences.
> (interview June 2018, Beijing)

Needless to say, establishing transnational professional networks of the kind outlined by my interview partner at CCPIT crucially relies on an open and enabling institutional environment in the host country. Host country governments have long been identified as active agents that have been instrumental in determining the actual forms in which foreign investment takes hold in local agri-food spaces (Wolford et al. 2013). Australia is no exception here. As we have seen in Chapter 3, shaped by a neoliberal doctrine of "open markets," Australia's policy environment has traditionally been open to and supportive of foreign investment in Australian agriculture. Even as concerns about "state-led" investment for food security reasons were running high, ultimately forcing the re-regulation of Australia's foreign investment regime, then Minister of Trade and Investment Andrew Robb had this to say in a foreword to the Chinese embassy's investment guide mentioned above: "We have a clear message to global investors – we unambiguously welcome investment from abroad. We are open for business. And we want to create the most stable and conducive investment environment possible." (Ma 2014, pp. v–vi). But Australian policymakers have not only been *welcoming* to foreign investment, they have been actively *attracting* foreign investment by promoting Australia, as a "land of opportunity [that] offers golden prospects for astute [foreign] investors" (Ma 2014, p. vi). Indeed, scholars examining the politics of foreign investment in Australia have argued that the mechanisms by which Australian state actors promote investment "are explicitly, and at times exclusively, identifying and targeting foreign [...] investors" (Rogers et al. 2015, p. 737).

One of the most salient institutions through which Australia promotes itself to foreign investors is its government-operated trade and investment agencies. On the national level, the Australian Trade and Investment Commission (Austrade) is a key actor. Established in the wake of Australia's neoliberal turn in the 1980s, Austrade became an expedient political institution through which to press foreign governments for better market access and win "productive" foreign investment into Australia's domestic economy. In 2021, Austrade operated 106 offices in locations around the world, with eight of them located in China alone (Austrade 2021). The increasing significance of bringing foreign investment to Australia is reflected in the agency's name change in 2016 that brought the word "investment" into the agency's previous official title as "Australian Trade Commission," signaling a "very strong commitment by the Australian government to investment attraction," as one Austrade official put it (interview March 2017, Canberra). Next to Austrade, trade and investment agencies also exist on the state and, at times, local levels, where they seek to develop investment promotion strategies specifically tailored to the characteristics of Australia's regional and local economies.

One of the central practices through which Australia's trade and investment agencies have sought to recruit foreign investment into Australia's agricultural sector is investment delegations. They typically involve a group of Australian agribusiness professionals and food exporters with investment and trade interests in the Chinese market to jointly travel to China for a number of days to follow a tightly packed agenda of meetings, site visits, and conferences. Investment delegations provide an opportunity for Australian agribusiness professionals to meet potential Chinese investors and explore export opportunities for Australian food and agricultural products in the Chinese market. Delegations also feature seminars and conferences where investment officers and industry experts give presentations with titles such

*Figure 5.1* Chinese agri-investment delegation attending a conference organized by the Victorian Trade & Investment Office, March 2017, Melbourne.

*Source:* Image by the author.

as "Investing in Australia – A Wealth of Opportunities" and "Australia: Agri-Food Success Stories" to selected Chinese business representatives invited to join the delegation. At times, such delegations are headed by Australian ministers and provide an arena for high-level official talks on trade and investment rules (see Table 5.1).

Within Australia, trade and investment agencies routinely act as hosts for delegations from China, providing a complementary program of presentations, trainings, and field visits to rural farms and agribusinesses. Such delegations are a testament to the often "mundane practices" (Fairbairn 2014, p. 252) through which Chinese investment in Australian agriculture is constituted: business people networking over conference lunches and handing out business cards to potential investors, sellers, or business partners; experts and investment professionals traveling back and forth between their Sydney or Melbourne offices and Chinese conference centers to present the latest investment success stories and market insights; or investment officers preparing glossy magazines and reports in Chinese language that present investment case studies and development trends in the Australian agricultural sector to prospective investors.

*Table 5.1* High-level political and industry events promoting Chinese investment throughout the 2010s

| | |
|---|---|
| May 2014 | **Australia China Food Summit**<br>*Conference held in Sydney and organized by the Australia China Business Council (ACBC) with a focus on Chinese investment in Australian agriculture, attended by Australian and Chinese political and business leaders.* |
| August 2014 | **ASA100 Partnership**<br>Signing into force of the private industry-led *Australia Sino One Hundred Year Agricultural and Food Safety Partnership* (ASA100) between Australian mining and beef magnate Andrew Forrest and Chinese agri-business tycoon Liu Yonghao of New Hope Group in Canberra. The partnership was signed with high-level political endorsement, marked by the presence of Chinese President Xi Jinping and Australian Prime Minister Tony Abbott. |
| September 2014 | **Australian business mission to China**<br>Business mission led by Minister of Agriculture Barnaby Joyce comprised of 38 industry representatives to meet with China's Minister of Agriculture Han Changfu and lobby for an agriculture-focused free trade deal with Australia. |
| September 2014 | **Australian Dairy Farm Investment Forum**<br>Conference organized by industry peak body Dairy Australia to attract Chinese investment into Australia's dairy industry, attended by Australian and Chinese political and business leaders. |
| June 2015 | **Signing of China-Australia Free Trade Agreement (ChAFTA)**<br>Comprehensive agreement to liberalize trade and investment between Australia and China with agriculture as a key industry, signed by Prime Minister Tony Abbott and Chinese Minister of Commerce Gao Hucheng in Canberra. |
| April 2016 | **Australia Week in China**<br>Largest ever trade delegation of Australian politicians and 1,000 business leaders visiting 150 locations across China to promote agriculture as part of the touted economic transition from the previous "mining boom" to food and agriculture. |
| November 2016 | **Australia-China Food & Agribusiness Summit**<br>Follow-up conference to the 2014 "Australia China Food Summit" by the ACBC, promoting Chinese investment in Australian farmland and agribusiness. |
| February 2017 | **Summit on "Chinese investment in the Australian agribusiness sector"**<br>Conference organized by the ACBC for senior Australian and Chinese executives from business and government, highlighting the opportunities and challenges surrounding Chinese investment in Australian agriculture. |
| March 2017 | **5th China-Australia Annual Prime Ministerial Meeting**<br>Visit of Chinese Premier Li Keqiang to meet Australian Prime Minister Tony Abbott in Canberra. During the meeting, a number of agriculture-related agreements were signed, including an agreement that would increase access of Australian chilled beef to export markets in China. |

*Source:* Elaborated by the author.

Efforts to promote Chinese investment in Australian agriculture are not only limited to government institutions but also involve industry peak bodies, such as the Australia China Business Council (ACBC). Founded in 1973, ACBC represents over 900 Australian companies doing business in China and promotes bilateral trade and investment between the business communities of both countries. Through regular networking and business matchmaking events, ACBC offers a platform for business executives from Australia and China to build transnational linkages and learn about new business opportunities. Arguably, the industry peak body has in some ways been instrumental in popularizing discourses about the new opportunities Chinese investment could offer to the Australian food and agriculture sector. Indeed, one of the earliest "Food Summits" on the topic—a large-scale conference bringing together hundreds of Australian and Chinese agribusiness professionals, investment advisors, as well as policymakers—was organized by ACBC in 2014 (see Table 5.1). "It was groundbreaking," a former ACBC staff member involved in putting together the conference told me. "I think no one else had done anything like it" (interview February 2018, Berlin). Growing Chinese investor interest in Australian food and agriculture has also spawned new industry initiatives such as the Australia Sino 100 Year Agricultural and Food Safety Partnership (ASA100)—an initiative involving major Australian agribusinesses with export interests in China as well as some high-profile Chinese investors such as private agribusiness corporation New Hope Group (see Table 5.1). Established in 2015 with endorsement from both Australian Premier Tony Abbott and Chinese President Xi Jinping, the initiative has been focused on building a unified branding strategy for Australian food exports to China, seeking to strengthen Australia's reputation as a supplier of safe, premium agricultural food products (Durkin 2019). Especially Australian industry groups have been eager to keep in close contact with the Chinese agri-business community, even as investment became more contentious and diplomatic relations became increasingly fraught with tension at the end of the 2010s, with annual industry summits remaining a fixture in the bilateral relationship between both countries.

## The role of transnational locals

Institutional arrangements such as bilateral investment conferences, business delegations, and industry initiatives are both an indicator of Chinese interest in Australian food and farming and a mechanism by which that interest is propagated. At the same time, however, their role should not be overemphasized. In fact, investment processes are rarely shaped through formal institutions alone but also involve transnational personal connections and entanglements. Asked about the processes through which Chinese investment actually materializes in specific Australian ruralities, a Chinese investment official working at CCPIT confirmed:

> There is a lot of information coming through but there is not so much information that is available broadly to everyone. Most of it is private

> information that people learn about through their personal channels. [...] A lot of the investment activity relies on personal recommendation or personal connections. And these types of referrals often happen without the involvement of the authorities or official [investment] institutions.
>
> (interview June 2018, Beijing)

This statement draws attention to the pivotal role played by a new group of transnational deal brokers in channeling transnational investment flows into actual investment deals on the ground. Conceptualized as "translocal actors" or "transnational locals," what sets them apart is their ability to articulate local sites with global networks. In other words, while these actors are closely integrated into border-crossing business and trade networks, they are also deeply embedded in local sites and their related knowledges and resources. Indeed, as my research confirmed, translocal actors play critical roles in enabling and implementing Chinese land deals. In what follows, I will look at three groups of transnational locals that are relevant in the Australian context—investment intermediaries/ advisory firms, agribusiness professionals acting as business partners, and investment fund managers—and examine the practices through which these actors enable and implement specific investment initiatives.

### *Investment intermediaries*

Investment intermediaries are Australian investment professionals who help Chinese agri-investors develop an investment strategy, identify investment opportunities, and broker deals with local farmers and agribusiness professionals. Some investment intermediaries are hired directly by a Chinese company to implement their Australian investment strategy while others work for Chinese investors as specialized, external consultants on a fee basis. While investment intermediaries do not necessarily have a background in agriculture, many emphasize their "cultural abilities" as the key feature qualifying them for their role. Indeed, many of the investment intermediaries I encountered were Australian business professionals of Chinese descent. Fluent in both cultures and languages, these individuals see themselves as uniquely equipped to bridge the gap between Chinese investors lacking a careful understanding of Australia's business culture and Australian agri-business professionals and farmers with little knowledge about the background and motivations of their Chinese counterparts. One such intermediary who had helped a large Chinese retail group to establish a significant portfolio of beef cattle farms in Australia explained:

> Where we [the Chinese retail group] stand apart probably for a lot of the other foreign businesses, particularly Chinese investors, is that we're bridging the cultural difference, okay? That cross-cultural management is what we're doing better than a lot of the other companies. So, what I mean by this is, really in the industry that we operate in

> there's three sets of cultures. There's Chinese culture, there's Australian city culture, and there's Australian farming culture. So, a big part of my job is to bridge that gap. [...] You have a lot of Chinese companies where the managing director here is Chinese, but from China, so they can't connect with their staff here locally. They are not on the same wave-length, okay? But then if you have a group of Caucasian Australians, they don't understand China. And it's finding that right balance to manage all of that. So that's where I think we're doing a good job. [...] Because if I go and speak to a vendor about a property that's for sale, they'll look at me differently. When they speak to me, they'll realize that I'm Australian, right?
>
> (interview September 2017, Sydney)

While transnational locals such as the manager quoted above typically take on senior management positions with the Chinese investor companies themselves, the need for transnational locals that help Chinese investors navigate the Australian agri-food landscape has also spawned a number of specialized investment advisory firms. I met the director of one such firm, Ling,[4] in her office in the Western Sydney business district. Born in China and with a degree in business management from the University of New South Wales, Ling had built a remarkable career in cross-border investment, first as a foreign direct investment specialist at the Chinese Ministry of Commerce in Beijing and later as an advisor for Chinese investment in the Australian mining sector at PwC in Sydney. Leveraging her networks and connections built during her time at the global consultancy firm PwC, Ling established her own specialist advisory firm in 2011, together with a partner from PwC. What sets Ling's company apart from similar businesses is its ability to "cut through the obvious language barriers and less obvious cultural differences that can have unforeseen detrimental consequences in business deals if not managed properly," as we can read on the company's website. Brokering a deal crucially revolves around "educating" Chinese investors and funneling their, at times, "unrealistic" expectations toward feasible investment strategies. As Ling explained:

> We help the client to understand what their strategy into agriculture is. What are they trying to achieve? How much money do they have? What sector do they want to invest in? And then, after we're clear on the strategy we help them to implement. Execution. We help them to find different possibilities and do due diligence and make an approach and make a purchase.
>
> (interview March 2017, Sydney)

It becomes clear that deal brokers such as Ling play a critical role in mediating, shaping, and transforming the sometimes vague and abstract investment intentions of Chinese businessmen into specific, materially grounded investment outcomes. Indeed, the new group of intermediaries emerging around Chinese capital inflows literally *translates* Chinese investor interest into on-the-ground acquisitions of agricultural land and businesses. For the investment intermediaries themselves, grounding Chinese investment flows constitutes an expedient avenue by which these actors propel themselves forward professionally. Whether it is by establishing themselves as key figures in the terrain of China's transnational capital flows or by obtaining a lucrative position as the Australian CEO of a China-based investor company, their activities enable investment intermediaries to firmly embed themselves within the transnational business elites that have been rising along with China's global agri-food expansion.

### *Agribusiness professionals*

Beyond deal brokers and investment intermediaries such as Ling, a second group of transnational locals that is of significance here are Australian agribusiness professionals who come to establish themselves as business partners of a Chinese agri-food investor. In contrast to investment intermediaries, agribusiness professionals do not have language and cultural skills to commend themselves in the eyes of Chinese agri-investors but have rich agribusiness expertise. Agribusiness professionals partnering with Chinese investors may have worked in top management positions for major Australian agribusiness and trade companies and have built valuable transnational business relationships. For these actors, partnering with a Chinese investor is first and foremost a means to personally capitalize on the growing trade and market opportunities China's global agri-food expansion promises. The story of Australia Baoniu[5] illustrates the ways in which a number of Australian agri-business professionals have been able to form partnerships with Chinese investors, thus enabling and structuring Chinese investment flows on the ground. Baoniu's story begins in 2013 with two Australian livestock veterans setting up their own livestock trade company. Originally focusing on the shipment of Australian live cattle to export markets around the world, the company soon began to diversify into livestock production. The vision was to acquire a string of Australian cattle stations, raise high-grade black Angus beef cattle, and sell the meat under the company's own brand to high-priced export markets in China and other Asian countries, as Phil, one of the company's founders and its general manager, explained. What was missing, however, was the capital necessary for expansion. With no money but a number of Chinese business contacts developed through the company's cattle trading activities, the two entrepreneurs set out to find a Chinese business partner. Their personal connections proved to be instrumental, Phil recalled:

> We had a vision, but we needed a significant contribution of equity. And through having dealt with China for a number of years, we developed strong relationships in China. And whilst we hadn't known our current

> business partners for that long, we had other relationships in China that had spanned for several years, and it was through those relationships that we were introduced with our current partner in China. [...] And, as I said, we hadn't known this chap for very long at all, but we've known other people that knew him and knew us that when the introduction occurred, he took us with the degree of trust because his close friends had made the introduction.
>
> (interview August 2017, Melbourne)

In 2016, the newly minted business partners formed a joint venture, Australia Baoniu, comprised of five Australian shareholders and their Chinese partner – Fuyao Group, an agri-food entrepreneur with diversified business interests in the chemical industry, real estate, financial services, trade and fishery, and shipping, among others. While Fuyao is the largest single shareholder of the venture, it is Phil and his business partner who are responsible for Baoniu's investment strategy and the company's daily operations:

> At the end of the day, the relationship only works because of the fact that our Chinese partner uses the skills and the knowledge that we bring to the table. So, whilst he is the dominant partner in the business, and in theory, could exercise his right to change the direction of the company, he has enough understanding of life and reality to know that he must accept our guidance and our knowledge in how to run this business because that's why we're here. [...] And so, as a company, it is the Australian principles [Phil and his Australian business partner] that set the overall strategy and make the key decisions on how the company will execute as a business on a day-to-day basis. And that works quite smoothly in that regard.
>
> (interview August 2017, Melbourne)

With significant financial support from Fuyao, within 12 months Baoniu had acquired five grazing and feedlot properties across Victoria and Western Australia, aiming to expand its export capacity to 100,000 heads of cattle by 2020. Phil acknowledges that the partnership with Baoniu's Chinese backer has been crucial for the speed and scale at which the company has developed:

> I would say that if we did not have the equity backing of the Chinese, we would not be as aggressive in our positioning, currently, [...] because I would probably have to question whether we want to take that risk independently as such. So, to a degree, the Chinese investment here has given us the confidence to grow in this sector [...].
>
> (interview August 2017, Melbourne)

At the same time, Phil insisted that not every Australian farmer can strike up a successful agribusiness partnership with a Chinese investor. Similar to the investment intermediaries I have encountered during this research, Australian agri-business professionals with Chinese equity partners emphasize the need to understand Chinese business culture and the realities of the Chinese market. As Phil summarized Baoniu's success story:

> I think the difference between the experience that we've had with our Chinese partners and probably 90 percent of the experiences between China and Australia in agriculture that have failed, is that fact that we've done business in China since 2009. And so, our understanding of Chinese culture was reasonably refined. Our understanding of Chinese business was quite strong. And our understanding of how Chinese society and business works in regards to state-owned enterprises, private companies, movement of funds, restrictions, all those sort of things, we weren't starting from a naive position. We were starting from quite an experienced position, which enabled us very quickly to have productive initial conversations.
>
> (interview August 2017, Melbourne)

The case of Baoniu is emblematic of the alliances between Australian agribusiness elites and Chinese agri-food capital that frequently propel cross-border agricultural investments in Australia. While Baoniu's Australian executives crucially rely on their Chinese partner for access to equity capital and distribution networks in China, Fuyao's investment would not have been thinkable in its current form without the involvement and guidance of two highly experienced Australian agribusiness professionals. With two Australian "faces" at the front line, Baoniu has also escaped the negative media coverage surrounding much of China's agricultural investment in Australia. Indeed, Baoniu may represent a perfect example of the type of "investment partnership" Australian policymakers have been envisioning when reregulating foreign investment in Australian farmland back in 2015 (see Chapter 3).

### *Fund managers*

In contrast to investment intermediaries and agribusiness professionals, one group of actors that has been conspicuously absent from grounding Chinese capital in Australian ruralities are the managers and financial experts in charge of Australian farmland/ agricultural investment firms (FAIFs). Since the late 1990s, a host of FAIFs have been set up to capture investor capital and funnel it toward agriculture and farmland. In Australia, the rise of FAIFs is closely connected to the dismantling of state support for agriculture as governments began to liberalize the sector from the 1970s onward, creating space for financial capital to fill the gap left by the state when in the interest of profit (Larder et al. 2018). Among the most prominent FAIFs are, for instance, Macquarie Pastoral Fund, launched by global investment bank Macquarie Group, Queensland-based Laguna Bay, or specialist agricultural asset manager Growth Farms Australia. The typical modus operandi of an FAIF is to pool investor capital with which to build a portfolio of farmland/ farm properties, diversified by geography and agricultural sector. FAIFs promise investors regular returns in the form of the immediate cash flow generated by operating or leasing farmland as well as the capital returns resulting from the expected increases in the value of the underlying farmland or farm property. In exchange for their service, investors pay the FAIF a management fee, at times coupled with a performance fee (see also Ouma 2018; Sippel et al. 2016; Magnan 2015; Fairbairn 2014).

Situated at the intersection of agriculture and finance and with extensive experience in attracting capital from both domestic and international investors, FAIFs would appear to be well suited to capture growing Chinese interest in Australian agriculture—particularly from Chinese agri-food entrepreneurs, who, as we have seen, tend to focus their investment strategies around the acquisition of Australian farmland. Yet, while Australia's FAIFs have channeled billions of dollars into the Australian farm sector, acquiring millions of hectares of farmland, they have had little success in engaging Chinese investors. My interviews with fund managers confirm that most Australian FAIFs have little to no capital from Chinese investors under management. When being asked about his experience with Chinese investors, one fund manager aired his frustration:

*Manager:* It's hard work. My view is with Chinese investors, I really don't want to deal with them. I've dealt with between 50 and 100 prospects over the last five years. One has invested.

*Interviewer:* What happened to the others?

*Manager:* They just took the information, they changed their minds, kicked tires. If an investor comes to us, we will help them once they start investing. With Chinese investors I now tell them, "You have to write out some money, a cheque upfront. If it goes ahead, we'll give you that money back in reduced fees for management and stuff like that. But you've got to put some money on the table." Because so many of them, to be blunt, just fuck around and we've got no idea what they're doing. And disappear after one meeting or two meetings and burn up our time. So, I'll take one meeting and I'll say to them, "If you want us to continue this work for you, you've got to pay us $20–30,000. We'll give a rebate if you go ahead. If you don't, it's gone." That sends them out the door very quickly.

(interview February 2017, Sydney)

There are two reasons why Australian fund managers play virtually no role in articulating Chinese capital with Australian agriculture. First, Chinese investors generally prefer to have direct ownership over agricultural assets (sometimes in collaboration with an Australian partner) rather than merely owning shares in a fund that pools capital from a broad base of investors. "Rarely do Chinese like to invest with other Chinese, they like to do their own investment," a former manager of Macquarie Pastoral Fund summarized this view (interview March 2017, Melbourne). While in his interactions with prospective Chinese investors, the manager found that many were keen to build a farmland portfolio similar to what the manager had done on behalf of Macquarie, "they don't want to do it with anybody else," he explained. A second issue relates to the degree of control investors have over production processes and the agricultural commodities produced by the farms/ agribusinesses they own. In the case of FAIFs, the returns investors receive are purely financial in nature and come in the form of income from operating/ leasing farms as well as from capital appreciation. In contrast, for the vast majority of Chinese investors, gaining control over the agri-food commodities grown on their farms in Australia is a critical element in their investment strategy. While investments have to be financially profitable, they also need to provide investors with a material return in the form of control over food supplies.

Some fund managers point to cultural differences and a lack of investment sophistication as the root causes of missing Chinese enthusiasm for FAIFs. As one frustrated fund manager told me, the Chinese investors he was dealing with had little regard for innovations such as geographical diversification and operational efficiency with which the manager's FAIF sought to recruit prospective investors:

> At the end of the day, the Chinese mentality is they want physical assets. They want something they can go out and feel and touch and know it's there, and they want to know they've got ownership to it. [...] All those things that are really the advantage of what we're trying to do [as FAIF], they don't want to see.
>
> (interview March 2017, Canberra)

While FAIFs may blame their failure to enroll Chinese capital on a simplistic Chinese investment mentality favoring tangible over abstract assets, such a perspective fails to recognize how the distinct nature of Chinese capital, i.e., the specific interests, logics of accumulation, and processes of valorization associated with it, can make it fundamentally different from financial capital. In other words, the investment model proposed by FAIFs may suit the needs of the financial investors from the Global North that FAIFs typically cater to, but it does not chime with the production-driven and commodity-focused characteristics of much of the Chinese investment capital that has been flowing into Australia—an issue we will return to in more detail in Chapter 6.

Despite the absence of FAIFs in the transnational networks that ground Chinese capital in Australian agri-food spaces, some fund managers have found ways to individually engage with and benefit from the inflow of Chinese investment into Australian agriculture, for example by using their knowledge and skill set to source farm properties on behalf of Chinese investors (without necessarily managing them) and to provide other advisory services. Others have gone further still, directly taking up management positions with Chinese investor companies. A case in point is the former manager of Macquarie Pastoral Fund mentioned above, who took on a role as senior executive at the Australian agribusiness arm of Chinese investor Zhefu Group[6] in 2014. Drawing on his networks, finance background, and longstanding experience in the Australian agricultural sector, the former fund manager helped Zhefu Group—a typical Chinese agri-food entrepreneur—to build a portfolio of 19 beef cattle properties consolidated into a number of larger operational aggregations and spread across various climatic and rainfall zones throughout Victoria and New South Wales. According to the manager, the farmland portfolio built under his management closely resembles a typical fund portfolio in terms of diversification and risk management logics. What has changed though, is that the capital is no longer pooled from a group of individual investors but provided directly by a single Chinese agribusiness entrepreneur. With some 600 million AUD to spend on behalf of the Chinese business tycoon behind Zhefu Group, this may be one of the most exciting projects he had worked on, the manager admitted (interview March 2017, Melbourne).

## Frictions and failures

So far, we have looked at the key role of national institutions and state actors, business elites, and individuals in co-producing Chinese agri-investment on the ground. These examples demonstrate how interests align and new alliances between investors, state and business elites are formed around the flows of Chinese agri-food capital. Yet, investment flows across national boundaries also invariably generate friction among these groups. In fact, the engagement of Australian state and business actors does not necessarily guarantee investment "success" but, on the contrary, may complicate or even endanger specific investment projects—intentionally or unintentionally. The last section highlights some of the tensions that arise among investors and the actors grounding Chinese investment as interests clash and different goals come into conflict with each other.

In the Australian context, friction often arises from the uneven relations of power between Chinese agri-investors and the transnational locals that actualize investment strategies on the ground. In contrast to how we may think of transnational capital—as a powerful force effortlessly moving across borders and extracting surplus from overseas landscapes unhindered—Chinese capital is not necessarily in a dominant position vis-à-vis the actors and interests it encounters in Australian ruralities. Unlike their counterparts from the global North, many of the Chinese investors I have encountered during my research have only begun to operate in the global arena and lack the experience, rigor, and professionalism of the North Atlantic-based agribusinesses and financial institutions acquiring Australian agricultural land and businesses. This is reflected by China's high agri-investment failure rate, supposedly the highest in the world, according to a 2014 report from the Chinese embassy in Australia

(Ma 2014, pp. 279–280). It is also a widely shared view among Australian business and investment professionals. As one outspoken fund manager put it when I asked about his perspective on Chinese investors in Australian agriculture: "I would describe them generally as being unsophisticated, naïve, and a lot of them are going to end up in trouble" (interview February 2017, Sydney). Naturally, this makes Chinese investors vulnerable to local actors seeking to profit from and take advantage of a group of investors perceived to be capital-rich but inexperienced.

According to the Australian investment professionals I interviewed for this research, the lack of investment sophistication among many Chinese investors is reflected, for instance, by a tendency to value land size over land quality. Many Chinese investors are attracted by the mindboggling size of Australian farms and cattle stations—particularly in comparison to China, where farms are small, scattered, and lack private property rights (Lin 2009). This focus on farm size often obscures the fact that much of Australia's land mass is low-grade land or simply "a big brown place" as one Australian agribusiness professional scoffed (interview February 2017, Sydney). Next to size, there also appears to be a "beauty factor" (Ouma 2020), whose significance should not be underestimated in accounting for investment decisions. I have heard countless stories of rich Chinese businessmen "falling in love" with a farm and rushing to buy it, sometimes without a clear understanding of how to turn that acquisition into a profitable investment. As one investment advisor at the Victorian Trade & Investment Office described it:

> We have had investors [from China] that just came here, drove around, and fell in love with a rural property. Perhaps they liked the scenery, or they liked the landscape. […] They buy it but then the question is: what are they going to do with it? It's more than buying the farm. It's about what am I doing with the farm? And then there might be a lot of issues that initially they wouldn't be aware of. Maybe someone bought a farm with plans to grow this and that and realized that there wasn't enough water. Or someone bought a farm thinking that it might be ideal to convert into a site for rural tourism and then being stuffed with the local Council because they didn't get the planning permit. So, we are trying to steer them into the right direction. Do proper due diligence. You buy a farm and before you get it you need to understand what's your plan and whether that's feasible.
>
> (interview March 2017, Melbourne)

This depiction is in stark contrast with the sober calculative practices and rigorous business considerations that we associate with the investment strategies of more "sophisticated" investors such as financial institutions or agribusinesses from the Global North. Yet, whether the "impulsive" investment approach observed for some Chinese agri-investors ultimately endangers investment projects is difficult to say. Particularly for the case of Chinese agri-food entrepreneurs—wealthy individuals with considerable autonomy over their companies' investment decisions—there is much to suggest that investments are, at least in part, "lifestyle acquisitions" where hard profit interests intersect with a desire to obtain "the fame and fortune of large landlord status" (Geisler 2015, p. 243).

A "naïve" fetishization of farmland size and beauty coupled with a lack of knowledge about local land markets and prices has meant that many Chinese investors overpay for the farms and cattle stations they acquire—a tendency readily exploited by some Australian farmers and investment professionals. As Ling, the investment intermediary we encountered above, explained:

> The reason [Chinese investors] pay a much higher price than their next-door neighbor would pay is because of information asymmetry. Lack of information. They don't know what they are doing. And the vendors happily take the money and run away, enjoying their retirement.
>
> (interview March 2017, Sydney)

Phil, the Australian business partner behind Chinese-Australian-invested Baoniu, had similar stories to tell about Chinese investors falling into the "traps" dishonest deal brokers had laid out for them:

> Australian individuals and groups that have assisted with investment of Chinese money in Australia for agricultural purposes [...] have taken advantage of the naivety of the Chinese in understanding Australian agriculture and sold them properties and done whatever else, and then quite happily sat back and watched the hard reality of life bite when the Chinese don't achieve what they had aspired to achieve.
>
> (interview August 2017, Melbourne)

For transnational locals like Ling, whose fortunes are closely bound up with the overall "success" of Chinese investment in Australia, this raises serious concerns:

> A lot of Chinese investors are losing money in Australian agriculture. That's not good for China, and that's not good for Australia. I want to see more success stories in agriculture so that people have the confidence to invest more.
>
> (interview March 2017, Sydney)

Chinese agri-investors themselves have been careful not to complain about their Australian business partners and deal brokers. Of the investors I spoke with personally, most cited overall regulatory uncertainty in Australia and China rather than unfair deal-making practices as their primary concern. When asked, nobody called into question earlier investment decisions, instead putting on the "show" of optimism and confidence so familiar in business and investor circles. The exception was an extremely frustrated manager in charge of a large-scale farmland investment by a Chinese state farm. Much seems to have gone wrong with the investment project. Yields were lower than expected for the price that had been paid, workers "cheated" knowing that the investor company had no experience farming in Australia, and other farmers with whom the company had signed offtake agreements refused to honor these agreements. The manager now had only one recommendation for anyone back in China interested in making investments in Australian agriculture: "Do not try to grow grain in Australia!" (interview August 2017, Geelong).

Moments of friction do not only come up with Australian business partners and deal brokers but also arise with Australian state actors operating at the subnational scale. Although Australia's national institutions and government work to attract Chinese investment, as we have seen in the first section of this chapter, the ability of Chinese investors to place capital into Australian agricultural landscapes depends on the commitments and actions of lower-scale state actors. These actors play a critical role in structuring and enforcing the specific terms of individual investment projects as they issue planning permits, set environmental policy, and administer employment and health-related regulations. In contrast to China's own experience as a destination of foreign investment and where local governments have usually gone to great lengths to help foreign investors succeed and smooth business risks (Brautigam 2015), local state actors in Australia may be less prepared to support foreign investment at all cost. The ambiguities generated by national-scale actors courting Chinese investors and local governments dragging their feet to accommodate investor wishes take many Chinese companies by surprise. As a high-ranking investment officer working for the New South Wales state government explained:

> In China, because business and government are so closely aligned, if you're not going to go anywhere, the government tells you right at step one, "You're not going to be able to do this." If there is a problem in the way and you have the right government connections, the government will fix the problem. That doesn't work like that here. So, what we sometimes find is that Chinese businesses will come to us as government expecting us to step in and solve the problem and move that town, or that river, or whatever it might be to make things work for them. And it just doesn't work like that in Australia.
>
> (interview February 2017, Sydney)

The tensions generated by conflicting development mandates espoused by state actors working at different scales of government are best illustrated by the story of Chinese investor Hengyu Dairy Group.[7] In the summer of 2014, Hengyu Dairy, a large milk producing and processing company from China's Zhejiang province, acquired a string of dairy farms in southern Victoria. The company had an ambitious vision: exporting 100,000 liters of fresh milk a day from its Australian dairy farms to its customer base in China. To achieve its goal, the company announced that it would intensify its farming practices by doubling its herd size, building a large barn in which to house its animals during much of the year, and to construct a nearby bottling plant from where its fresh milk would be collected on a daily basis and transported to the nearest airport from where the milk would be airfreighted to China. But things soon turned sour for Hengyu Dairy. Hundreds of local farmers filed complaints about the potential environmental and health impacts the project might engender for the local community; protest meetings were staged at which participants agitated against the "industrialization" of the local dairy industry by an overseas company; and the local council was suddenly dragging its feet about approving the company's planning application. Concerned about the future of the investment project, company executives began making concessions: the company would dispense with building a barn and only construct a bottling plant; milk production targets were reduced from 100,000 liters a day to 30,000 liters and day; and instead of collecting milk daily for transport to China, the company would now only charter one weekly flight, selling its milk to local processors on the remaining six days of the week. In August 2015 after more than a year of debating, petitioning, and waiting, the local Council summarily rejected Hengyu Dairy's planning application, making clear that the company would not be able to go ahead with any of its development plans. Company executives were confounded by the decision. The unwillingness of the local government to support investor interests was all the more incomprehensible to the company executives since they had been encouraged by the Victorian state government "to be here [...], and to expand dairy production and exports" the company's Australian chief executive explained to an Australian newspaper outlet (Neales 2015c). "It seems like the national government is saying it wants foreign investment and welcomes Chinese companies here, but then when we do what they encourage us to, local councils really have more power," the bewildered executive stated (Neales 2015c). Today, the company appears to have abandoned its ambitious dairy export plans. All the while, its Australian dairy farms have fallen into disrepair, symbolically underlining the failure of an ambitious investment endeavor.

*****

The Chinese government may well have a strategy to help its agri-food companies "go out" and invest in overseas food and farming, but turning abstract strategy into concrete investment opportunity is a different story altogether. As this chapter has shown, a multiplicity of actors is implicated in grounding Chinese capital in Australian ruralities—from investment promotion agencies to deal brokers, advisors, and Australian agribusiness professionals looking to raise investment capital from Chinese businesses. As transnational locals, these actors leverage their transnational networks, interpersonal connections, and multicultural backgrounds to boost investment from China. It is through their initiatives, commitments, and activities that high-level policy pronouncements are translated into specific investment projects on the ground. Far from being a homogenous force advancing on Australian communities unhindered, Chinese agri-food capital crucially relies on the support and guidance of transnational locals to articulate with Australian farms and food businesses. Moreover, the way in which investor interests turn into investment deals points to the somewhat contingent and haphazard nature of Chinese capital flows. Not every Chinese investor comes to Australia with a solid plan. A conversation with a savvy deal broker at a business conference, an organized tour through beautiful vineyard landscapes, or a passionate investment pitch delivered by a charismatic agribusiness professional may well sway a Chinese agri-food entrepreneur to rethink his investment strategy, shift focus from one agricultural sector to another, or reconsider the region in which to invest. Any land deal, then, is the contingent outcome of multiple actors and their interests coming in alignment with each other rather than the faithful execution of a strategy cooked up by the Chinese state. Finally, the stories in this chapter make clear that many Chinese businesses are, in fact, newcomers to the world of farmland investment and sometimes surprisingly naïve in their approach. For investment intermediaries and fund managers, whose own success is predicated upon investors closing successful deals, the unrealistic expectations and amateurishness characterizing the behavior of some Chinese investors create a real headache, and there is good reason to believe that the number of prematurely aborted or botched deals is far greater than we would ever read in the papers. Unlike the totalizing portrayals of China's land rush, the account presented here draws our attention to the profound unevenness with which Chinese capital works through Australian agricultural landscapes.

## Notes

1 The vignette is based on a personal interview in July 2018 in Shanghai. The company name used here is a pseudonym.
2 A regularly updated "country guide" for foreign investment in Australia presents a pertinent example here (MOFCOM 2017).
3 China's major state-owned commercial banks comprise the Bank of China (BoC), China Construction Bank (CCB), Agricultural Bank of China (ABC), and the Industrial and Commercial Bank of China (ICBC), all of which have established branches in Australia over the past two decades. The local presence of these banks is largely driven by increasing demand for debt facilities by Chinese investors coming to Australia.
4 The name is a pseudonym.
5 The name of the company and its managers are pseudonyms.
6 Again, I use a synonym here.
7 The company name is a pseudonym. The case of Hengyu Dairy Group has been assembled from a number of sources, including media reports, company documents, and personal communication with a member of local Council (see e.g., Neales 2014, 2015a, 2015b, 2015c; Ningbo Dairy Group 2014; Poole 2015).

## References

Austrade (2021): Annual Report 2020–2021. Available online at https://www.transparency.gov.au/publications/foreign-affairs-and-trade/australian-trade-and-investment-commission-austrade/australian-trade-and-investment-commission-annual-report-2020-21, checked on 7/22/2024.

Brautigam, Deborah (2015): *Will Africa Feed China?* Oxford, New York: Oxford University Press.

Durkin, Patrick (2019): How Twiggy Built an All-Star Team to Sell Australia to the World. In *Australian Financial Review*, 5/9/2019. Available online https://www.afr.com/work-and-careers/leaders/how-twiggy-built-an-all-star-team-to-sell-australia-to-the-world-20190408-p51c48, checked on 09/12/2020.

Fairbairn, Madelaine (2014): Just Another Asset Class? Neoliberalism, Finance, and the Construction of Farmland Investment. In Steven A. Wolf, Alessandro Bonanno (Eds.): *The Neoliberal Regime in the Agri-Food Sector. Crisis, Resilience, and Restructuring*. London: Routledge, pp. 245–262.

Fairbairn, Madeleine (2013): Indirect Dispossession: Domestic Power Imbalances and Foreign Access to Land in Mozambique. In Wendy Wolford, Saturnino M. Borras, Ruth Hall, Ian Scoones, Ben White (Eds.): *Governing Global Land Deals. The Role of the State in the Rush for Land*. Chichester, West Sussex: John Wiley & Sons, pp. 141–161.

Geisler, Charles (2015): Trophy Lands: Why Elites Acquire Land and Why It Matters. In *Canadian Journal of Development Studies* 36 (2), pp. 241–257. DOI: 10.1080/02255189.2015.1041881.

Hofman, Irna (2016): Politics or Profits along the "Silk Road": What Drives Chinese Farms in Tajikistan and Helps them Thrive? In *Eurasian Geography and Economics* 57 (3), pp. 457–481.

Klinger, Julie Michelle; Muldavin, Joshua (2019): New Geographies of Development: Grounding China's Global Integration. In *Territory, Politics, Governance* 7 (1), pp. 1–21. DOI: 10.1080/21622671.2018.1559.

Larder, Nicolette; Sippel, Sarah R.; Argent, Neil (2018): The Redefined Role of Finance in Australian Agriculture. In *Australian Geographer* 49 (3), pp. 397–418. DOI: 10.1080/00049182.2017.1388555.

Lee, Ching Kwan (2018): *The Specter of Global China. Politics, Labor, and Foreign Investment in Africa*. Chicago, London: The University of Chicago Press.

Lin, George C. S. (2009): *Developing China. Land, Politics and Social Conditions*. London, New York: Routledge.

Ma, Chaoxu (Ed.) (2014): *赴澳大利亚投资指南 [How to Invest in Australia]*. Beijing: 中国商务出版社 [China Commerce and Trade Press].

Magnan, André (2015): The Financialization of Agri-Food in Canada and Australia: Corporate Farmland and Farm Ownership in the Grains and Oilseed Sector. In *Journal of Rural Studies* 41, pp. 1–12. DOI: 10.1016/j.jrurstud.2015.06.007.

MOFCOM (2017): 对外投资合作国别（地区）指南 [Country (Region) Guide for Foreign Investment Cooperation]. 澳大利亚 [Australia]. Beijing.

Neales, Sue (2015a): China's Ningbo Dairy Group Looks to Greener Australian Pastures. In *The Australian*, 4/4/2015. Available online at https://www.theaustralian.com.au/business/in-depth/global-food-forum/chinas-ningbo-dairy-group-looks-to-greener-australian-pastures/news-story/8c32e3a6c3a85fb635b7a3ac6ab7cf26, checked on 5/17/2017.

Neales, Sue (2015b): Chinese Relent on 'Barned' Dairies in Gippsland. In *The Australian*, 4/16/2015. Available online at https://www.theaustralian.com.au/business/in-depth/global-food-forum/chinese-relent-on-barned-dairies-in-gippsland/news-story/1a775ed3fc2fab7f3ed379fd6d92775f, checked on 5/12/2017.

Neales, Sue (2015c): Dreams Blocked as Council Cries over Milk Spilling to China. In *The Australian*, 9/5/2015. Available online at https://www.theaustralian.com.au/nation/foreign-affairs/dreams-blocked-as-council-cries-over-milk-spilling-to-china/news-story/b4740d9e002aa6fc6e63ff21a37a5a01, checked on 5/12/2017.

Neales, Sue (2014): China's Dairy Churn: We Can Get More Milk Out of Your Cows. In *The Australian*, 9/17/2014. Available online at https://www.theaustralian.com.au/news/nation/chinas-dairy-churn-we-can-get-more-milk-out-of-your-cows/news-story/a498515daf600f4cc2e02adea4b31c3a, checked on 5/12/2017.

Ningbo Dairy Group (2014): 宁波牛奶集团再次收购3家澳洲牧场澳洲报纸头版大篇幅报道 [Ningo Dairy Group Acquires Yet Another 3 Australian Dairy Farms and Makes it on to the Front Page of Australian Newspaper]. Available online at https://www.nbnn.com.cn/, checked on 11/12/2017.

Oliveira, Gustavo de L. T. (2018): Boosters, Brokers, Bureaucrats and Businessmen: Assembling Chinese Capital with Brazilian Agribusiness. In *Territory, Politics, Governance* 7 (1), pp. 1–20.

Ouma, Stefan (2020): *Farming as Financial Asset. Global Finance and the Making of Institutional Landscapes*. Newcastle upon Tyne: Agenda Publishing.

Ouma, Stefan (2018): Opening the Black Boxes of Finance-Gone-Farming: A Global Analysis of Assetization. In Hilde Bjørkhaug, André Magnan, Geoffrey Lawrence (Eds.): *The Financialization of Agri-Food Systems. Contested Transformations*. Abingdon, Oxon, New York, NY: Routledge, pp. 85–107.

Poole, Laura (2015): Gippsland Community Celebrates Win over 'Farming Industrialisation' as Yo You Dairy Expansion Stalls. In *ABC News*, 10/22/2015. Available online at https://www.abc.net.au/news/rural/2015-10-22/yo-you-dairy-at-kernot-stalls/6875822, checked on 3/20/2020.

Rogers, Dallas; Lee, Chyi Lin; Yan, Ding (2015): The Politics of Foreign Investment in Australian Housing: Chinese Investors, Translocal Sales Agents and Local Resistance. In *Housing Studies* 30 (5), pp. 730–748.

Sippel, Sarah R.; Larder, Nicolette; Lawrence, Geoffrey (2016): Grounding the Financialization of Farmland. Perspectives on Financial Actors as New Land Owners in Rural Australia. In *Agriculture and Human Values* 34 (2), pp. 251.

VC Group (2016): Profiling Chinese Agribusiness (Beef) Investment in Australia. Available online at https://www.agric.wa.gov.au/sites/gateway/files/Profiling%20Chinese%20agribusiness%20beef%20investment%20in%20Australia%20-%20VC%20Group%2C%202015_0.pdf, checked on 3/5/2018.

Wolford, Wendy; Borras Jr., Saturino M.; Hall, Ruth; Scoones, Ian; White, Ben (2013): Governing Global Land Deals: The Role of the State in the Rush for Land. In Wendy Wolford, Saturnino M. Borras, Ruth Hall, Ian Scoones, Ben White (Eds.): *Governing Global Land Deals. The Role of the State in the Rush for Land*. Chichester, West Sussex: John Wiley & Sons, pp. 1–22.

# 6 Accumulation

## Rendering farmland investment profitable

A mild December day on the northwestern tip of Tasmania—Australia's southernmost island. I am sitting in a car with the farm manager of a large local dairy farm. As we drive past the lush pastures of the farm property, I can see small herds of Friesian and Jersey dairy cows, grazing peacefully under the steel blue sky. I have come here to visit one of the largest Chinese farmland investments that have occurred over the past few years in the Australian dairy sector. The farm manager, an experienced dairy farmer from the local community, has taken time out from her busy schedule to show me around the property. As we inspect the new pasture management methods, upgraded milking sheds, and raw milk collection points, I learn more about the investor company's ambitious plans to set up an integrated supply chain that will deliver fresh liquid milk from the company's Australian dairy farms to supermarkets and households in China's eastern cities. As the day draws to an end, the farm manager points out that there is still one place I absolutely must see if I am to understand what the investor company is trying to achieve in Australia. It is the most important part of the whole farm, she insists. We drive up one of the many hills, and a spectacular view across the South Australian coastline opens up before our eyes. "This is literally the edge of the world," the farm manager explains to me, and, pointing to the weather station installed on top of the hill, "the place where the cleanest air is, right up here. So, we actually boast the healthiest cows, breathing the healthiest air, producing the highest quality milk." "This," the farm manager concludes, "is obviously a huge selling point in China, and some people will pay a premium for that."

***

In the previous chapter, we examined the actors and processes through which Chinese agri-investments are grounded in specific Australian ruralities. This chapter shifts the perspective to a second dimension necessary for understanding China's global agri-food integration: the forms of accumulation through which Chinese investors seek to derive profits from their ownership of Australian farmland and food businesses. As I have argued earlier and as the

DOI: 10.4324/9781003474661-9

opening vignette suggests, profit accumulation is key to the overseas investment activities of Chinese agri-food companies. Even state-owned companies that are often thought of as pursuing predominantly strategic aims have to generate corporate profits to ensure the financial viability of their overseas ventures (see Chapter 4). This raises questions with respect to the particular arrangements through which different qualities of agriculture, or more broadly speaking, nature, are translated into profits. In particular, my focus here is on the ways in which Chinese agri-food capital circulates through the biophysical elements of food and farming – soils, water, nutrients, and the food commodities themselves – to generate profits—or maybe even "premium" profits—for investors. Which strategies do Chinese investors use to render profitable the farms and food businesses they have acquired in Australia? How do they leverage different biophysical elements of the farm and its natural environment in this process? How successful are they? And how do these stories decenter common understandings of China's food security?

To be sure, there is nothing new about the idea that agriculture and farming are organized around the imperative of profit-making. Processes of agricultural commodification have a long history, particularly in developed economies, where they pertain to both farmland and the food produced from it. Yet, understanding where, for a Chinese investor, the value of an Australian farm or food business comes from is crucial if we are to make sense of the dynamics driving China's land rush in Australia.

This chapter identifies three distinct and partially overlapping modes of accumulation: first, a *productive* mode of accumulation where profits accrue from practices of commodification, i.e., from the production and sale of agri-food commodities; second, a *valorization-based* mode of accumulation where productive revenues are enhanced by practices that valorize agricultural resources by mobilizing imaginaries of quality and safety associated with the Australian farming environment; and third, a *financial* mode of accumulation whereby agriculture is transformed into an asset from which investors derive an income stream in the form of rents, dividends, or capital gains. Most investors I met during my research aspired to obtaining premium profits from the place-based valorization of the food they produced on their Australian farms, but a small group of investors appeared to value the farmland they had bought for its financial rather than its productive qualities. While these modes of accumulation do not only render profitable different aspects of the biophysical processes underpinning agricultural production, they also have diverse transformative impacts on the spatialities and temporalities of food and farming, thus co-producing new and distinct agricultural landscapes (see Table 6.1).

The categorization provided in Table 6.1 is, of course, a stylized one and does not necessarily capture the messy realities of Chinese agri-investments on the ground. In practice, as my examples will demonstrate, different modes and logics of accumulation often overlap and intersect within one and the same investment project. The stories I present here highlight that Chinese

*Table 6.1* Accumulation strategies of Chinese agri-investors

| *Mode of accumulation* | *Type of investor* | *Spatio-temporal features of investment* |
|---|---|---|
| *Productive:* Seeking profits from food production | All investors, but particularly agribusiness SOEs and state farms | – Long-term investment horizons<br>– Own-operate approach<br>– Intensification of production with a focus on output and productivity |
| *Valorization-based:* Commanding premium prices by leveraging the symbolic meanings associated with the farming environment (clean, green, safe) | Private agribusiness corporations and agri-food entrepreneurs (in cooperation with Australian agri-business partners) | – Long-term investment horizons<br>– Own-operate approach<br>– Material increases in output and productivity combine with a focus on discursive value construction |
| *Financial:* Speculating on capital gains from IPOs or strategic buyouts of an acquired farm or food business | Large private agribusiness corporations and agri-food entrepreneurs (in cooperation with financial capital from China and global investors) | – Mostly in the context of agribusiness investments<br>– Short-term investment horizons<br>– Speculative, risky, volatile investments flows from global sources of capital; stability and profitability of agricultural operations are secondary |

*Source:* Elaborated by the author.

farmland investors do not simply respond to growing demand for high-quality food imports but seek to actively *construct* demand by valorizing Australia's natural environment and discursively linking Australian food products to meanings of health, success, and the good life. Seen from this perspective, the inflow of Chinese capital into Australian food and farming is not the causal outcome of a "natural" shift toward the consumption of high-quality and animal-based foods by Chinese eaters. Rather, farmland investment and shifting consumption patterns mutually shape and reinforce each other.

In contrast to financial actors such as the farmland and agricultural investment funds (FAIFs) that have mushroomed in Australia in recent years, the Chinese investors I encountered during my research have focused on the productive rather than financial qualities of farmland. In general, Chinese investment projects generate profits from controlling the flow of food through supply chains that connect Australian farms with high-end consumer markets in China and by shaping consumers' understandings of these food products. Financial income from farmland in the form of rents and capital gains (that can be securitized and traded on financial markets) is of secondary interest to most Chinese owners of Australian farmland. Yet, some of the most risk-taking Chinese individuals have gone beyond a valorization-based mode of accumulation, attempting to "sell" the environmental and cultural meanings ascribed to Australian farmland and food to financial markets. The results have often been sobering, as we will see below, but they underscore the profit-driven nature of China's land rush, even as investors themselves mobilize a "feeding China" narrative to legitimize their investments. In what follows, I examine each of the three modes of accumulation individually, drawing on case studies from my fieldwork.

## Investing in the productive qualities of farmland

At first glance, Chinese agri-investment in Australia is predominantly shaped by a logic of production. In other words, investors generate profits from the production and sale of agri-food commodities rather than from financial income streams generated by land ownership. As a matter of fact, all Chinese investment projects I encountered during my research were functional agricultural projects and the centrality of production was palpable not just on the farms and in the processing plants I visited but also in the office buildings and conference rooms where I met with top-level managers. During our discussions, investment managers often revealed an astonishing level of insight into the daily operations of their agricultural businesses—from annual crop yields to cattle breeding principles to the technical complexities of dairy or meat processing.

In general, agricultural production undertaken by Chinese investors is shaped by two goals. The first is to increase output and production capacity. Indeed, many Chinese investors have ambitious production targets—whether this involves the number of cattle to be exported to the Chinese market, increases in annual raw milk output, or tons of grain to be produced. Enhancing productive capacity is seen as key to ensuring the consistency and stability of supply required to secure contracts with Chinese retailers and distribution outlets, to establish a new food brand in the Chinese market, and to build a customer base. As a representative of a Chinese investor company with interests in the Australian beef industry phrased it: "[...] there's very little point in trying to deliver to China if you're talking about a couple cartons of meat [...]. To do trade, you need volume." (interview August 2017, Melbourne).

The second goal revolves around cost-cutting and efficiency. Such measures are undertaken to improve the competitiveness of the farm or agri-business and increase profits from production. Increasing production capacity and efficiency generally requires Chinese investors to make substantial investments into the farms or agri-businesses they own as we can see from the account of an investment manager in charge of a Chinese-owned beef cattle farm in Australia:

> We've done a lot in getting the farms operational. We've been focused on improving, making sure that we've got good reproductive rates, making sure that we're growing enough grass, making sure that we invest in fertilizer to continue growing enough grass, changing the infrastructure in terms of the fencing, and the water, and the yards [...]. But we've also got to go to the next stage. What are our cattle's weight gains on the backgrounding farm? And then how do our cattle perform for those people that buy them from us? And feeding that information back into the system so that we can make the right decision when we're breeding.
>
> (interview May 2018, Shanghai)

To understand the production-oriented logic underpinning much Chinese agri-investment, a comparison with finance-driven investment is instructive. While financial investors (e.g., FAIFs, pension, or hedge funds) base their investment calculus, at least in part, on capital appreciation, Chinese investors primarily focus on consumer demand. When I asked a representative of a Chinese investor company about the role that appreciating farmland prices played in the company's investment model, the representative bluntly stated:

> I think land appreciation is the last metric we would use. The first metric is absolutely [...] the rising middle class in China. There will be huge demand for high-quality, imported goods from New Zealand, from Australia.
>
> (interview February 2017, Sydney)

Another Chinese investment manager explained his company's production-oriented investment logic in the following terms:

> We don't do anything unless we know where the demand is. So, we always start with demand. If we don't know where the demand is going to go and how we're going to grow the demand, we don't make an investment. So, the first criterium is, where is the market for these products and how are we going to grow them?
>
> (interview August 2017, Melbourne)

As the manager saw it, this was different from most finance-driven agricultural investments in Australia. "Most of them are actually more real estate style of transactions than true agriculture style of transactions," he explained. "So, when they're looking for some sort of land asset backing or capital [gains], they're very real estate in their thinking" (interview August 2017, Melbourne).

The demand-driven nature of Chinese agri-investments also means that Chinese investors cannot simply sit back and wait for their agricultural assets to generate income, as a wealthy individual owning shares in an FAIF might do. To capture value from demand, Chinese investors must tightly control the food production process and the flows of agri-food commodities from their Australian farms and agribusinesses to their target markets in China or elsewhere. As one investment manager phrased it when I asked him to compare the operations of his company to those of an FAIF:

> We need to produce the product that drives the profitability of what we do. [...] Whereas the fund, generally, so long as the investors in the fund are getting their returns, they are not that focused on the products.
> (interview May 2018, Shanghai)

A focus on agricultural products means that top-level managers at Chinese investor companies (at times all the way up to the ultimate business owner or chairperson) involve themselves closely in questions concerning the types of agri-food commodities to produce, the organization of production and processing processes, as well as the markets and consumer segments to target. Organizing supply chains around new spatialized value relations that connect Australian food production with geographically and socio-economically specific consumer markets (located in China or elsewhere) thus becomes one of the key characteristics of production-oriented logics underpinning Chinese agri-investments.

Direct involvement in the operations of their overseas farms does not mean that Chinese investors use their own workers and experts from China, as is sometimes feared in the Australian public and media discourse. On the contrary, the vast majority of Chinese investors I have encountered rely on local Australian expertise, for example, in the form of Australian farm managers or an Australian joint-venture partner with a background in Australian agriculture to provide expert knowledge and help reduce the considerable risks associated with agricultural production in an unfamiliar environment. Nonetheless, the top-level managers or the chairman at the Chinese head office retains final decision-making power and will not always heed the recommendations of their local management teams. For Chinese investors owning Australian agricultural farms, the prerequisite to be tightly involved in the farm's operations also means that those investors invariably choose an own-operate approach rather than the own-lease out model common among many institutional investors. As one manager of a Chinese state farm told me when reflecting on the particular challenges that come with running a large-scale Australian farming venture: "We don't just need the *return*, that would be easy. We need the *product*." (interview August 2017, Melbourne). It is the necessity to control the physical product instead of simply pocketing the financial return which also explains why the managers of Australia's farmland and agricultural investment funds (FAIFs) have been so spectacularly unsuccessful in enrolling Chinese investor capital, as we have seen in the previous chapter.

The production-oriented logic of Chinese agri-investments deviates from the *modus operandi* of financial capital not just with respect to the spatialized value relations it engenders but also with regard to the time horizon of the investment. Institutional investors must offer some kind of exit strategy, for example, in the form of an initial public offering (IPO) or a strategic sale, that will allow the fund to return capital to its end investors and compensate the fund managers. A typical time frame for an institutional investor such as a private equity fund, for instance, is between seven and ten years (Fairbairn 2014b, p. 792). Chinese agri-investment, on the other hand, takes a relatively long-term investment outlook, at least in theory. Indeed, no investor I spoke to had a defined exit strategy, and many emphasized the stable and long-term nature of their investments. Investing for agricultural production inevitably requires an open-ended time frame—a feature that sets Chinese investors apart from global financial investors, the Chinese investment managers with whom I spoke insisted. In the words of one manager in charge of the Australian agri-investments of a large Chinese private agri-business corporation:

> The investment horizon is super important. We really buy to hold. Most fund managers, they need to transact, they need to exit their investments to realize their returns for their shareholders. [...] But we're doing it as a corporate, we're doing it for production. If you look at Macquarie [a major institutional investor in Australia], their timeline is finite. They're doing it for the purpose of getting returns for their investors. We're doing it because we want to make money, of course, but we're doing it as a corporate active in this space, producing for our consumers.
>
> (interview February 2017, Sydney)

Seen from this perspective, Chinese agri-investors have little need for a defined exit strategy. As the quote suggests, for as long as consumer demand is growing, companies can make profits from investing in overseas food production.

Astonishingly, a production-driven accumulation logic appears to be dominant despite the potentially high capital gains farmland owners can capture from rising land prices. All Chinese investors I interviewed insisted that capital gains from land appreciation played no or, at best, a secondary role in their investment strategy. As one investment manager phrased it:

> We accept the fact that right now in Australian agriculture, our land assets are probably going to increase in value at about five to seven percent. That's just where agriculture's going. But that's a secondary or a different view of where our company's heading for its overall value. We don't use that to prop up our trading margins as such.
>
> (interview August 2017, Melbourne)

Even in cases where investors had undertaken significant improvements to "upgrade" and "transform" farmland, a strategy commonly used to enhance the value of the underlying farmland (Fairbairn 2014a, p. 254), investment managers insisted on the production-oriented nature of these endeavors:

> We do [land improvements] not to increase the value of the asset but to increase our production capability. Because, no doubt, naturally you have that positive flow-on effect anyway. So, if you're increasing the capital value of your assets through investments, the value's going to go up anyway. But really, I'm more operationally focused to make sure that I can increase the running capacity and the production capabilities.
>
> (interview September 2017, Sydney)

Another investment manager went even further, suggesting that agriculture in and of itself was an unlikely place for investors to look for capital gains:

> If you want to make money from capital gains, it's better to go to Sydney and invest in some real estate, like office buildings or apartment blocks. These are also going up in value. No need to invest in cattle farms, to spend all that time and energy on raising cattle, that's such hard work. [...] After all, we are a livestock company, we are not a real estate company.
>
> (interview March 2017, Hangzhou)

The subordinate role capital gains play in the accumulation strategy of Chinese farmland investors does not mean that they are entirely oblivious to land's appreciating qualities or, at a minimum, its ability to store value. For example, several industry insiders who had been involved in brokering or structuring Chinese land deals in Australia suggested that part of land's attractiveness lay in its ability to act as a safe storage of wealth—a characteristic that is of particular importance to private Chinese business owners who bring their "own" money when making overseas investments. As one investment advisor put it, "[land] is one place of parking some money outside of China that the Chinese government can't get its hands on" (interview February 2017, Sydney). Another investment advisor explained that many Chinese agri-investors saw land as a form of "buffer" that would insulate them, at least partially, from the high risks related to agricultural production (interview March 2017, Shanghai). Hence, it is fair to assume that considerations about capital gains do enter the calculus of Chinese investors. Yet, here these gains do not serve as an end in themselves but as a means to enable production.

### Seeking premium profits from practices of place-based valorization

Even as Chinese investors emphasize the production-oriented nature of their Australian farm and food ventures, there is more to the ways in which Chinese investors generate value from their investments. In fact, many investors do not simply obtain profits from the straightforward production and sale of agri-food commodities but through practices of agri-food valorization. Valorization refers to strategies whereby producers seek to gain premium profits (sometimes referred to as "excess profits" or "superprofits") for products that are perceived as higher value by consumers (Guthman 2004, p. 66). To valorize agri-food products, Chinese investors leverage popular imaginaries of Australia as clean, green, and safe. By drawing on and adding to existing imaginaries that associate Australian food and farming with meanings of quality and safety, so the theory goes, Chinese agri-investors can enhance the desirability of their Australian-produced food products in Chinese consumer markets and secure a price premium.

Practices of valorization based on claims about the origins of food and the socio-environmental conditions of production are not new and have been discussed at length within the literature on organic food production (Morgan et al. 2008; Guthman 2004), alternative food networks (Goodman 2010; Goodman et al. 2010), or discourses of *terroir* shaping the wine industry (Murray & Overton 2016; Overton & Murray 2016). Within the literature on China's land rush, however, the role of food safety and quality is routinely overlooked. Observers of China's domestic agri-food transformation, in contrast, have long highlighted how growing concerns about the safety and quality of food are leading to a restructuring of consumer markets in China. Countless food scandals—from "gutter oil" to milk contaminated with chemicals—have led to a "crisis of trust" in domestically grown food products among Chinese consumers (Hanser & Li 2015; Klein 2013; Yan 2012). Particularly more affluent urban consumers have begun to "opt out" (Hanser & Li 2015) of the Chinese food system in favor of imported foods from countries and places of production associated with higher levels of quality and safety. Against this background, it is the accumulation of opportunities associated with *food safety* rather than *food security* that provide an impetus for many Chinese companies to invest in overseas farmland.

The extent to which Chinese investors rely on practices of valorization for their profits depends on a number of factors: for one, investment geography plays an important role. Particularly countries such as Australia and New Zealand enjoy a reputation for their clean, green, and safe farming environments among Chinese consumers. According to a report by consultancy firm KPMG and the University of Sydney, imported agri-food products from Australia—meats, dairy products, vegetables, and wine—are perceived as premium foods by the Chinese middle class and enjoy far higher levels of trust than domestic food brands (Ferguson & Hendrischke 2013). As a result, acquiring agricultural resources in Australia or New Zealand yields a higher potential to reap premium profits from the valorization of agri-food commodities than, say, investing in a farm or agribusiness located in Latin America. Second, the type of commodity is crucial. Clearly, agri-food products marketed directly to end consumers—for example, an infant formula product or a packaged beef brand—lend themselves more to practices of valorization than bulk commodities, such as wheat or sugar, that serve primarily as inputs for other food products. Consequently, practices of valorization are most common among Chinese agri-food investors focused on developing consumer brands and niche market opportunities, i.e., among private agribusiness corporations and agri-food entrepreneurs. Lastly, I have found farmland investors to be more deeply engaged in practices of valorization than investors owning food businesses. This does not mean that a Chinese-invested beef processing company will not leverage Australia's reputation as a clean and safe source of food. Yet, practices of valorization are most pronounced in cases where investors can link their agri-food products with the local environmental characteristics of a particular place, farm, or location of production over which they exercise control.

Importantly, practices of valorization are not only anchored in the actual biophysical properties of the production environment but also, to an equal measure, draw on the commonly shared perceptions and imaginations of these environments. Thus, "elements of the material and the imagined" (Overton & Murray 2016, p. 800) become inextricably intertwined. In other words, the place-based claims through which Chinese investors embed "extra quality" into food products are closely attuned to Chinese public imaginaries of Australia as a clean, green, and safe environment for food production, even as these perceptions may deviate from the actual local environmental conditions of production on the farm.

### *Zhejiang Shengda Investment Group: investing in the "purest milk on earth"*

The ways in which Chinese farmland investors mobilize place-based claims of food safety and quality to capture premium profits from agricultural production are best illustrated by the case of Zhejiang Shengda Investment Group.[1] As a Chinese manufacturing company with no previous experience in agriculture, Shengda made headlines in 2016, when it acquired one of Australia's most iconic dairy businesses for 280 million AUD. With 25 individual farms, 17,890 cows, and more than 7,062 hectares of farmland, the dairy company is one of Australia's largest raw milk producers. What has contributed to the company's iconic imaginary, however, is not so much its size but its scenic landscape and rich history. Founded in 1825 by royal charter, the farm was granted 350,000 acres (143,500 hectares) of land by King George IV of England in the fledgling British colony that was to become Tasmania. Initially established as a wool and sheep farming business, a long and winding history saw the royal charter company move through various stages of commercial development, including wool, beef cattle, and goat farming, before the company's principal land holdings were converted to dairying in 1993. Since then, the company has operated as a dairy, raising cows on lush pastures located on the windswept northwestern coast of Tasmania.

Prior to its acquisition by Shengda in 2016, the dairy's operations had been focused on supplying raw milk to local processors to make cheese and other dairy products for the Australian market. But Shengda had a bigger vision. A few months after acquiring the Tasmanian dairy business, the company announced bold plans to airfreight fresh, liquid milk from Tasmania to China's major cities. The company's executives set to work to set up the necessary supply chains. At the time of my interactions with the company in 2018, raw milk was trucked once a week in a seven-hour journey from the farm to a processing plant near Tasmania's capital Hobart, where it was pasteurized and packaged. After that, the milk was transported by ship to Melbourne and then placed on an airplane for a nine-hour flight to Guangzhou in southern China. Following clearance by the Chinese customs authorities, the milk would travel further to Shengda's main China offices in Shanghai, Hangzhou, Ningbo, and Beijing, where local sales teams ensured its timely distribution to retail outlets and private Chinese households that had subscribed to regular home deliveries. This arduous journey took no more than four days—not much longer than the time it would take for fresh milk to reach Australian supermarket shelves.

Volumes were small but set to increase rapidly. In late 2018, Shengda delivered around 15,000 liters of fresh Tasmanian milk to China every week. The volume accounted for roughly 10 percent of the company's raw milk production, but executives were working to boost delivery to 100,000 liters a week. In addition to fresh liquid milk, the company was in the process of expanding the range of premium dairy products destined for the Chinese market. Three of its Australian farms had recently undergone organic certification, producing organic ultra-high temperature (UHT) milk for the Chinese market. In addition, the company was working on adding adult and baby milk powder to its range of products destined for China.

It goes without saying that delivering fresh milk from the fringes of Australia to China's Eastern coast is a highly risky endeavor. As one of the world's most perishable foods, milk, especially in its fresh liquid form, is inherently limited in how far it can last over time and space. Fresh milk will spoil within hours if not refrigerated. Given its perishable nature, the geography of dairy farming has traditionally been highly localized, making milk "the most local of all supermarket staples" (Freidberg 2009, p. 198). Overcoming fresh milk's natural biophysical limits has thus required a series of remarkable technological and logistical feats, from seamless cold chain management to rigorous food safety testing, smooth transportation links within and across national borders, as well as tightly coordinated inspection procedures to avoid import delays that would impact fresh milk's most precious attribute—its shelf life. These logistical efforts have their price. When I visited Shanghai during fieldwork in the summer of 2018, a one-liter carton of Shengda's premium fresh milk would sell at the mindboggling price of 70 RMB (roughly 10 USD) in high-end supermarkets, making it three to four times more expensive than comparable fresh milk brands produced in China and up to 10 times more expensive than the fresh milk sitting on Australian supermarket shelves.

To convince consumers that Shengda's fresh milk is worth its hefty price premium, the company employed a marketing strategy that placed farmland at the center. Emphasizing the farm's remote location "at the edge of the world," images of the natural and pure farming environment combined to convey meanings of quality, safety, and freshness to Chinese consumers. On their social media accounts, the company's marketing specialists provided consumers with a constant flow of images and stories about the farm's "happy cows" and "superior environment." By narrating specific locational and environmental characteristics, these images and texts reinforced the perceived contrast between Shengda's natural and, by extension, presumably safe dairying practices and a Chinese dairy industry characterized by intensive and agro-industrial dairying methods that are seen to put the health of both people and animals at risk. Beyond the rich soils and lush pastures of Shengda's farming environment, attributes related to air and atmosphere played a key role in projecting quality and safety onto the company's products. Indeed, Shengda marketed its fresh milk product as "milk from the purest place on earth"—a clear reference to the low levels of air pollution characteristic of the Tasmanian island state. The company's focus on purity speaks to popular anxieties in China about the impact of smog on nature, health, and the safety of food. During a tour of the farm, as we were gazing across the rolling hills and coastline opening up before our eyes, a company executive explained the link between images of purity and meanings of quality in the following words:

> This is literally the edge of the world, the place where the cleanest air is, right up here. So, we actually boast the healthiest cows, breathing the healthiest air, producing the highest quality milk. And this is obviously a huge selling point in China, and some people will pay a premium for that.
> (interview December 2018, Smithton)

To convey an image of locational embeddedness to consumers living thousands of miles away from where their fresh milk is produced, Shengda relied on traceability technology. By scanning a bar code on the milk carton with their mobile phones, consumers could trace the carton's entire journey from the fields of the farm to the shelves of a Chinese supermarket. Each step of the supply chain was meticulously documented, providing consumers with a "complete grass-to-glass experience" for every glass of milk they drink, as one company executive described it (interview September 2017, Sydney). By thus tying food products to places imbued with images of naturalness and purity, the company hoped to reinforce perceptions of quality and safety among consumers.

Shengda provides a pertinent example that Chinese agri-investors appreciate Australian agriculture not only for its productive capacity—i.e., as a

*Figure 6.1* View from the most north-western tip of Shengda's farming property—the "purest place on earth."

*Source:* Picture taken by the author during a field trip to Shengda's dairy farm, December 2018.

biophysical combination of soils, nutrients, atmosphere, and water necessary to grow food—but also for a set of local, environmental, and cultural features that can be leveraged to unlock value from agricultural production beyond its "normal" rate of return. Yet, almost a decade after Shengda's bold expansion into the Australian dairy industry, the company's vision lies in tatters. Already in 2018, the company was struggling to find a market for its significantly overprized fresh milk. Even rich urbanites in China's most advanced metropoles were thinking twice whether to spend ten dollars on a small carton of milk. "The tricky part is [...] to convince consumers that our products are very, very premium and worth their price," as one manager admitted to me (September 2017, Sydney). Appealing to imaginaries around the naturalness and purity of Shengda's dairy farm might conjure up meanings of quality and safety in the minds of anxious Chinese consumers, but this does not necessarily guarantee premium profits for the company. After all, as Overton & Murray (2016) remind us, the apparent value of food products imbued with meanings of quality and safety remains "imaginary until it is made real by the purchase of a place-based commodity at a premium price by consumers" (p. 806). At the time of this writing, more than half a decade after Shengda's foray into China's high-end dairy market, there is no trace left of the company's dairy products on Chinese supermarket shelves. Shengda spectacularly failed to unlock excess value from the locational-environmental characteristics of its Australian farms. But from the perspective of the Chinese funders behind Shengda, the story gets even worse, as we shall see below.

## Financialized modes of accumulation

As we have seen so far, in Chinese investment projects, profits predominantly accrue from agricultural production and practices of valorization that leverage Australia's image as clean, green, and safe environment for the production of food. The preponderance of a production-oriented mode of investment, however, does not mean that financial logics of accumulation are entirely absent. In relation to farmland, financialization generally refers to the processes and actors that turn farmland from a simple commodity to be bought and sold into an asset class, generating *financial* profits in the form of rents and capital gains that can then be securitized and traded on financial markets (Fairbairn 2020; Ouma 2020; Clapp et al. 2017; Ducastel & Anseeuw 2017).

This final section traces the emerging assetization of farmland by Chinese capital. In particular, I focus on the small but growing role of private equity in underwriting Chinese agri-investment as well as the ongoing efforts of Chinese agri-investors to list their overseas agri-food assets on the stock market via an initial public offering (IPO). What both trends have in common is that they seek investment returns primarily through financial channels (e.g., capital gains from land appreciation or dividends from trading farmland assets on the stock market) while productive revenues from the production of agri-food commodities are of relatively less importance. In this process, farmland and its capacity to produce agri-food commodities are transformed from a natural resource and commodity, whose market value may have been heightened by practices of territorial valorization, into a financial asset, i.e., into a "property that yields an income stream" (Birch 2017).

### *Private equity funds*

Of all the investment deals I have come across during this research, not a single one was undertaken directly by a financial investor from China. Yet, a closer look reveals some emerging "behind-the-scenes" intersections between the worlds of food and finance. One key channel through which finance capital links up with the Chinese companies and businesses spearheading China's overseas agricultural engagement is private equity funds. Private equity funds are a relatively new financial instrument in Chinese capital markets and have only been legally sanctioned in 2007, when the Chinese government passed a revised Partnership Enterprise Law (Robertson 2015). Modeled after their Western-style counterpart, Chinese private equity companies are typically set up as limited partnerships between a general partner (GP) responsible for sourcing and managing investments and a number of limited partners (LPs), who invest capital into the fund in exchange for financial returns. Private equity funds have short investment horizons of around seven to ten years. At the end of each investment cycle, capital and dividends are distributed to investors, along with a fee for the fund manager. Today, there are more than 6,000 private equity firms operating in China which raise capital in both RMB and USD from domestic and foreign investors, including pension funds, sovereign wealth funds, banks, local Chinese governments, and high net-worth individuals from within and outside of China (Robertson 2015).

Given China's outbound investment restrictions, private equity funds are limited in their ability to acquire foreign assets directly. As a consequence, their investments often take the form of a partnership with a Chinese company strategically positioned to expand overseas through cross-border investment. In this model, the private equity firm takes an equity stake in a Chinese company which then uses the capital raised by the fund (usually combined with other sources of equity and/or debt) to acquire an overseas company and integrate it into its business operations. As the market value of the company increases following its successful overseas expansion, two main exit options present themselves to the fund. It can either divest its equity stake through a strategic industry buyout in which another buyer takes over its stake in the company, or, if the company is publicly listed, it can sell its shares directly on the Chinese stock market. The profits obtained from the sale of the fund's equity stake are then used to pay out the end investors and compensate the fund manager. An alternative way to bypass outbound investment restrictions involves setting up an offshore legal structure. In such an arrangement, the private equity firm is registered in the domestic Chinese economy, while the financial entity itself is separated and registered in an offshore jurisdiction, usually a tax haven such as the Cayman Islands or Jersey. Offshore funds provide the dual advantage of tax benefits and easy access to US dollar-denominated funding (Robertson 2015, p. 49).

In the Australian context, the emerging intersections between financial markets and China's overseas agricultural engagement are best illustrated by the case of Hosen Capital (*Housheng Touzi* 厚生投资)[2]—the private equity firm spun off by Chinese agribusiness giant New Hope Group which we already encountered in Chapter 4. The firm focuses its investment activities on food and agribusiness-related companies in and outside of China. It exclusively targets the food processing sector and does not own farmland. Since 2010, Hosen Capital has established three funds with a combined 2.3 billion USD under management and, in 2019, was raising another round of capital for its fourth fund, Hosen Investment Fund IV, expected to close at 600–700 million USD. In addition to Hosen Capital's investments in a number of independent food and agribusiness companies, the private equity firm also cooperates closely with New Hope Group and has been underwriting key steps in the group's international expansion. In 2013, for example, the firm facilitated New Hope Group's acquisition of one of Australia's largest meat processing companies, Kilcoy Pastoral, for nearly 100 million AUD.

Since the acquisition, the processing capacity at Kilcoy has been upgraded significantly, and the business has been integrated into the group's new global animal protein business Kilcoy Global Foods. In 2019, plans were announced to float the new business platform on the Hong Kong stock exchange. Importantly, the capital with which the private equity firm has been backing New Hope Group's global expansion primarily derives from international institutional and commercial investors, including World Bank's International Finance Corporation (IFC), Singaporean sovereign wealth fund Temasek, US-based grain trader Archer Daniel Midlands (ADM), and Japanese trading company Mitsui.

Another example is provided by Heilongjiang-based livestock production and processing company Hengyang Cattle (*Hengyang Niuye* 恒阳牛业) and CDH Investments (*Dinghui Touzi* 鼎晖投资)[3]—one of China's first and most renowned private equity firms. In 2014, Hengyang teamed up with CDH Investments to acquire Australian beef processing company Tabro Meats. Around the same time that Hengyang was making investments in Australia, it began expanding into Uruguay, Argentina, and Brazil, where it rapidly acquired a number of beef processing and meat packing plants. In 2017, Hengyang listed its portfolio of overseas beef processing assets on the Shenzhen stock exchange through a reverse merger with Chinese mining and motorbike company Sundiro Group, realizing an estimated 1.5 billion RMB in net profits from its public listing. While there is no public information about the amount of equity financing Hengyang obtained from CDH Investments, the pace and scope of Hengyang's investment spree suggest that CDH Investments has been instrumental in promoting the company's global expansion. As with Hosen Capital, CDH Investments has been able to enroll an impressive universe of international institutional investors, including Singapore's sovereign wealth fund GIC, US-based pension funds, and well-known global asset management companies such as Swiss-based LGT Capital Partners.

The above examples illustrate the growing role of financial capital in facilitating the global expansion of Chinese agri-food corporations. Indeed, as one industry insider told me, private equity firms have become a major channel of finance for China's leading private agribusiness corporations and their overseas investment ambitions (interview June 2018, Beijing). With China's banking system primarily aimed at guaranteeing the provision of cheap funding to state-owned agribusinesses and state farms, private agribusiness corporations increasingly rely on linkages with the non-bank financial sector to finance cross-border acquisitions of agri-food processing firms and brands. Naturally, only the largest and most successful private agribusinesses have the capacity to tap private financial markets for their global expansion "because they are close to the funds. [...]. There are at most 200 companies who know how to run this," my interview partner claimed (interview June 2018, Beijing).

A surprisingly large share of private equity capital derives from major bi- and multilateral financial institutions and institutional investors located outside of China. Private equity firms from China thus serve as an important vehicle through which global capital is channeled into some of the individual investment projects constituting China's global agri-food expansion. In other words, China's emerging global agribusiness firms are increasingly enmeshed in global circuits of capital. This raises important questions about the interests and power relations inscribed in China's overseas agricultural engagement, ultimately calling into question the very "Chineseness" of some of China's cross-border agricultural deals. As Klinger and Muldavin (2019) remind us, "[...] financial institutions of [Europe and North America] are financing China's overseas activities and therefore have a tangible stake in China's banks and firms making a return on their investments" (p. 11). From the perspective of global financial institutions, the appeal of Chinese private equity funds lies in their ability to offer exposure to China's fast-growing consumer market for food products. China's private equity firms do not engage in overseas farmland deals and thus do not offer investors exposure to agriculture *per se*. Instead, their "investment thesis" is to capture value from China's fast-growing demand for quality foods. "We seek to leverage our extensive experience investing and helping Chinese companies become leaders in China's fast-growing domestic consumption sectors," the chairman and founder of CDH Investments Wu Shangzhi explained in a media interview, thus providing the firm's international investors with a "unique China angle" that financial institutions from the global North cannot offer (Wu quoted in Mendoza 2017).

Finally, growing linkages with private equity capital suggest that the production-oriented mode of accumulation that has so far been characteristic of Chinese agri-investors may gradually be superseded by a financial logic as profits increasingly accrue through financial channels rather than through commodity production. Chinese agri-investors backed by private equity financing differ from the production-driven investments outlined in the first two sections of this chapter in that, ultimately, they base their investment strategy on the prospect of capital gains from the eventual sale or public share offering of their company, even as such gains will continue to depend, to a certain extent, on the company's ability to generate revenues from agri-food production and the development of new market opportunities. Take the case of Hengyang Cattle and CDH Investments as an example. In just three years, Hengyang was able to amass a global agricultural portfolio and successfully list its assets on the Shenzhen stock exchange. The perceived success of its global expansion enabled the company to generate windfall financial gains for itself and its backers from China's capital markets even as its production revenues were plummeting. In Australia, for example, Hengyang's beef processing operations have been loss-making since 2016 and have forced the company to put its Australian beef abattoir back on the market for sale (Condon 2020). Yet, for Hengyang's financial backers, the company's rapid global expansion and subsequent stock exchange listing have generated handsome dividends. One industry insider summarized the speculative logic at the heart of the new alliance between private equity capital and China's leading agribusiness firms in the following words:

> When you look at the news, all these companies [making investments] abroad, their stock prices are increasing, it's looking really beautiful. But if you look inside, they always have big losses, big problems with management. But they are hiding behind financial numbers.
>
> (interview June 2018, Beijing)

### *Initial public offerings (IPOs)*

While private equity-backed deals may be out of reach for all but the largest agribusinesses, initial public offerings (IPOs) represent another strategy through which Chinese agri-investors can potentially generate financial returns. Indeed, many of the smaller private agribusinesses or agri-food entrepreneurs I met during my research entertained ideas to publicly list their Australian farms and agribusiness assets, even though many insisted that it was not a current concern but a consideration "for a bit further down the track." It is indeed noteworthy that of all the investment projects I tracked during this research, none has been publicly listed as of yet. Nonetheless, IPOs are attractive for investors as a fast way to make money. By listing their overseas assets on the stock exchange, investors can immediately raise large amounts of capital, which results in faster returns on their investment than they could obtain from productive revenues.

There are three ways for Chinese investors to list their assets on the stock exchange. First, investors can aggregate their overseas assets into a separate company and issue shares for investors to buy. Listing a new company on the stock exchange is subject to approval from China's stock market regulators and requires high levels of financial transparency and regulatory compliance. A second option is to "inject" assets into an existing listed company and issue a new round of shares to reflect the increased value of the company. Such asset injections must also meet a number of regulatory requirements and, obviously, are based on the precondition that the investor already controls an exchange-listed company in China. The last option involves the so-called backdoor listing or reverse merger, in which a private company requires a listed company. Following the acquisition, the buyer may merge both companies' operations or alternatively create a shell company that allows both entities to operate independently from one another. Backdoor listings constitute a prominent way for private companies to go public even if they do not meet the requirements to list on the stock exchange. Having gained access to the stock exchange, the company can then inject its assets into the listed vehicle and issue another round of shares. As we have seen above, a backdoor listing was precisely the way in which private equity-backed Hengyang Cattle listed its beef processing assets on the stock exchange, thereby generating windfall profits for its shareholders.

Another key question facing investors who plan to spin off their assets via an IPO is the country in which to list their company. In theory, Chinese investors could undertake an IPO on any stock exchange around the world. Practically, however, most investors consider listing either in Hong Kong or in one of the two stock exchanges in mainland China—Shenzhen or Shanghai. Hong Kong is attractive to many investors because it is tightly integrated with global financial markets and it functions as a safe haven for companies that want to place assets outside the reach of the Chinese government. In contrast, the main advantage provided by the stock exchanges in Shenzhen or Shanghai is the high average prices listed companies can obtain for their shares. High share prices are the result of high (retail) investor demand for a limited amount of shares available on China's stock markets—and this is despite the fact that average earnings per share are lower in China than elsewhere (Walter & Howie 2011, p. 128). This peculiar feature of China's stock markets enables Chinese agri-investors who list their assets in Shenzhen or Shanghai to benefit from the arbitrage of the relatively low prices they paid for their agri-food assets in Australia and the high valuations listed companies receive in China. "China's domestic stock market is the best choice," one Chinese investment advisor confirmed. "Here you can maximize your transaction value. You can obtain P/E ratios[4] of 50 or even 100, as long as you can maintain high investor expectations" (interview March 2017, Sydney).

However, the trend among Chinese companies to speculate on financial returns from the spread of overseas asset prices and domestic valuations has not remained without criticism. Some industry insiders even consider the practice fundamentally unsustainable.

*Insider:* The problem of this is the sustainability. It's not sustainable. So, in order to make money you have to sell the business. Take the money, and walk away. That's the trick. And that's what people have been focused on doing. And that's the problem because then the business they invest in is not the true potential business. They will pick up any story that can excite the market. And they will pledge all their shares, [...] borrow all that money to invest in that [business]. And when they have made money on the project, they'll sell the business and walk away. That's their game, right? And unfortunately, that's a lot of Chinese business men's succession plan today. And that creates a big issue.

*Interviewer:* Which issues?

*Insider:* It creates chaos in the [stock] market because people don't know any more what to invest in. At the end of the day, it's the small investors that suffer. These people suffer because they follow the trend and might see their money disappear in the stock market.

(interview December 2018, Sydney)

Similar concerns are shared by China's regulatory authorities and have recently led to a crackdown on companies and individuals seeking to simply "dump" their overseas assets on the Chinese stock markets and walk away with the gains. Since 2016, the profitability requirements of the business to be publicly listed have been drastically increased. This makes it harder to list a "mismanaged" or barely profitable overseas company on the Chinese stock market. As stock market listings of overseas assets are becoming more difficult, the speculative excesses of Chinese companies investing overseas with the sole aim of cashing in on high valuations in China have been somewhat tempered. As one investment advisor scoffed when she explained the effects of tighter IPO rules on the overseas investment behavior of Chinese companies:

> Now the companies are becoming more and more rational when making [overseas] investments. Investment decisions are not just driven by the wish to make fast money on the stock exchange. In the past, Chinese companies would invest quickly and without much due diligence because they knew they could make a lot of money from [listing their overseas assets on the domestic stock market]. But now it's getting more and more difficult to get money back from the stock market. You have to use your own money. You have to be cautious.
>
> (interview March 2017, Shanghai)

Yet, not everyone has yielded this advice. One investor whose IPO ambition has fallen victim to the tightened regulations on China's stock markets is, yet again, Zhejiang Shengda Investment Group. As we have seen above, the company has pursued an investment strategy based on the production of premium Tasmanian milk. Yet, behind the company's efforts to leverage its pure farming environment in order to obtain excess profits from affluent Chinese consumers, there is an entirely different accumulation logic at play. A close look at the way the investment was structured reveals how, at its core, Shengda's entire investment strategy was based on a risky (and ultimately failed) stock market gamble.

The main actor behind Shengda is a rich Chinese businessman, Xu Tianfeng[5], who is the founder and majority owner of a publicly listed materials company based in Zhejiang province. The acquisition was financed by three bank loans: a 56 million USD loan from Australian-based Rabobank, a 74 million USD loan from the Industrial and Commercial Bank of China (ICBC), and a 22 million USD loan from the China Zhesheng Bank.[6] The loans were guaranteed by Xu's publicly listed company, which in turn was backed by the value of the Tasmanian dairy assets. Additionally, Xu began to pledge the shares he personally held in his listed company to raise more capital. The businessman handed over blocks of shares to other lenders as collateral for more loans, eventually pledging 96 percent of his shares. Having raised a mindboggling 200 million USD in debt, Xu then channeled these

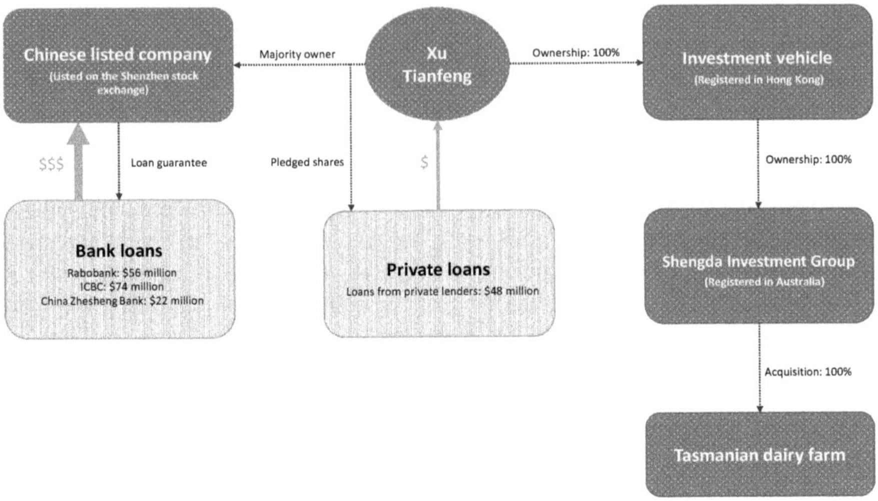


*Figure 6.2* Deal structure of Shengda's dairy investment.

*Source:* Reconstructed by the author based on company information and financial reports.

funds through a Hong Kong-based investment vehicle he controlled to the newly founded Zhejiang Shengda Investment Group—a company founded with the explicit purpose of acting as the primary buyer of the Tasmanian dairy farm Xu had been pursuing (see Figure 6.2).

The Shengda deal caused a stir among Australian investment professionals and dairy industry insiders. Not only had Shengda significantly overpaid for the acquisition, offering some 20 USD more than the second highest bidder, but the fact that one of the largest farmland deals in recent Australian history had been financed entirely by debt was unheard of. How was it that an unknown Chinese manufacturing company without any experience in the agricultural sector would be able to secure 200 million USD in loans for the purchase of an Australian dairy farm, many in the Australian agri-investment industry wondered? How was Shengda able to make a return on its investment, even as it was working to establish a market for a premium milk product at 10 dollars a liter in China?

As Shengda set to work to develop market opportunities for its premium liquid milk product in China, behind the scenes, Xu was busy preparing a major company restructuring. Through a financial sleight of hand, the restructuring would have seen the Australian dairy assets injected into Xu's publicly listed company, Xu significantly increasing his controlling share in the company, and the cash raised from issuing a second round of shares to stock market investors to pay off loans. In this scheme, Shengda's claim to provide Chinese consumers with the "purest milk on earth" would have functioned as an exciting "investment story" with which to boost investors' expectations of the company's future profit potential and growth prospects.

In other words, in Xu's "economy of appearances" (Tsing 2005), the spectacle of bringing "milk from the purest place on earth" to an aspirational consumer class in China was a necessary prerequisite to attracting investor interest on the Chinese stock market. To an Australian deal broker with whom I discussed Shengda's hidden stock market gamble, such an investment strategy made perfect sense and, indeed, seemed to be the only explanation that would justify that the deal had come to pass in the first place:

> If he is able to borrow 100 percent of the money at a low cost of funds and his objective is to then retail it, if you like, by doing an IPO [...], that might be able to explain where they [Chinese investors] are all seeing the value that they can unlock by buying an asset here in Australia.
>
> (interview March 2017, Melbourne)

Yet, none of this happened. Just around the time Shengda had finalized its investment, dairy industry conditions within Australia deteriorated. Milk prices fell and the region experienced one of its worst dry spells on record. As a result, the dairy farm's already razor-thin profit margins shrunk further. Shengda's dairy business in China was expanding, but the high costs associated with airfreighting fresh milk to China did not help profitability either. At the same time, China's regulatory authorities had begun to tighten regulations for companies wishing to list or inject assets on China's stock markets. In December 2016, China's stock market regulator rejected Xu's move to inject Shengda into the publicly listed company, given that the dairy business did not meet the recently introduced profitability requirements. Xu's investment gamble had failed.

Since then, Xu's business interests in China and Australia have been faced with uncertainty. The listed company's share price has fallen precipitously in recent years and the company has been repeatedly forced to stop trading on the stock exchange. Barred from re-capitalizing itself on the financial markets, Shengda has been struggling to service its loans and honor its promises to Australian government officials that the investment deal would bring in new funds to create jobs and upgrade farm facilities. As one industry insider described the situation to me back in 2018:

> Shengda had a good story, but the timing they picked was wrong. They [the Chinese regulators] refused Shengda's application [for an IPO] in the stock market. [...] If the IPO had been granted, I don't think Shengda would be in today's situation.
>
> (interview December 2018, Sydney)

In the meantime, Shengda has gone from bad to worse. In 2021, widely publicized effluent issues as well as alleged animal welfare and farm management problems saw Shengda's Australian board of directors resign, while the recent cancelation of a 25-million-liter offtake agreement with Fonterra, the farm's major dairy processor in Australia, has forced the farm to reduce its herd size by over 10 percent (Powell 2024).

When Shengda first appeared in Australia, it had a story to sell: bringing "milk from the purest place on earth" to Chinese consumers concerned about food safety and quality. The story was meant to resonate not just with affluent Chinese urbanites but, above all, with financial investors looking to profit from China's emerging "dining boom." Discursive spectacle was expected to generate an investment frenzy, yet regulatory changes on China's stock market forestalled the venture. With its finances in dire straits, Shengda has been forced to sell off half of its farms to other buyers, slowly whittling down the historic property it acquired back in 2016. Xu Tianfeng, the Chinese businessman behind Shengda might have banked on the dining boom, but today, Shengda is above all a tale of a Chinese dairy dream gone sour.

*****

The focus on the involvement of the state in China's land rush has obscured the capitalist nature of Chinese overseas land and food deals. By contrast, my research shows that generating profits is a prerequisite for any Chinese investment deal to succeed. By expanding the production and output of food products that are in high demand among Chinese consumers, investors seek to profit from a new "dining boom" as the task of feeding China has been expanding from producing basic staple foods to providing diversified and more Westernized diets. But Chinese investors do not simply profit from this dining boom; they actively *construct* it, together with their Australian and international partners, through images and narratives that imbue Australian food products with environmental and cultural meanings. Notions of health, safety, and success play a key role in this regard. By associating a carton of fresh, Australian milk from pasture-fed cows with a modern, successful, and healthy lifestyle, or by appealing to Chinese mothers worried about providing the best nutrition possible for their children to succeed in China's highly competitive society, investors, to a certain extent, create the demand for food they are claiming to serve.

Creating stories about the positive qualities of Australian-grown food is necessary not only to convince consumers but also to attract capital from investment partners and financial markets. Spectacular narratives that "conjure" up future profits (Tsing 2005) are an important feature in how Chinese investors seek to generate profits from their Australian land deals, but unlike stories that construct farmland as a financial asset class, it is not the land-based capital gains as such—e.g., from land appreciation or rents—that make Australian farmland attractive to Chinese investors. Rather, it is the promise to extract place-based premium profits from Australian-grown food with a reputation as safe, green, and clean that Chinese investors draw on to raise additional capital from investment partners or financial institutions. This means that simply owning Australian farmland and producing food on it is not enough for Chinese investors seeking to maximize profits from their investment deals. Instead, investors must show that they are able, at least theoretically, to connect the food they produce on their Australian farms with the Chinese consumers willing to pay a premium for it. This puts the issue of supply chains at center stage. The making of supply chains is the final piece in the puzzle of Chinese land deals in Australia to which we must now turn.

## Notes

1 I have anonymized all names of companies and people relating to this case. The case study is based on a series of interviews conducted with various company representatives as well as a field visit to the farm.
2 Based on company websites and newspaper articles, including Carter (2019), Cheesley (2019), Burwood-Tayler (2017), and Hosen Capital (2016).
3 Based on company websites and newspaper articles, including Gonzalez (2016), Yue (2016), and CDH Investments (2011).
4 The price-to-earnings ratio (P/E ratio) is commonly used to value a publicly listed company. It measures a company's current share price relative to its per-share earnings. High P/E valuations mean that a company's share price is high even as the per-share earnings it offers are low.
5 All names of persons and business entities have been anonymized.
6 The deal structure of Shengda's dairy investment has been reconstructed based on company filings, financial reports, and Internet databases, including Knaus (2018), Grigg (2018), Miller (2018), Ningbo Xianfeng (2018a, 2018b, 2018c), Grigg (2017), Perlez and McMorrow (2017) as well as Chinese corporate research databases Tianyancha (https://www.tianyancha.com/) and Qichacha (https://www.qcc.com/).

## References

Birch, Kean (2017): Rethinking Value in the Bio-Economy: Finance, Assetization, and the Management of Value. In *Science, Technology, & Human Values* 42 (3), pp. 460–490.

Burwood-Taylor, Louisa (2017): China Will Produce 4 of Top 10 Global Food Companies by 2027, Says Leading Food Investor. In *AgFunderNews*, 4/26/2017. Available online at https://agfundernews.com/china-will-produce-4-of-top-10-global-food-companies-by-2027-says-leading-food-investor.html, checked on 5/7/2019.

Carter, Bridget (2019): New Hope to List Meat Processor Kilcoy Pastoral in Hong Kong. In *The Australian*, 9/4/2019. Available online at https://www.theaustralian.com.au/business/dataroom/new-hope-to-list-meat-processor-kilcoy-pastoral-in-hong-kong/news-story/699e55f355da71266e0891beed134aba, checked on 4/17/2020.

CDH Investments (2011): Company Website. Available online at http://www.cdhfund.com/index.php?m=content&c=index&a=english_index, checked on 4/17/2020.

Cheesley, Amanda (2019): Hosen Capital to Launch $700m Agribusiness Fund. In *AgriInvestor*, 2/1/2019. Available online at https://www.agriinvestor.com/hosen-capital-launch-700m-agribusiness-fund/, checked on 10/16/2019.

Clapp, Jennifer; Isakson, S. Ryan; Visser, Oane (2017): The Complex Dynamics of Agriculture as a Financial Asset: Introduction to Symposium. In *Agriculture and Human Values* 34, pp. 179–183.

Condon, John (2020): Victoria's Troubled Tabro Beef Processing Plant May Have Found a Buyer. In *Beef Central*, 2/27/2020. Available online at https://www.beefcentral.com/processing/victorias-troubled-tabro-beef-processing-plant-may-have-found-a-buyer/, checked on 4/22/2020.

Ducastel, Antoine; Anseeuw, Ward (2017): Agriculture as an Asset Class. Reshaping the South African Farming Sector. In *Agriculture and Human Values* 34 (1), pp. 199–209.

Fairbairn, Madelaine (2020): *Fields of Gold. Financing the Global Land Rush*. Ithaca, New York: Cornell University Press.

Fairbairn, Madelaine (2014a): Just Another Asset Class? Neoliberalism, Finance, and the Construction of Farmland Investment. In Steven A. Wolf, Alessandro Bonanno (Eds.): *The Neoliberal Regime in the Agri-Food Sector. Crisis, Resilience, and Restructuring*. London: Routledge, pp. 245–262.

Fairbairn, Madelaine (2014b): 'Like Gold with Yield': Evolving Intersections between Farmland and Finance. In *The Journal of Peasant Studies* 41 (5), pp. 777–795. DOI: 10.1080/03066150.2013.873977.

Ferguson, Doug; Hendrischke, Hans (2013): Demystifying Chinese Investment in Australian Agribusiness. Important Choices to Be Made. In *KPMG and The University of Sydney*. Available online at https://hdl.handle.net/2123/23164, checked on 6/2/2016.

Freidberg, Susanne (2009): *Fresh. A Perishable History*. Cambridge, Massachusetts: Belknap Press.

Goodman, David (2010): Place and Space in Alternative Food Networks: Connecting Production and Consumption. In Michael K. Goodman, David Goodman, M. R. Redclift (Eds.): *Consuming Space. Placing Consumption in Perspective*. London: Routledge, pp. 189–211.

Goodman, M. K.; Goodman, D.; Redclift, M. (2010): Introduction: Situating Consumption, Space and Place. In Michael K. Goodman, David Goodman, M. R. Redclift (Eds.): *Consuming Space. Placing Consumption in Perspective*. London: Routledge, pp. 3–40.

Gonzalez, Emma (2016): Foresun Buys Latin Beef-Processing Units. In *China Daily*, 4/9/2016. Available online at http://www.chinadaily.com.cn/business/2016-04/09/content_24394644.htm, checked on 4/17/2020.

Guthman, Julie (2004): *Agrarian Dreams. The Paradox of Organic Farming in California*. Berkeley, London: University of California Press.

Grigg, Angus (2018): Chinese Investor at Mercy of Bank over $280 Million Tasmanian Dairy Play. In *Australian Financial Review*, 6/7/2018. Available online at https://www.afr.com/business/agriculture/chinese-investor-at-mercy-of-bank-over-280-million-tasmanian-dairy-play-20180607-h113az, checked on 2/26/2019.

Grigg, Angus (2017): Chinese Billionaire Tried to Sell Van Diemen's Land Company before Buying It. In *Australian Financial Review*, 8/2/2017. Available online at https://www.afr.com/companies/agriculture/the-chinese-billionaire-who-tried-to-sell-giant-tasmanian-dairy-before-buying-it-20170802-gxnq4m, checked on 3/11/2019.

Hanser, Amy; Li, Jialin C. (2015): Opting Out? Gated Consumption, Infant Formula and China's Affluent Urban Consumers. In *The China Journal* (74), pp. 110–128.

Hosen Capital (2016): Company Website. Available online at https://www.hosencapital.com, checked on 4/22/2020.

Klinger, Julie Michelle; Muldavin, Joshua (2019): New Geographies of Development: Grounding China's Global Integration. In *Territory, Politics, Governance* 7 (1), pp. 1–21. DOI: 10.1080/21622671.2018.1559.

Klein, Jakob A. (2013): Everyday Approaches to Food Safety in Kunming. In *The China Quarterly* (214), pp. 376–393.

Knaus, Christopher (2018): Mass Resignations at Chinese Owner of Australia's Largest Dairy Farm Cast Doubt on Investment. In *The Guardian* 4/25/2018. Available online at https://www.theguardian.com/australia-news/2018/apr/25/mass-resignations-at-chinese-owner-of-australias-largest-dairy-farm-cast-doubt-on-investment, checked on 1/29/2019.

Mendoza, Carmela (2017): Privately Speaking with CDH's Wu Shangzhi. In *Private Equity International*, 11/30/2017. Available online at https://www.privateequityinternational.com/cdh-is-here-for-the-long-haul/, checked on 4/17/2020.

Miller, Andrew (2018): Chinese-Owned Tasmanian Dairy Farms Crisis. In *Stock & Land*, 4/26/2018. Available online at https://www.stockandland.com.au/story/6229033/chinese-owned-tasmanian-dairy-farms-crisis/, checked on 5/2/2018.

Morgan, Kevin; Marsden, Terry; Murdoch, Jonathan (2008): *Worlds of Food. Place, Power, and Provenance in the Food Chain.* New York: Oxford University Press.

Murray, Warwick E.; Overton, John (2016): Investing in Place: Articulations and Congregations of Capital in the Wine Industry. In *The Geographical Journal* 182 (1), pp. 49–58.

Ningbo Xianfeng (2018a): Annual Report 2017 [2017年年度报告]. Available online at http://data.p5w.net/stock/lsgg.php?code=sz300163 checked on 5/2/2019.

Ningbo Xianfeng (2018b): Half-Year Annual Report 2018 [2018年半年度报告]. Available online at http://data.p5w.net/stock/lsgg.php?code=sz300163, checked on 2/15/2019.

Ningbo Xianfeng (2018c): Investor Platform. Available online at http://rs.p5w.net/c/300163.shtml, checked on 7/26/2018.

Ouma, Stefan (2020): *Farming as Financial Asset. Global Finance and the Making of Institutional Landscapes.* Newcastle upon Tyne: Agenda Publishing.

Overton, John; Murray, Warwick E. (2016): Fictive Place. In *Progress in Human Geography* 40 (6), pp. 794–809.

Perlez, Jane; McMorrow, Ryan (2017): A Deal for an Australian Dairy Wrapped in Layers of Chinese Loans. In *The New York Times*, 8/2/2017. Available online at https://www.nytimes.com/2017/08/02/world/australia/china-australia-dairy.html, checked on 5/9/2018.

Powell, Meg (2024): Tasmanian Farm the Size of Gibraltar Sells for $15m in 'Good Deal' for Management Fund. In *ABC Rural*, 3/26/2024. Available online at https://www.abc.net.au/news/rural/2024-03-26/chinese-owned-tasmanian-dairy-farm-returns-to-australian-hands/103553226, checked on 4/14/2024.

Robertson, Justin (2015): *Localizing Global Finance. The Rise of Western-Style Private Equity in China.* Basingstoke: Palgrave Pivot.

Tsing, Anna Lowenhaupt (2005): *Friction. An Ethnography of Global Connection.* Princeton: Princeton University Press.

Walter, Carl E.; Howie, Fraser J. T. (2011): *Privatizing China. Inside China's Stock Markets.* Second edition. Hoboken, New Jersey: John Wiley & Sons.

Yan, Yunxiang (2012): Food Safety and Social Risk in Contemporary China. In *The Journal of Asian Studies* 71 (3), pp. 705–729.

Yue, Jillian (2016): CDH-Backed Hengyang Cattle Plans Backdoor A-Share Listing. In *China Money Network*, 1/27/2016. Available online at https://www.chinamoneynetwork.com/2016/01/27/cdh-backed-hengyang-cattle-plans-backdoor-a-share-listing, checked on 4/17/2020.

# 7 Articulations

## Remaking agri-food chains

In late February 2017, Chinese news media reported a small sensation: China's first-ever ship-based consignment of live beef cattle from Australia had arrived by sea at the port of Shidao in China's eastern Shandong province. On February 4, a vessel loaded with 1,200 grass-fed Angus cattle left Portland in Victoria, Australia, and reached Shidao after a 16-day journey across the Pacific Ocean. Following inspection and quarantine upon arrival, the cattle were to be slaughtered, processed, packaged, and then shipped south again for another 1,000 kilometers where the high-end beef cuts were to end up on the dinner tables of wealthy Shanghai consumers. The company behind the shipment was Furui Group[1], a large real estate development group from Shanghai that had ventured into the Australian beef cattle industry a few years earlier, where it had since become one of the largest owners of pastoral land for the production of beef cattle in Northern and Western Australia. The company was no stranger to the public. It had made an earlier media splash in 2016, when it succeeded in taking a 33 percent minority stake in one of Australia's largest cattle empires in a joint venture with an Australian mining firm-turned-agribusiness. As the single largest landholding in Australia covering some 100,000 square kilometers and with a herd of 185,000 head of cattle, the beef business was a major prize in the eyes of the company's key executives and immediately catapulted the little-known Chinese investor to the top echelons of the Australian beef cattle industry. The live cattle shipment following just a few months later appeared to present the next logical step in an ambitious plan to turn the real estate group into a prominent player in the Chinese beef market. Furui celebrated the arrival of the cattle consignment with a large media event and ceremony at the company's shiny Jinyi Plaza building in Shanghai. Speaking to an audience of high-level representatives from the Australian consulate general, the Australian Trade and Investment Commission, and the Chinese food industry, Furui chairman and billionaire Wang Yiwen praised the shipment as a new era in China-Australia agri-food relations. By managing the import of Australian beef cattle right through arrival at port, slaughtering, and packaging, Furui Group would bring the freshest, highest quality meat to its discerning

DOI: 10.4324/9781003474661-10

customers in China—the chairman proudly declared—thus taking the beef trade between the two countries to the next level.

*****

The story of Furui exemplifies a vision shared by many Chinese agri-investors: controlling the flow of food from the farms and factories these investors own in Australia all the way to the dinner tables of consumers in China or elsewhere. Indeed, few Chinese companies would start an investment project without developing an idea of the market(s) with which they aspire to connect. This, in turn, requires investors not only to manage the flows of capital through agricultural landscapes but also to control the flows of food emanating from these landscapes. What this amounts to in practice, then, are attempts to reorganize agri-food chains and to forge new market connections. To understand how investors seek to reconfigure agri-food chains and connect to markets, this chapter zooms in on a third aspect of Chinese agri-investment in Australia: the movement of agri-food commodities along supply chains that connect Australian farms with Chinese consumers located thousands of miles away. By following agri-food commodities through different stages of the supply chain—from production to processing to distribution to consumption—this chapter asks how China's land rush in Australia reconfigures market connections across countries.

Drawing on other critical accounts investigating the making of global market connections (see e.g., Ouma 2015; Tsing 2005), I argue that the agri-food supply chains necessary to turn Chinese investment projects into economically successful endeavors do not simply exist "out there," ready to be utilized by savvy Chinese agri-food entrepreneurs or well-resourced Chinese agribusiness corporations but, instead, are assembled through messy encounters between investors, regulators, importers, farmers, and eaters. For a live cattle consignment to succeed, investors like Furei do not only rely on demand from Chinese consumers, but they must also ensure that they meet trade protocols and health standards and have access to the quarantine, slaughtering, processing, and logistics infrastructure required to send a live animal from Western Australia all the way to the dinner table of a high-end restaurant in Shanghai. Formed through "materially entangled" (Ouma 2015, p. 190) relations involving capital, nature, logistical infrastructures, technological devices, and regulatory regimes, the agri-food chains along which we can trace the movement of food are, thus, neither "given" nor "natural," but rather the contingent outcome of a diverse set of elements and practices that are subject to disruptions and uncertainties. Indeed, following Tsing (2005), the closer we look at the commodity chain, the more every step can be seen as an arena of friction where different elements are linked together, sometimes awkwardly.

This chapter draws on empirical material from my fieldwork to shed light on the material practices and visions through which Chinese agri-investors turn into enablers of new and sometimes global commodity chains that connect food production and consumption across national borders. This chapter traces the making of these market connections, the links they establish, and the obstacles they face. By zooming in on the new production-consumption linkages that Chinese investors establish (or fail to do so) when they seek to connect their overseas farms and agri-businesses with consumer markets elsewhere, I highlight both the complex work that is necessary to do so and the uncertainties surrounding many such projects.

My examples focus on supply chains in the beef and dairy sectors, given the dominant role of these two types of commodities in China's land rush in Australia. I begin my account with a brief overview of a stylized journey of a beef and dairy commodity, respectively, along the commodity chain connecting Australia and China and the regulatory, infrastructural, and socio-technical elements that sustain this journey. In the following two sections, I look more closely at a set of examples from my fieldwork, highlighting both how Chinese investors successfully draw together the various elements necessary to link up their farms and agribusinesses with consumer markets and how they fail to do so as they encounter unforeseen obstacles and face the recalcitrances of "nature."

## Forging market connections: agri-food chains in the beef and dairy sectors

To an affluent Chinese urbanite shopping at a high-end supermarket, a package of Aussie beef, a carton of milk imported fresh from Australia, or a tin of Australian-branded infant formula are familiar sights. They are so familiar, indeed, that few shoppers would stop to think about the "messy materialities" (Ouma 2015) through which these foods have ended up in their hands as a commodity ready for consumption. But what does it take for a food commodity to move from an Australian farm to a Chinese supermarket shelf?

Figure 7.1 and Figure 7.2 illustrate the movement of beef and dairy all the way through the commodity chain until they arrive at the consumer. Despite Australia's image as a "natural" farming environment, the process through which beef and dairy products become available to consumers as commodities is an industrial one, shaped by efforts to measure, optimize, and streamline the biophysical properties of animals and landscapes alike. The typical beef production process begins with the breeding of calves. At around four to nine months, calves are weaned from their mothers and enter the so-called backgrounding phase where animals spend their days grazing pastures until they reach slaughter weight. Cattle production may look deceptively simple, but, in fact, it is a highly optimized process. From daily feeding routines, to the distances animals have to walk to reach water and feed, to the types of grasses and supplementary rations they are fed—all are designed to achieve efficiency or, in other words, to obtain maximum growth rates in the shortest possible time at the lowest possible cost.

*Figure 7.1* Stylized beef commodity chain.

*Source:* Elaborated by the author based on Meat & Livestock Australia 2018a/b/c, Edwards et al. 2016, PwC 2011a, as well as field interviews.

After 12 and 18 months, animals reach slaughter weight. Some animals may enter a feedlot before slaughter, where they are fed a specially formulated grain-based diet designed to produce cattle with brighter, whiter fat and more marbling than grass-fed beef—attributes that are associated with premium quality in markets such as China. Most animals are slaughtered in Australian abattoirs and reach the Chinese market as frozen or chilled cuts of meat which then pass through the hands of certified importers and wholesalers before they end up in Chinese supermarkets, hotels, or restaurants. Additionally, a live export agreement with China signed in 2015 gives Australian producers the option to export living animals to be slaughtered and processed overseas. While the transport of living animals across national borders is commonplace in economically integrated parts of the world such as the European Union, it assumes a new dimension in the case of Australia. The continent's geographical location means that animals are transported

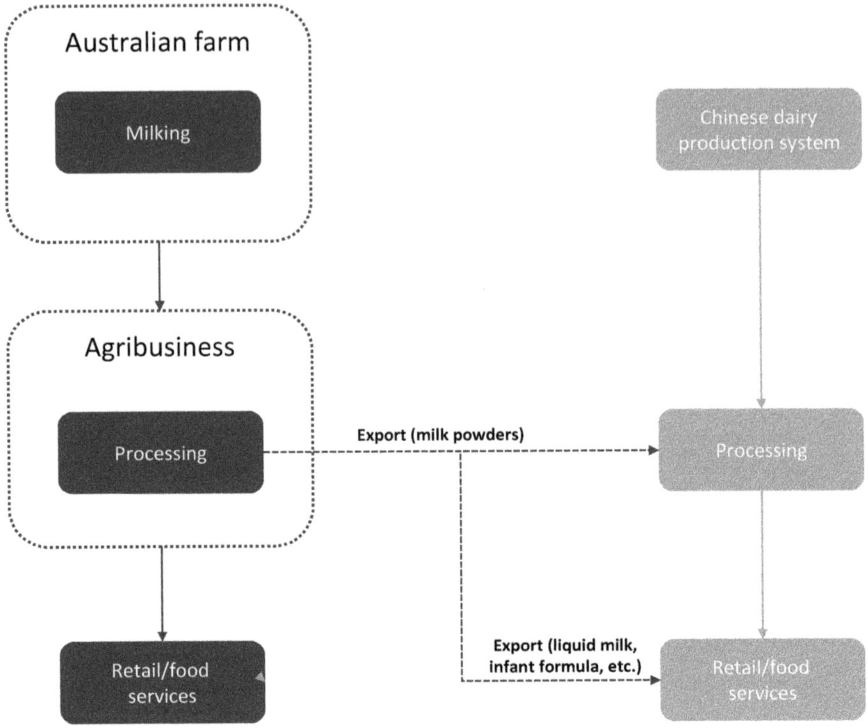


*Figure 7.2* Stylized dairy commodity chain.

*Source:* Elaborated by the author based on Dairy Australia 2018; PwC 2011b, and field interviews.

in week-long journeys across the ocean or, in some cases, even by airfreight, adding considerable logistical (as well as moral and ethical) complexity.

Similar to the beef commodity chain described above, for milk to become available as food, dairy production relies on the efficient transformation of "nature" into a commodity. Production starts with the harvesting of raw milk produced by cows on dairy farms. With 5,699 dairy farms and an average herd size of 273 cows, the Australian dairy industry is still characterized by relatively small producers. However, there are increasing numbers of large farms milking over 1,000 cows. Many farms operate pasture-based production systems where cattle graze pastures between milkings, but there is also a growing number of barn-style farms. Here, animal herds are confined in dairy sheds and kept on commercially prepared feed to achieve productivity increases and economic gains. The raw milk produced on dairy farms then moves to the manufacturing stage to be processed into a range of dairy products, including whole milk powder and skim milk powder, drinking milk, yogurts, infant formula, cheese, and others. Unlike milk production, the dairy manufacturing sector is dominated by agribusiness companies, some

Australian and other large multinational corporations, and is considerably more concentrated.

Dairy manufacturing companies produce two types of dairy products for export. First, there are so-called dairy ingredients such as milk powders that are used by dairy manufacturing companies overseas in the production of consumer dairy products. The second category includes dairy products ready for consumption, such as liquid milk, yogurts, or infant formula. While milk powders exported to China serve as inputs for China's domestic dairy manufacturers, finished dairy products are destined for Chinese consumers and distributed through supermarkets and other retail channels. Milk powders take the form of bulk commodities as they can be stored over long periods of time and transported in large volumes. By contrast, finished dairy products, particularly in their "fresh" form, are highly perishable foods that rely on modern technological infrastructures and fast transportation links.

To be sure, these are two highly stylized accounts. In practice, the journey of beef and dairy commodities through the agri-food chain relies on a host of carefully coordinated technologies and regulatory procedures, from seamless cold chain management to rigorous food safety testing, smooth transportation links, as well as tightly coordinated inspection procedures to avoid costly import delays and harbor fees. At the same time, the elements required to stabilize supply chains are constantly at risk of falling apart, threatening to slow down or hamper the movement of food along the chain. Chinese regulators may suddenly slap tariffs on Australian imports or revoke import licenses, citing health and hygiene concerns—as last happened during the COVID-19 pandemic, when Chinese authorities imposed a ban on beef imports from several Australian abattoirs amid heightened political tensions between both countries. Moral outrage over animal welfare, such as in the case of live cattle exports, may call the legitimacy of certain flows of food into question. And price and exchange rate fluctuations may make Australian food less attractive to Chinese consumers, particularly in the case of "lifestyle products" such as beef and dairy for which demand is volatile and highly price-sensitive.

Reflecting on the case of one Australian beef producer hoping to enter the Chinese market, a representative of the Australian Chamber of Commerce in Beijing described how quickly export dreams can fall apart as the beef producer was struggling with unrelenting regulators and recalcitrant food properties:

> They [...] had a wrong test result and they had their license suspended for six months or so. [...] Their beef was fine, but they had to do a full audit of their supply chain, their license was suspended by the Chinese government, they had to satisfy the Chinese government that it wasn't their fault, and all of that process took, I think, round about six months and a lot of money. And there's a lot more things that can go wrong.
>
> (interview May 2018, Beijing)

Beyond such challenges, widespread practices of food counterfeiting and adulteration in China routinely disrupt the movement of food along the supply chain. Evidently, for a Chinese investor seeking to carve out a niche in the Chinese agri-food market based around notions of food safety and quality, the diluting, mixing, or mislabeling of food commodities by third parties involved along the supply chain presents an essential business risk. Describing his interactions with Chinese importers and wholesalers, one Chinese investor running an Australian beef export business bluntly stated: "We can't trust other people. So even if we give them the product, once they have it in their possession, we don't know what they're going to do." (interview September 2017, Sydney). The widely held belief that "you can't really trust anyone but yourself to do the job," as the manager put it, has meant that control over the entire supply chain from "farm to fork" has become a key element in the export strategy of Chinese investors (Sippel & Böhme 2019). The next section examines how Chinese agri-investors seek to reduce uncertainties along the agri-food chain through various strategies of vertical integration.

## Building agri-food chains from "farm to fork"

According to Heffernan (2000), "vertical integration occurs when a firm increases ownership and control over a number of stages in a commodity system" (pp. 68–69). In other words, vertically integrated agri-food companies do not simply engage in primary production or in the processing of agri-food commodities but control the commodity chain "from farm to fork." Control is achieved by either owning assets at different stages of the commodity chain (e.g. owning the farm, the processing plant, the retail outlet) or, more commonly, via long-term contracts and offtake, supply, or processing agreements with companies operating in upstream and downstream segments of the commodity chain. One investor described the importance of vertical integration for his company's investment strategy in the following words:

> We recognize that to really achieve our ultimate vision [...] we need to retain ownership of that product in our supply chain right through to the end point in China, whether the sale is on Alibaba, or whatever. We need to deliver it right through if we can. [...] By controlling it the whole way through, working with a focus on maximizing profit in the entire company, we have the best opportunity to make it work.
>
> (interview August 2017, Melbourne)

Vertical integration is thus often seen as a fundamental investment principle underpinning the activities of Chinese investors in Australian agriculture. Asked about the significance of vertically integrating across various stages of the commodity chain, one investor with interests in the Australian dairy industry bluntly stated:

> We have to be able to see a path to vertical integration. We do not invest in commodities. We don't invest in one segment of the value chain. It has to be the whole value chain.
>
> (interview August 2017, Melbourne)

Vertical integration is a buzzword not only among Chinese investors acquiring farms and food companies overseas but also within China itself. In fact, over the past years, vertical integration has been promoted by the government as the principle mechanism for modernizing China's domestic agriculture sector (Schneider 2017). By integrating primary production with processing and marketing, usually under the leadership of the so-called dragon-head firms, Chinese policymakers seek to address a whole range of domestic rural concerns, such as increasing incomes of China's peasant population, modernizing and scaling up agricultural production, and integrating rural and urban industries (Schneider 2017). In the dairy industry, policies promoting vertical integration have resulted in an industrial restructuring where processing companies have come to control an increasing part of the primary production stage, either by acquiring existing dairy producers or through investment in the construction of large-scale, modern dairy farms. For example, Chinese dairy processor Mengniu holds a majority share in both China Modern Dairy, China's largest producer of raw milk, and Shengmu High-tech Dairy, China's leading organic milk producer (PwC 2019). Similar developments have been documented in the meat industry, where a growing number of leading national companies are now involved in more than one stage of the commodity chain (Schneider & Sharma 2014). These domestic transformations form an important backdrop to the overseas strategies of Chinese agri-investors. Indeed, as Schneider (2017) argues, "[t]he same logics of vertical integration that propel agricultural development for national-scale developments also condition global strategies" (p. 15).

Vertical integration is popular among Chinese companies operating in the food sector because it promises greater control over the commodity chain, thus preventing food adulteration by upstream or downstream actors as a food commodity moves through the supply chain. It is often seen as the only way for a food business to ensure the stringent application of food safety regulations throughout the entire production process and as a safeguard against food scandals. "If you want to get into the food business in China," an investment advisor from PwC China told me, "in order to provide safer food, you need to have better control over the supply chain." (interview March 2017, Shanghai). Adopting a "fully integrated supply chain strategy" is crucial for any Chinese company seeking to bring overseas food supply to the Chinese market, the advisor emphasized. I heard similar views expressed in interviews with Chinese investors, as this statement by an executive of a Chinese company with investments in the Australian beef industry demonstrates:

> Food safety is the NUMBER ONE concern. In China, when a consumer buys something, their number one thought is: "Is this real?" Even if they go to Louis Vuitton and they buy a bag, they need to ask themselves the question: "Is this product real?" Now, when you're talking about non-food products, it doesn't matter as much. Because the worst thing is that you lose some money. But if you eat something fake, it can actually pose serious health risks to you. So, that's the number one concern. And that's part of the reason why we're creating a supply chain "from paddock to plate".
>
> (interview September 2017, Sydney)

Beyond food safety concerns, vertical integration also helps investors to reduce costs and improve their often-times very tight margins. By controlling various stages of the commodity chain, investors seek to ensure the regular supply of a given commodity at a relatively fixed price—two factors that are important for setting up and expanding distribution networks in the Chinese market. As the PwC investment advisor told me when describing the motivations of one of her clients to invest in an integrated beef commodity chain from Australia to China:

> For some products like beef, especially two or three years ago, it was very difficult to get imports from the market at a good price. You can of course always get beef, but not at a good price. By having greater control over the supply chain, you can get rid of price fluctuations. You can also get a better margin if you own and control the supply chain.
>
> (interview March 2017, Shanghai)

While vertical integration along the commodity chain is a common strategy among Chinese investors, decisions vary with respect to the production stage at which investors enter the chain. Reflecting on the flexibility with which Chinese companies have begun to integrate commodity chains, one investor told me:

> Some of them own farms, some don't, and some of them own the cattle from the feedlot but have contracted growers. It's a bit like building Lego, you can almost do it any way you want.
>
> (interview May 2018, Shanghai)

To be sure, where to invest in the commodity chain is not as arbitrary a decision as the comment above might suggest. In fact, my discussions with investors and industry insiders have shown that different factors, including overall business strategy, role and position of the investor in China's agri-food system, as well as investment opportunities and market cycles, determine whether an investor will acquire primary production, processing, and/ or retail assets and in which combination. Primary production and processing require fundamentally different sets of expertise, monetary resources, and operational skills. While the acquisition of an agri-food processing business, at times including its associated food brands, often involves the transaction of hundreds of millions of dollars as well as the management of large teams of staff, farms may sell for as "little" as a few million dollars, necessitating but a handful of people to manage farm operations. Consequently, as we have seen in Chapter 4, to date, acquisitions of Australian beef and dairy processing companies have predominantly been undertaken by China's large agribusiness corporations, both state owned and privately owned, which source supply through offtake agreements with primary producers. In contrast, agri-food entrepreneurs and state farms tend to focus investment on the upstream stages of the commodity chain, achieving control over the downstream stages of the production chain through contractual arrangements with processing companies.

Another important factor that determines at which stage of the production chain investors acquire assets are commodity cycles. For example, in the beef sector, farm prices tend to be low during drought years as farmers are forced to sell off cattle, thus depressing the prices paid for their farm properties. In contrast, abattoir prices increase as ample supply of cheap cattle during drought years means that meat plants can grow their profits and margins. As one investor told me, it was precisely a shift in the commodity cycle that made the company change its investment strategy from an initial focus on beef processing plants to a focus on beef farms, although he concluded that, ultimately, the company's goal was to invest "in all stages of the supply chain, otherwise the risk is too high" (interview March 2017, Hangzhou).

#### *"It's all about vertical supply chain integration ... backwards"*

Chinese investors' ambitions to become vertically integrated businesses are beginning to produce material outcomes. While in 2015, an industry report on the Australian beef sector stated that "currently, no Chinese beef investor has an end-to-end supply chain investment in Australia" (VC Group 2016, p. 11), by 2017, branded beef and dairy products originating from Chinese-invested farms and processing plants in Australia had started to appear on Chinese supermarket shelves and e-commerce stores. To understand what had happened, stories like that of agri-food entrepreneur Feihe Group[2] provide an instructive example.

In China, Feihe Group is a well-known retail company, operating a range of department stores as well as supermarkets across cities in China's north-east. The group completed its first Australian agri-investment in 2015, when it acquired a 30,000-hectare beef cattle farm in central New South Wales. Since then, Feihe has acquired more than 100,000 hectares of Australian farmland throughout New South Wales and Queensland, mainly for the production of "elite" Wagyu and black Angus cattle, as the company's executive manager told me during an interview (interview September 2017, Sydney). The group

*Figure 7.3* Imported beef from Feihe Group's Australian beef operations at a company retail outlet in Beijing's Fengtai district.

*Source:* Author's own picture taken during fieldwork in 2017.

does not own Australian beef processing facilities, but it has contract arrangements with Australian feedlot and processing firms in place and exports chilled and frozen beef products under its "Hunter Valley" brand to its own retail stores in China (see Figure 7.3). Feihe Group also promotes and sells its branded beef products through the company's own WeChat[3] store but, so far, has stayed away from the popular e-commerce platform Alibaba for fear that food adulteration somewhere within Alibaba's network will compromise Feihe's brand image. "We don't want to put our brands out there to other people," the manager emphasized the company's strict focus on supply chain control. To complement its beef line, Feihe also owns a number of vineyards in France and Australia and recently acquired two fruit orchards in Tasmania. Inasmuch as its beef operations are concerned, the company is proud of "owning the supply chain all the way through," as its Australian-based executive manager explained to me:

> We own the farm, we own the cattle. We produce them, then we put [the meat] in a box or we do live cattle exporting. Then [the meat] gets

> sent to China and we sell it in our own supermarkets. So that, I think, is a real definition of "paddock-to-plate" for consumers.
>
> (interview September 2017, Sydney)

Controlling the supply chain from "paddock to plate" is important for Feihe Group primarily to create consumer trust. With food safety being a key concern among Chinese consumers, creating a brand with a "clean and green" reputation is crucial for the company, the manager told me, and seamless management throughout the whole supply chain is the only way to ensure that the brand image is not damaged by practices of food counterfeiting or adulteration. Feihe's "paddock to plate" story is not only about supply chain management but also about consumer communication. When I visited one of Feihe's retail stores in Beijing in the spring of 2017, a copy of an origin certificate placed at the meat counter caught my attention. The certificate was issued in the English language with the words "Certificate of Australian Origin" prominently displayed on it, signaling authenticity to the shoppers scrutinizing the various beef products on offer.

Yet, supply chain control is not only about traceability, food safety, and quality but also about controlling prices. Indeed, to be profitable in China's challenging market environment, Chinese retailers need to ensure they can offer beef products at competitive prices. Owning one's own source of supply is hence often seen as a way to control the beef price and, consequently, the profit margin. In the words of Feihe's general manager:

> Retail is tough because there's so much competition. So, the margins generally are quite similar [between different retail companies] and transparent. If you're only going to be able to sell a product for so much, for you to extract more profit out of it, what do you do? You have to reduce your cost of input. And the best way for you to do that is for you to be able to own and control that.
>
> (interview September 2017, Sydney.)

The manager described the company's supply chain model as "vertical supply chain integration … backwards". Starting from its retail business in China, backward vertical integration has meant for the company to expand into segments further upstream of the commodity chain, ultimately with the goal of providing a stable and safe supply of beef at a predetermined retail price. Meanwhile, in Australia, investor strategies based on "backward" vertical integration have attracted criticism. The notion that such supply chain arrangements could turn Australia into a cheap provider of food to the Chinese, "cutting out all the milk" for Australia—as one manager described it—has not gone down well with some stakeholders in Australian politics and business. Rather than linking Australian farms and agribusinesses into existing retail channels in China, these critics argue, investors should integrate "forward" through the supply chain. This, it is hoped, will open up entirely new market segments at higher margins. Baoniu's story exemplifies this approach.

### *"'China first' but not 'China exclusive'"*

In Australian agribusiness circles, Baoniu[4]—the Chinese-Australian beef cattle joint venture we encountered in Chapter 5—is considered a quintessential example of what a successful Chinese agri-investment project may look like. Similar to other agri-food entrepreneurs, Baoniu's investment calculus is based on the assumption of rising Chinese demand for (imported) beef and the business opportunity this presents to savvy investors able to carve out a niche in this quickly expanding market. "They're going to want more red meat," a top Baoniu manager described the company's straightforward investment vision. "If we can control supply from the farm in Australia right through to after processing in China, everything says that we should be able to make money out of this process" (interview August 2017, Melbourne). Unlike investors such as Feihe Group, however, Baoniu began its investment spree entirely from scratch, with no Chinese retail stores to provide an entry point into the Chinese market. To the manager, this has not been a drawback but, on the contrary, the key to Baoniu's apparent success. "It's actually allowed our company to develop in a more sustainable way," the manager explained. In contrast, doing the "Chinese retrofit" like Feihe is bound to fail "because of the fact that the cost is a cost is a cost," the manager insisted (interview August 2017, Melbourne). In other words, rather than fitting its Australian beef operations into pre-defined, tight retail margins in China, Baoniu's supply chain strategy is aimed at opening up new market segments that promise larger profits.

Equipped with the above strategy brief, Baoniu's Australia management team set to work to establish one of the most seamlessly integrated beef supply chains connecting Australia and China. By mid-2018, when I last interviewed a Baoniu representative, the company did not only own a string of grazing properties and feedlot facilities in Western Australia and Victoria, but, as one of the very few investors, it had also expanded into the beef processing sector, acquiring a Victorian-based abattoir from a troubled Chinese private agribusiness corporation which, at that time, was seeking to divest its Australian assets. On the Chinese side, the company had acquired a beef processing facility and a well-known Chinese meat brand "Qingdao Snowdragon" with an existing distribution network. In addition to selling Australian beef under the "Qingdao Snowdragon" brand, which, as the Baoniu manager told me, is "high-end" but remains decidedly "Chinese," the company had developed a second brand designed to be perceived as "authentically" Australian in the Chinese marketplace (interview May 2018, Shanghai). Somewhat ironically, the plan was to supply both brands from Baoniu's Australian beef cattle business—a testament to the significance of "narrating" food to consumers (Goodman et al. 2010).

Moreover, Baoniu had emerged as a key actor in the nascent live cattle trade with China. Through its Chinese majority partner—Fuyao—the company had become involved in a joint venture with Chinese state-owned logistics companies Sinotrans Group and China Merchants Group, which own and operate two ships approved for the export of live cattle from Australia to China. This arrangement, the manager told me, provided the company with regular time charters at fixed and predictable costs, a crucial advantage in the live cattle export component of its business model. Indeed, since December 2017, Baoniu has been sending several live cattle consignments to ports in China for slaughter and processing, including to the eastern Chinese port city of Qingdao, where Baoniu's Chinese beef processing assets are located and the "Qingdao Snowdragon" brand is headquartered. And while export volumes were still low at the time of our conversation, the manager was optimistic to see exports grow sharply over the next months.

The case of Baoniu exemplifies the complex work that is needed to draw together the different elements underpinning the frictional movement of commodities along the agri-food chain: from "ramping up" animal production to generating the export volumes necessary for carving out a position in the Chinese market; to juggling a set of intricate sourcing, vaccination, and quarantining rules that must be observed when preparing live cattle shipments to China; and to leveraging brand image effects in order to "place" beef commodities in the right, that is—most profitable—way with Chinese consumers. But although it has taken Baoniu a considerable amount of effort to reconfigure beef supply chains with China, its level of engagement is highly contingent on favorable market conditions in China. In the words of Baoniu's Australian manager:

> Our company's focus is "China first", but not "China exclusive". So, in reality, what does that mean? That means that, yes, our target is to deliver meat or live animals to China, but only if China's paying the right amount of money. If the better market is Indonesia or Vietnam or Korea or domestic or whatever, then that will take the focus, but China is first.
>
> (interview August 2017, Melbourne)

This strategic calculus is not unique to Baoniu. Indeed, the desire of most Chinese agri-investors to link their Australian farming assets with markets in China is driven by the allure of extra-high profits to be had in the Chinese market and, thus, relies on growing demand and high prices for food commodities from specific origins such as Australia. Ultimately, Baoniu's business logic of "'China first' but not 'China exclusive'" reminds us that the market connections forged by Chinese agri-investors and their Australian partners are not immutable and can easily find themselves disrupted, selectively transformed, or disarticulated under changing global market conditions.

### *"It's an issue of trust"*

Strategies of vertical integration are also prominent in the dairy sector. This is perhaps best illustrated by Tianrun Dairy[5]—a little-known Chinese agri-food entrepreneur operating a dairy supply chain that stretches all the way from its Australian dairy farms to the dinner tables of Chinese consumers. At a time when highly spectacular and speculative investment projects such as Shengda Investment Group's Tasmanian dairy gamble (see Chapter 6) were gripping the attention of the Australian public and media, Tianrun was quietly assembling an end-to-end supply chain that would bring high-end Australian dairy commodities to affluent Chinese consumers.

When I arrived at the company's dairy manufacturing plant located on the outskirts of Sydney on an early December morning in 2018, the place was already bustling with activity. Trucks were driving up and down the gateway leading to the factory gate located behind a non-descript, one-story office building. Some appeared to deliver raw milk collected at the farm gate and ready for processing at Tianrun's dairy plant. Others would pick up large containers filled with packages of milk and yogurt that would now begin their journey to the consumer. I was there to meet with Andrew Chen—a smart, Western-educated Chinese business man that was running Tianrun's Australian dairy operations as its executive director. Andrew invited me on a tour through the company's manufacturing plant—an offer I gladly accepted. As we were walking in our white lab coats and hairnets through the factory, carefully maneuvering around polished tubes, massive tanks, and conveyor belts churning out a steady flow of milk cartons and other dairy products, Andrew explained to me what the company had been trying to achieve in Australia.

Tianrun is a prototypical agri-food entrepreneur. Founded in 1983, it made a fortune in the industrial label printing industry, eventually listing on the Shanghai stock exchange in 2012. But cutthroat competition and shrinking margins have put the company under pressure. In search of new business opportunities, Tianrun decided to diversify into China's fast-growing consumer market, identifying dairy as a major growth sector. According to Andrew, there was little chance the newcomer was ever to compete with China's leading dairy businesses. To carve out a niche, then, in the highly competitive Chinese market, Tianrun was to focus on high-end dairy products for China's rising middle class:

> We have our opportunities compared to these big guys. Because they have the majority of the market, which is the lower-end products. [...] Most of the products they sell are three yuan a unit. That's what the majority of Chinese consumers will spend on dairy. But our customers will be different, will be rising middle class. By 2020, China will have more than 100 million middle class people. And that group of people is our market. So, we cannot compete with the production costs [of

> China's dairy giants]. They are significantly cheaper because of economies of scale. [...] We have to target a different group of people, and that's where we see our opportunity.
>
> (interview December 2018, Sydney)

With this vision in mind, the company has focused on the production of high-quality, imported dairy products ready for consumption by aspirational end consumers in China. In 2016, Tianrun made its first foray into the Australian dairy sector, acquiring an out-of-business dairy manufacturing facility at the north-western outskirts of Sydney. Following the upgrading of the processing equipment, the company brought the facility back into operations at the end of the same year. "There are currently three production lines," Andrew explained to me as he was showing me around the factory floor, "one for UHT milk, one for fresh milk, and one for drinking yoghurt." There were also plans to extend the product range to other high-end dairy products such as lactose-free milk.

As one of the world's most perishable commodities, the movement of fresh dairy, particularly fresh liquid milk, poses its own set of logistical challenges. To ensure that its products travel smoothly through the supply chain, Tianrun has established a fast customs clearance procedure with the local government of Wuxi in southern Jiangsu province, where the company's dairy products enter Chinese customs control. Thinking about how to organize the material flow of fresh food commodities between airports, customs, and supermarket shelves is a logistical and technological challenge. Wuxi not only boasts advanced cold chain infrastructure but also enjoys a favorable geographical location. Because Wuxi sits in the middle of many cities in Eastern China, "it's a lot more economical when you ship product from Wuxi," Andrew laid out the intricacies of Tianrun's supply chain organization to me. As the company has worked to optimize product handling and workflows to ensure no precious shelf life is lost during transport, it has been able to greatly speed up the time for a carton of milk to move through the commodity chain. "We have progressed a lot," Andrew proudly explained. "It only takes ten hours now to clear customs and complete the checks. So, the best time we have achieved was 48 hours to send our milk from the farm to the shelf in China." Yet, despite the company's efforts to bring into alignment the technical, logistical, and regulatory elements needed to build a robust supply chain, transforming milk from Australian cows into dairy commodities enjoyed by Chinese consumers thousands of miles away remains a costly and risky endeavor. When I asked Andrew about the difference between exporting a food commodity such as dry milk powder and fresh liquid milk, I was told that this was hardly comparable. Obviously, the latter presented unique challenges to producer-exporters:

> [...] the logistics costs are quite high and it's a lot harder to do the job correctly. You must be more precise in terms of controlling the

> temperature, the time. You must be really strict about picking up the milk, dropping off the milk, when to deliver, and when to pick up. Very strict. You make one mistake...
>
> (interview December 2018, Sydney)

In the positive event when no mistakes are made and the commodity emerges safely at the other end of the chain in China, more work is needed to "place" it in the market. To ensure that the dairy products reach the type of affluent customer around which Tianrun has built its investment strategy, the company has entered into supply agreements with a range of high-end retail stores in China and popular Chinese e-commerce platforms. It has also been experimenting with the so-called experience stores—brick-and-mortar shops that exclusively sell Tianrun-branded dairy products and "educate" Chinese consumers about their pristine origins, safe supply chains, and superior health benefits.

Tianrun's control over the supply chain, however, is not limited to dairy processing and retail, but extends further upstream to include raw milk production. In addition to its Sydney-based manufacturing plant, the company owns and operates two dairy farms in the Gippsland region of Victoria. With no more than 580 hectares and a combined herd of 950 dairy cows, the farms are relatively modest in size. Indeed, they are so modest that their raw milk output is insufficient to sustain the operations of Tianrun's dairy manufacturing plant. Consequently, Tianrun has been collaborating with other farmers in the region to supply raw milk to its factory. This came as a surprise to me. Why would an investor company choose to confront the biophysical vagaries of raw milk production only to have most of its raw milk supplied by other Australian farmers? But when I suggested the company might be better off just focusing on dairy manufacturing, Andrew adamantly replied: "You don't just sit in the middle. You need to control the whole industry chain."

The desire of Chinese agri-food investors to "control the whole industry chain" was nothing new to me, and, as we have seen above, there are many reasons for investors to pursue such a strategy, from increasing profit margins to safeguarding against practices of food adulteration and counterfeiting to secure supply at a defined cost. The case of Tianrun revealed yet another dimension of that investment calculus: producing authenticity. The premium profits to be had from selling an "authentically Australian" dairy commodity are based on claims about controlling the life of the commodity all the way to its source—the green, lush pastures of an Australian dairy farm. It is about there being something "behind the brand," Andrew explained, something that goes back all the way to "the farm" and to "the grazing model of the cows." To Andrew, "it's an issue of trust." Consumers will only trust the commodity if they believe in its authenticity. Authenticity in turn means that the food company must control the chain "all the way through." In other words, reorganizing supply chains from "farm to fork" becomes a means of achieving authenticity, upon which high food prices in the Chinese market are premised.

The significance of authenticity also explains why Tianrun's reorganization of supply chains has focused not only on China but on Australia as well. In fact, Tianrun is not just an aspiring niche provider in China's high-end dairy market but also a major supplier of Aldi Australia, with whom it signed a retail agreement for the retailer's one-liter milk range in 2016. Operating as a milk supplier to one of Australia's top retail chains was not a business decision dictated by mere financial necessity. Rather, it was quintessential to the company's investment logic as it would make Tianrun look more authentic in the eyes of discerning Chinese consumers, Andrew believed:

> [Chinese consumers] want a product that's imported from other countries. They don't want somebody to go out there and make a brand and distribute it back to China. This is considered "fake". It's a Chinese-made foreign brand rather than a foreign brand imported from Australia to the Chinese market. So, we need to distribute the product here in Australia in order to get the customer's interest.
>
> (interview December 2018, Sydney.)

The case of Tianrun reminds us that the flow of commodities from "farm to fork" relies on both the material and the imaginary or, in the words of Ouma (2015), on a set of "material-cum-discursive" practices. Thus, what turns milk from an Australian cow into a high-end, authentically Australian commodity in the hands of Chinese consumers are not only the materially grounded configurations of technology, infrastructure, and regulatory regimes that enable the movement of milk from Australian farms to Chinese dinner tables but also the stories through which the milk is sold.

### *"You don't put all your eggs in one basket"*

While most agri-food entrepreneurs have been reorganizing supply chains around the export to high-end niche markets in China, some of the largest Chinese agri-investors have sought to position themselves at the center of a global network of market connections. Take Zhongnong Group[6]—one of China's largest private agribusiness corporations in the Chinese livestock industry—as an example. In the past one and a half decades, Zhongnong Group has transformed itself into a veritable multinational agribusiness that owns production, processing, and distribution assets for animal protein products (meat, dairy, and seafood) around the globe. The group explicitly describes itself as a global business. "We're not a Chinese company. We're global. We run our business globally.", the company's key executive for business operations in Australia and New Zealand emphasized, when I referred to Zhongnong Group as a "Chinese company" during an interview (February 2017, Sydney).

In the beef sector, the group's transition toward becoming a globally integrated business began in 2013, when Zhongnong acquired a large Australian beef processing plant. Like other investors I spoke to, Zhongnong executives have confirmed to me that the meatification of Chinese diets has provided a powerful incentive to invest in Australia's beef cattle industry, but the group's ultimate vision goes far beyond supplying the Chinese market with beef. As one China-based executive stated:

> Chinese people are starting to consume beef, but you cannot really produce that in China because for beef, you need a lot of land, you need the right environmental conditions. Australia is very suitable for beef [production]. So, we are partnering with Australia. But we don't just want to bring all the beef back to China. We partner with Australia, but we want to grow our beef business globally.
>
> (interview April 2017, Beijing)

In 2014, Zhongnong Group expanded further, this time acquiring a US-based meat production plant specializing in branded "meal solutions" for supermarkets and fast-food restaurants, such as pre-cooked meals and portion cuts. The US company is the single largest Northern American customer of beef slaughtered at Zhongnong's Australian abattoir which it then processes further into "value-added products" for the food service industry in the United States. Another strategic deal followed in 2015, when Zhongnong Group acquired a Chinese meat portioning, value-adding, and distribution business located in China's eastern Shandong province. The meat business is a leading supplier to fast food restaurants in China, particularly international chains such as McDonald's, KFC, Pizza Hut, or Burger King. As Zhongnong Group was expanding its global footprint, the group also made capital investments into its Australian beef abattoir, modernizing equipment and increasing plant capacity from 750 to 1,200 head of cattle to be slaughtered per day.

In 2018, a corporate restructuring then brought the abattoir's two foreign sister companies under a common management umbrella (see Figure 7.4). The newly formed venture is a "nature-to-plate food solutions enterprise" that "partner[s] with the world's food industry to relentlessly pursue new and better ways to source, prepare and serve wholesome meat and seafood that the world loves to eat," a company brochure informs potential customers. Zhongnong's meat plants in the United States and China now absorb about 30 percent of the group's expanding Australian beef exports, while the remainder is sold to customers in over 20 countries worldwide, including in the Australian market. In 2019, Zhongnong Group's global beef business announced its first plans to list on the Hong Kong stock market, expecting to raise 300 to 400 million USD in the process—a plan which, however, is still pending at the time of this writing.

Zhongnong Group sees its approach toward global integration as being fundamentally different from what other Chinese investors in the Australian beef industry are seeking to accomplish. As one company executive explained:

> Many Chinese companies go out to just buy resources overseas and bring them back to China. That's not smart. The Chinese government could cut off market access any time it wants. You don't put all your eggs in one basket. [...] [Zhongnong Group] sees the larger picture. It considers Australia a good place for resources but wants to connect them to the global beef production system. The basic logic is to turn [its Australian beef assets] into a global protein provider rather than just an Australian abattoir.
>
> (interview May 2018, Shanghai)

The company's stated goal of becoming a "global protein provider" is reflected in an investment strategy that goes beyond a focus on controlling vertical linkages in the beef commodity chain between Australian growers and Chinese consumers. By integrating one of Australia's largest beef processing companies with two major meat businesses in the United States and China, Zhongnong Group has positioned itself as a leading beef producer globally, controlling the supply of beef commodities across multiple borders, countries, and regions. Arguably, this approach has shielded the company from the manifold regulatory and market risks characterizing bilateral agri-food trade with China, such as the wave of beef import bans targeting abattoirs across Australia—including Zhongnong Group—amid a diplomatic row between China and Australia over the origins of the pandemic in early 2020. Indeed, despite curtailed exports to China, Zhongnong Group has been able to further expand its Australian footprint, acquiring several other distressed processing assets across Australia between 2021 and 2023. At the same time, the global approach the company has taken also increases complexities within the supply chain as executives have to manage multiple regulatory and legal regimes, technological and infrastructural conditions, as well as consumer preferences. Hence, pathways toward becoming a "global" agribusiness have been open but to the largest Chinese agri-investors able to mobilize massive amounts of investment funds, including state and international finance capital. The self-identification of Zhongnong as a global company, however, should not gloss over the fact that the group's globality is much more messy and incomplete than its rhetoric suggests. For example, while Zhongnong is deeply integrated through the upstream and downstream stages of the meat value chain in many parts of China, in the context of Australia, the group only controls the processing stage. In other major beef-producing countries such as Brazil, Zhongnong Group does not play a significant role. In short, then, Zhongnong's global ambitions may have made possible the production of globe-crossing agri-food chains, but these chains are constituted by uneven links.

## Disruptions along the agri-food chain

One aspect that has figured consistently in my field research is the gap between investor ambition and reality. Whether it is about identifying feasible investment opportunities, convincing consumers to pay premium prices, or creating the right stories to mobilize funding from investment partners and capital markets, there are many junctures at which investment endeavors can go spectacularly wrong. The market connections linking investor-owned Australian farms to Chinese (or other global) consumers are no exception. Indeed, as Chinese agri-investors set to work to reorganize agri-food supply chains, they often encounter unforeseen obstacles and uncertainties that put at risk and, at times, derail entire investment projects. In the final section of this chapter, I present a couple of case studies from my research that highlight how material flows of food from investor "farms" to consumer "forks" can be easily disrupted by regulatory and infrastructural obstacles and, indeed, by "nature" itself where investors fail to effectively control the biophysical dimensions of agricultural production. These examples remind us that Chinese investors' control over flows of food is not a fait accompli but requires hard work. The agri-food chains established in this process (or not) are thus not "natural" economic entities that exist *a priori* (Berndt & Boeckler 2011) but, rather, the outcome of specific sets of practices, policies, and technological infrastructures that need to come into alignment with one another.

### *Cattle export visions falling apart*

When Chinese agri-food entrepreneur Furui Group announced it would send a consignment of Australian-sourced live cattle to the Chinese market in early 2017, the company created somewhat of a stir in both the Australian and the Chinese media. Furui's endeavor marked the first time ever that a ship would deliver live animals from Australia for slaughter in China. Exporting live cattle and sheep from Australia to markets in China has been somewhat of a holy grail in the evolving agri-food relationship between the two countries. With Australia being one of the few countries worldwide allowed to export live cattle for breeding and slaughtering purposes to China since both countries signed an export deal in 2015, politicians have enthusiastically promoted the live cattle export trade as an opportunity for Australian producers, promising windfall profits for the Australian beef cattle industry and annual export volumes on the order of 1 million head of cattle (Borrello 2015). According to an Australian industry expert I interviewed in the fall of 2017, live export holds many promises to stakeholders in the beef cattle industry. Cattle producers in Australia's remote north hope to increase efficiency by selling cattle directly from northern ports rather than trucking animals over long distances—sometimes up to 48 hours—to have them slaughtered in Australian abattoirs. Others see live cattle exporting as an opportunity to market a "fresh" (as opposed to chilled or frozen) beef product to Chinese consumers. Live exports also offer the possibility to make money from the animal's entire carcass, including parts such as intestines and tripe that are considered specialty cuts in China but, for regulatory reasons, cannot be exported if an animal is slaughtered in Australia (interview September 2017, Sydney).

The promises of the live export trade are not lost on Chinese investors. Indeed, many investors with interests in the Australian beef cattle industry told me that live cattle exporting was part of their broader supply chain strategy. However, when pressed for more details, investors often admitted that they were not exporting any live animals yet and that this presented more of a vision than a reality. Because live exports involve the movement of living animals in shipping containers and airplanes over long distances, a complex array of technical (but also moral and ethical)[7] issues surround the trade. From the perspective of industry experts, differing age, quarantine, transport, and slaughter rules make the trade unnecessarily complex and risky for exporters. As one representative of industry peak body, Meat & Livestock Australia (MLA) told me at the sidelines of a Chinese food expo in Shanghai, "the protocol is not going to work. It's impractical, overly complex, and reflects a lack of understanding [...] by regulators," particularly on the Chinese side, he complained (interview May 2018, Shanghai). Indeed, according to a report by MLA, two years after the live cattle export deal had come into effect, Australian producers exported only around 25,000 live cattle annually for slaughter to China, a far cry from the "one million head each year" rhetoric advanced earlier by Australian politicians (Meat & Livestock Australia 2018b).

Against this background, it seemed only logical that Furui would celebrate its pioneering role in the live export trade with an elaborately staged press conference and media event. But when I met with Furui's managing director in Australia some six months later, I was surprised to find out that the company's live cattle shipment in February had been a one-off event and no further consignments were planned. "We're still at a very early stage," the manager told me when asked about the company's export experience and future plans (interview September 2017, Adelaide). Sending a consignment of live cattle to China earlier that year was part of the company's strategy to be "the first" engaged in the trade but did not signal any commitment to further live exports, the manager insisted. It was a bit of a "publicity piece" undertaken to establish market presence in China and highlight Furui's leading role as one of the country's overseas agri-investors. What the manager did not tell me, however, was that the shipment appears to have gone spectacularly wrong. When I later met Furui Group's main Australian business partner, an agribusiness company with whom Furui operates another beef joint venture not related to its own farms and live export endeavors, the business partner gave me some insight into what had happened:

> Earlier this year, they [Furui] exported some 1,200 cows from Victoria and sent them to China. And they tried to work out how to get them

> into China, process them, and sell them in supermarkets. [...] They couldn't do it, they had to throw the meat out, sort of. They simply couldn't work out the supply chain.
>
> (interview September 2017, Melbourne)

As it turned out, the complex logistical challenges surrounding the organization and coordination of the movement of live animals along the supply chain had overwhelmed Furui, turning the live cattle shipment into somewhat of a logistical nightmare for the company. "They hadn't worked with the supply chain yet," their Australian joint venture partner explained. "They still have to work out how to do the business, just like anybody else." (interview September 2017, Melbourne). To make matters worth, the Chinese market turned out to be more price-sensitive than originally envisaged, an issue Furui's managing director had hinted at during our earlier conversation: "The market in China is big, but it's not accepting the fact: 'this is what you have to pay!'," she told me. "So, we need to slowly open up the market. We start from the very high end because Australian beef, compared to other countries' beef, is very very expensive." (interview September 2017, Adelaide).

Indeed, high cattle prices (following the decimation of the national herd by drought) combined with an unfavorably high exchange rate have made Australian beef less competitive in the Chinese market, despite the fact that a free trade agreement between both countries has reduced import tariffs over the past years. This reminds us that the notion of inexorably growing Chinese demand often invoked by Chinese investors and Australian agri-food elites alike is not a fait accompli but may rely substantially on "educating" the market, to use the term with which Furui's managing director had described the company's struggle—and ultimate failure—to obtain a viable retail price for its costly Australian beef. Markets for high-end Australian beef do not simply exist, they must be made. Unbeknownst to the wider public, in the Australian live cattle export scene, Furui had turned from a success story to a business nightmare. As the MLA executive mentioned above summed up Furui's export endeavor: "It was a huge loss economically. They said they couldn't have found a better way to lose more money" (May 2018, Shanghai).

To avoid the fate of Furui, its Australian business partner stressed how for their own live export plans they would pursue a different approach. Unlike Furui, they were working to establish an import partnership in China whereby the company would control animal quarantine and processing facilities right at the port in China. This, the manager hoped, would allow his company to better handle the regulatory and logistical challenges involved in sending live animals to China. "We own the farms in Australia, and we do it as a partnership," he said. "So, we have export facilities in Australia, import facilities in China, we have partners in China along the supply chain to get into the market," the manager explained to me (interview September 2017, Melbourne). Whether Furui's Australian joint venture partner will be able to "crack" the live cattle export market remains to be seen. During my last field trips to Australia and China throughout 2018, there were rumors among industry experts that the project might be doing less well than initially envisaged.

As the case of Furui's failed export ambition highlights, agri-food chains that articulate flows of food from "farm to fork" cannot simply be wished into existence but require hard work. Drawing together the logistical infrastructures, animals, prices, exchange rates, volatile demand, and supply chain linkages presented a gargantuan and, ultimately, insurmountable challenge to Furui. In the end, then, the material reality of agri-food flows may stubbornly resist investor ambitions to open up the famed Chinese market to high-quality Australian food imports.

### *A supply chain plan thwarted by "nature"*

My final example highlights how the biophysical nature of farming itself can present an obstacle to the supply chain ambitions of Chinese investors. I draw on the story of Zhefu Group[8], a Chinese agri-food entrepreneur that had been engaged in one of the most spectacular "investment sprees" in Australian agriculture before unexpectedly announcing plans to divest its entire farming portfolio in mid-2019. Zhefu's plan had been to build an integrated cattle supply chain that would capitalize on growing Chinese demand for high-quality beef and sheep meat, but the plan never materialized. So what went wrong?

Originally a Chinese textile machinery manufacturing company, Zhefu Group made its appearance as an agri-investor in Australia in 2014, when the company acquired one of Australia's most prestigious sheep estates located in the state of Victoria. From there, the company quickly expanded, investing some 150 million AUD to build a beef cattle and sheep business comprised of 19 individual farming properties consolidated into larger aggregations and spread across different rainfall regions in Victoria and New South Wales (NSW). To manage its Australian investment strategy, the company hired Rick—a well-known former Australian fund investment manager with excellent connections in the worlds of both farming and finance. When I met Rick in early 2017 in his Melbourne office to learn more about the agri-investment strategy he was pursuing on behalf of Zhefu Group, it quickly became clear that Rick was following a "tried and tested" investment scheme with which he had made his career in the Australian farmland and agricultural investment fund (FAIF) scene. As I was told, it was all about buying cheaply and improving the farm asset through capital investment, as well as about geographical diversification to minimize weather-related risks from drought (interview March 2017, Melbourne).

Rick's formula for success was based on his close connections with the Australian farming sector, allowing him to identify smaller, undervalued farms that were not marketed nationally and aggregate them into larger holdings. In the eyes of Rick, what made this project particularly rewarding was the fact that the capital made available by the Chinese parent company was both

*Figure 7.4* Zhefu cattle property with newly installed water system intended to increase stocking rates and drought resistance, Gwydir Shire, NSW.

*Source:* Picture taken by the author during a field visit, September 2017.

plentiful and patient, allowing the company to build a profitable and efficient meat business that would prove resilient to the cyclical downturns routinely afflicting the Australian agricultural sector.

From the Chinese perspective, the plan seemed promising as well. The company's ultimate goal was to establish a large Australian beef business from where to export stable supplies of high-quality Australian beef to the meat processing plant and beef brand the company had recently established in China. Rick's acquisition strategy would allow the company to steadily grow its beef interests without risking to overpay for the relatively fewer large-scale beef farms that, at times, became available on the market. That such a business plan would require a long-term investment outlook was taken for granted, as the Chinese company representative in charge of managing the company's overseas agri-investment strategy told me during an interview:

> The ultimate goal is to produce meat products from our herd in Australia and sell them in the Chinese market. But you need to build sales channels and a customer base here in China before you can do that. You need to slowly build that up.
>
> (interview March 2017, Hangzhou)

In the meantime, Zhefu made headlines in Australia as it was adding more and more farming properties to its portfolio. But as Zhefu was continuing its Australian investment spree, cracks soon began to appear in the company's investment story. When I met another company representative half a year later for an informal conversation on the sidelines of a business event in Melbourne, I was surprised to learn that Zhefu was facing profitability problems (interview August 2017, Melbourne). According to my interview partner, at a recent board meeting, Zhefu's Chinese owners had complained that the company was not generating sufficient cash flow from its Australian beef business. On the books, the business was looking well as the value of its farmland and that of its "biological assets," i.e., its cattle herd, was appreciating, but profitability from the production and sale of beef was low. Moreover, the company had not made any progress in building a supply chain in the Chinese market. All cattle were sold on the Australian market, I learned, even though local commodity prices for beef were depressed because of a severe drought that was developing across much of eastern Australia. As a consequence, the Chinese headquarters had stopped supplying its Australian subsidiary with further equity capital. Meanwhile, a 36 million AUD loan facility from the Commonwealth Bank of Australia had been depleted. With no further financing forthcoming, Zhefu Australia had been ordered by its Chinese parent to focus on becoming a "healthy business" first before expanding further, the representative told me.

Not long after that conversation, I learned that Rick had left Zhefu Australia to take a new position as the CEO of a major Western pension fund with farmland investments in Australia. This was supposedly because Rick wanted to take on a new professional challenge, but it does not seem far-fetched to assume that his departure from Zhefu had something to do with the company's growing cash-flow challenges. As luck would have it, though, I knew his successor, Chris, from my fieldwork in Australia and was able to catch up with him on the company's overall development during one of his business trips to Zhefu's headquarters in Hangzhou. As I found out during our conversation, the company had not made much progress in the past few months to improve profitability and reorganize supply chains:

> [Our chairman] wants to see that the business is running well before we go and start spending a lot more money. So, we've invested somewhere over 150, 170 million dollars, which is a sizeable investment. He wants to see that starting to perform and provide a return before we start to look at significant additional acquisition sort of strategies or branching out in a whole lot of other areas, you know. We gradually will start to do more in terms of the supply chain, in terms of understanding our livestock, and where they fit, and how they perform, so we've got a fair bit of work to do there, because really up until October, November last year, which is just before Rick departed, the focus was all on acquisition

> and building. Now we're taking a breather from that and the focus is now really on performance, consolidating what we've got.
>
> (interview May 2018, Shanghai)

Despite Chris' efforts to project optimism, it was clear that Zhefu was facing an uphill battle. Australian cattle prices were still low, margins extremely tight due to ongoing conditions of drought, and the company still had not figured out a profitable way to integrate Australian beef production with its meat brand in China. As it turned out, acquiring farms and scaling up quickly was one thing, producing a stable cash return from integrating those assets into Zhefu's Chinese meat interests was quite another.

In the end, Zhefu's vision to establish a multi-million-dollar beef business to capitalize on growing Chinese demand did not materialize. In the summer of 2019, the company announced it would sell its entire Australian portfolio. As reported by the Australian financial press, the ongoing drought then experienced across much of Australia had resulted in two successive loss-making years for the company. Burdened with debt and with no opportunity in sight to put its operations on a sound basis, Zhefu Group was simply no longer willing to sink money into its Australian beef cattle business. Vulnerable to the vagaries of "nature," ultimately, Zhefu's investment in building a beef cattle supply chain proved to be neither as "patient" nor as "resilient" as envisioned.

Was the eventual failure of Zhefu's investment project surprising? Perhaps not. Indeed, my fieldwork has shown that there is often a significant gap between the supply chain ambitions of Chinese agri-investors and the realities on the ground. Sometimes, an aggressive investment strategy may belie the fact that, in reality, investors are struggling to generate profits from the farms and agribusinesses acquired. It is fair to assume that this was, at least in part, among the reasons for the collapse of Zhefu's investment project. "Rapid growth strategies at times mask the effective productive capacity," Chris was musing about Zhefu's earlier investment spree when I met him in China, but "at some point, it always catches up" (interview May 2018, Shanghai).

There were other warning signs, too. During an earlier field trip to one of Zhefu's cattle properties in the fall of 2017, the farm manager had expressed serious doubts concerning the feasibility of the company's broader strategy. I met with the farm manager at a moment when the drought had just started to bite and the manager was nervous that he might have to buy in expensive fodder as the feed crops he had planted earlier in the year were withering under a steel blue sky. At the same time, company targets to improve farm infrastructure and increase stocking rates further squeezed the manager's tight budget. Struggling to reconcile challenging weather conditions on the farm with demanding productivity targets from the company's head offices in Hangzhou and Melbourne, the farm manager admitted that, under the current conditions, they were simply unable to supply meat at a competitive price point to their Chinese parent company:

> The margins are so narrow and things are so tight, here and in China, and I just think at the moment the Australian beef is just too expensive for them [the Chinese parent company], quite honestly. [...] They're going to look at their profit margins, and they're going to say: 'Alright, we can't import the product at that figure.' It's as simple as that.
>
> (interview September 2017, Gwydir Shire).

As it turns out, the farm manager's appraisal of the situation was quite accurate, leading the company to eventually abandon its agricultural ambitions in Australia. While at the time of writing it was unclear under which conditions Zhefu would be able to divest its Australian farming assets (e.g., to which extent capital gains would make up for the operating losses the company had incurred in the past two years), what is clear, however, is that Chinese agri-investors may be far less willing (or able) to "weather" the challenging biophysical conditions of Australia's farming environment than celebratory accounts of "long-term" Chinese agri-investment suggest. In the end, Chinese capital may struggle to establish the agri-food supply chains necessary to drive a new "dining boom."

*****

As this chapter has shown, strategies of vertical integration constitute an essential part of the investment logic driving China's land rush in Australia. By increasing direct ownership or indirect control over various stages of the agri-food supply chain—from production to processing, retail, and marketing—investors endeavor to increase retail margins, ensure stability of supply, and enhance control over product quality in the face of recent food safety scandals and consumer scares. Bolstered by such efforts, beef and dairy products from Chinese-owned Australian farms and food businesses have begun to emerge on the shelves of Chinese supermarkets, as if untouched by the messy materialities of agri-food trade. This chapter has shown how the seemingly natural and taken-for-granted movement of food commodities along supply chains from "farm to fork" in fact depends on a multiplicity of socio-technical, legal, logistical, infrastructural, regulatory, and biophysical elements. Bringing together these heterogenous elements in stable configurations is by no means an easy task, as my examples suggest.

It would be wrong to assume that the making of such market connections is exclusively driven by the efforts, practices, and aspirations of Chinese agri-investors. In fact, the supply chain linkages I describe here are co-produced by numerous actors involved along the chain—from Australian and Chinese policymakers creating the regulatory framework for bilateral trade, to Australian peak bodies such as Meat & Livestock Australia promoting "brand Australia" to the wider Chinese public, to agribusiness professionals and industry experts bolstering discourses about a new Chinese "dining boom."

In the Australian context, the making of such market connections has been welcomed by political and business elites alike. Indeed, "opening up the Chinese market" to premium Australian food products has been one of the key promises mobilized to legitimate China's land rush. Likewise, from the perspective of Chinese investors, connecting Australian agricultural production with rising Chinese demand for safe, clean, and green food is often a quintessential premise of their investment calculus. Yet, my examples have shown that flows of Chinese investment capital do not naturally engender the types of market connections envisaged by optimistic investors, agribusiness professionals, and politicians. Whether it is about building a "one million head a year" live cattle export business to China or about creating a massive new export market for Australian dairy, a closer look at the materially entangled practices shaping the movement of food from "farm to fork" suggests that the making of new market connections might be more vulnerable to disruption and (geopolitical) friction as some might have hoped for. The three-year freeze affecting much of Australia's agricultural trade with China from 2020 to 2023 proved to be a powerful reminder of just how easily market connections can be unmade.

What do the above stories tell us about how Chinese agribusinesses reposition themselves in the global agri-food system? Insofar as investors are successful, vertical integration places them and their Australian partners at the center of supply chains reshaping regional and, at times, global markets for beef and dairy products. Leveraging expectations about an Australian "dining boom," Chinese agri-food investors have been instrumental in opening doors to the famed China market, thereby not only benefitting themselves and their direct Australian partners but, by deepening relationships with Chinese regulators, importers, and other actors along the supply chain, also profiting Australia's agribusiness sector at large. On the flip side, vertical integration, particularly in its "retrofit" form practiced by investors like Feihe, also risks increasing pressure on Australian producer prices as investors seek to fit Australian supply chains into existing, tight retail margins in China. Importantly, though, this potential price pressure is not driven by a non-commercial, state-mandated logic of Chinese agri-investments, as many Australian critics have feared (see Chapter 3), but, on the contrary, is the outcome of cutthroat competition as Australian food producers, whether Chinese or domestically owned, vie for market share in China. What is more, the fact that Chinese regulators have no qualms about slapping import bans on Chinese-invested agri-food businesses, as happened in Australia's beef sector in 2020, further highlights that, while profits from investment are overwhelmingly private so are the risks that come with the acquisition of farms and food businesses overseas. Australian beef and dairy products may well be a source of profits for Chinese investors and their partners seeking to tap the new "dining boom," but for Chinese decision-makers tasked with "feeding China," these are "non-essential" lifestyle foods that can be cut or replaced by other import sources if the geopolitical environment so requires.

## Notes

1 The names of the company and its executives quoted here have been anonymized. Information drawn from media reports (Wang 2017; Hu 2017), press releases (Shanghai Government 2017), company materials, and field interviews.
2 The company name used here is pseudonym. The case study has been reconstructed from field interviews and company materials.
3 WeChat is a popular Chinese communications app. It allows companies to run corporate accounts that function akin to a website and have largely eliminated the need to maintain a web presence for many Chinese companies, particularly those focused on the domestic market, where WeChat is ubiquitous. Chinese companies also use WeChat as their primary e-commerce channel to sell and market products to consumers.
4 All names used here are pseudonyms. The case study has been reconstructed from field interviews and company materials.
5 All names used are pseudonyms. The case study has been reconstructed from field interviews, company materials, and information collected at agricultural expos and trade shows in China during the summer of 2018.
6 The company name used here is a pseudonym. The case study has been reconstructed from field interviews, company materials, as well as reports published in the media.
7 In Australia, animal welfare concerns have led to heated debates about the legitimacy of the trade and infractions against animal health protocols routinely lead to the suspension of individual consignments or, at times, to trade suspensions with entire countries.
8 The company name and the names of all individuals quoted here have been anonymized. In the reconstruction of this case study, I rely on successive interviews I conducted with different company representatives in both Australia and China between 2017 and 2018 as well as undisclosed company materials.

## References


Berndt, Christian; Boeckler, Marc (2011): Performative Regional (Dis)Integration: Transnational Markets, Mobile Commodities, and Bordered North - South Differences. In *Environment and Planning A: Economy and Space* 43, pp. 1057–1078. DOI: 10.1068/a4381.

Borrello, Eliza (2015): Live Cattle Trade: Australia Could Earn $2b from Exports to China, Agriculture Minister Barnaby Joyce Says. In *ABC News*, 7/20/2015. Available online at https://www.abc.net.au/news/2015-07-20/australia-to-earn-242b-from-live-cattle-exports-to-china3a-jo/6635030, checked on 9/10/2020.

Dairy Australia (2018): Australian Dairy Industry in Focus. Available online at https://www.dairyaustralia.com.au/dairysa/industry-reports/australian-dairy-industry-in-focus, checked on 6/10/2020.

Edwards, Brooke; Waldron, Scott; Brown, Colin; Longworth, John (2016): The Sino-Australian Cattle and Beef Relationship. Assessment and Prospects. Sydney: Australia-China Relations Institute (ACRI).

Goodman, Michael K.; Goodman, David; Redclift, Michael R. (2010): Introduction: Situating Consumption, Space and Place. In Michael K. Goodman, David

Goodman, Michael R. Redclift (Eds.): *Consuming Space. Placing Consumption in Perspective*. London: Routledge, pp. 3–40.

Heffernan, William D. (2000): Concentration of Ownership and Control in Agriculture. In Fred Magdoff, John Bellamy Foster, Frederick H. Buttel (Eds.): *Hungry for Profit. The Agribusiness Threat to Farmers, Food, and the Environment*. New York, Breinigsville, PA: Monthly Review Press, pp. 61–75.

Hu, Ying (2017): 3月市民即可尝"鲜"澳洲活牛牛肉 [In March Citizens Can Taste "Fresh" Australian Beef from Live Cattle]. In *Sina Finance*, 2/28/2017. Available online at http://news.sina.com.cn/c/2017-02-28/doc-ifyavrsx5341494.shtml, checked on 6/25/2020.

Meat & Livestock Australia (2018a): Australia's Beef Industry. Available online at https://www.mla.com.au/globalassets/mla-corporate/prices--markets/documents/trends--analysis/fast-facts--maps/mla_beef-fast-facts-2018.pdf, checked on 6/10/2020.

Meat & Livestock Australia (2018b): Market Snapshot China. Beef. Available online at https://www.mla.com.au/globalassets/mla-corporate/prices--markets/documents/os-markets/export-statistics/oct-2018-snapshots/mla-beef-market-snapshot---china---oct-2018.pdf, checked on 9/10/2020.

Meat & Livestock Australia (2018c): Why Chilled Beef Is a Hot Market in China. Available online at https://www.mla.com.au/prices-markets/market-news/2018/why-chilled-beef-is-a-hot-market-in-china, checked on 6/12/2020.

Ouma, Stefan (2015): *Assembling Export Markets. The Making and Unmaking of Global Food Connections in West Africa*. Chichester, West Sussex: Wiley-Blackwell.

PwC (2019): The Ongoing Modernisation of China's Dairy Sector. Available online at https://www.pwccn.com/en/industries/food-supply-and-integrity/publications.html, checked on 5/18/2020.

PwC (2011a): The Australian Beef Industry. In *The Basics*. Available online at https://www.pwc.com.au/industry/agribusiness/assets/australian-beef-industry-nov11.pdf, checked on 4/29/2018.

PwC (2011b): The Australian Dairy Industry. In *The Basics*. Available online at https://www.pwc.com.au/industry/agribusiness/assets/australian-dairy-industry-nov11.pdf, checked on 6/10/2020.

Schneider, Mindi (2017): Dragon Head Enterprises and the State of Agribusiness in China. In *Journal of Agrarian Change* 17 (1), pp. 3–21. DOI: 10.1111/joac.12151.

Schneider, Mindi; Sharma, Shefali (2014): China's Pork Miracle? Agribusiness and Development in China's Pork Industry. In *Institute for Agriculture and Trade Policy (Global Meat Complex: The China Series)*. Available online at https://www.iatp.org/documents/chinas-pork-miracle-agribusiness-and-development-chinas-pork-industry, checked on 11/14/2017.

Shanghai Government (2017): 首次通过海运方式进入中国　澳洲活牛牛肉3月10日首发 [First Sea Consignment to China. Australian Live Beef Trade to Be Launched on March 10]. Available online at https://read01.com/02j3Bx.html, checked on 6/25/2020.

Sippel, Sarah R.; Böhme, Michaela (2019): Dis/Articulating Agri-Food Spaces: The Multifaceted Logics of Agro-Investments. In Steffi Marung, Matthias Middell (Eds.): *Spatial Formats under the Global Condition*. Boston MA: De Gruyter Oldenbourg (Dialectics of the Global, 1), pp. 334–359.

Tsing, Anna Lowenhaupt (2005): *Friction. An Ethnography of Global Connection*. Princeton: Princeton University Press.

VC Group (2016): Profiling Chinese Agribusiness (Beef) Investment in Australia. Available online at https://www.agric.wa.gov.au/sites/gateway/files/Profiling%20Chinese%20agribusiness%20beef%20investment%20in%20Australia%20-%20VC%20Group%2C%202015_0.pdf, checked on 3/5/2018.

Wang, Yongsheng (2017): 澳大利亚向中国海运活牛 首批1500头 [Australia Ships First Batch of 1,500 Head of Live Cattle to China]. In *Finance Sina*, 2/7/2017. Available online at https://finance.sina.com.cn/stock/usstock/c/2017-02-07/us-ifyafcyw0536250.shtml, checked on 5/02/2020.

# Conclusion

# 8 Beyond the land rush

## China, Australia, and the global agri-food system

In recent years, news headlines about China's "epic race" around the world to feed the "booming appetites" of its population of 1.4 billion people have put the country in the spotlight as a global hub of agri-food capital and a major investor in overseas food and farming. These stories conjure up images of a monolithic Chinese state engaging in a global scramble for resources to satisfy its insatiable demand for food—an abstract force that is transforming agricultural landscapes unhindered as it continues its relentless advance upon farms and food businesses around the world. In an effort to complexify these images of China's global land rush, I have begun my inquiry elsewhere: in the messiness of encounters between investors, state actors, deal brokers, farmers, eaters, and nature that shape the ways in which individual Chinese investment projects materialize on the ground. Against the grain of the dominant imaginary, I examine these encounters neither in the corn fields of Africa nor in the soybean plantations of the Amazon rainforest but rather in the cattle stations, dairy farms, and the food processing factories of rural Australia. This investment context has drawn significant amounts of Chinese agri-food capital, yet it has been largely overlooked in global media, activist, and scholarly discourses. By bringing into view the transnational connections and multiscalar linkages through which Chinese investment capital has coupled with rural Australia—a specific historical landscape shaped by the sedimented histories of settler colonialism, export agriculture, productivism, and neoliberalism—this book has explored the unfolding of Chinese investment projects in their historio-geographical concreteness and contestedness.

Research for this book has relied on a theoretical and methodological toolkit developed by global ethnographers such as Michael Burawoy (2000), Gillian Hart (2002), and Anna Tsing (2005). What such an approach has allowed me to do is to connect the heterogeneity of micro-level investment practices with the macro-level forces of agri-food globalization.[1] This is an attempt, then, to bring into relation with one another grounded practices and global forces, the specific and the general, the individual Chinese investment projects in Australia and the broader structures of a globalizing agri-food system that is becoming ever more interconnected with China's domestic agriculture and food sector. Such a lens has also been critical for moving beyond

DOI: 10.4324/9781003474661-12

a state-centric toward a transnational understanding of China's global land rush. Rather than portraying China's overseas agri-investments as a national, coherent, and unified strategy, I highlight the cross-border linkages and alliances that unite (and sometimes divide) different groups of powerful actors in pursuit of profits, power, and business success while marginalizing small farmers, the poor, and nature in both countries.

The overall objective of this book was to understand the drivers of China's overseas land rush, its relationship to national food security, and its consequences for the agri-food relationship between China, Australia, and the global agri-food system. Moving beyond aggregate statistics and abstract data points, I wanted to uncover the specific investment projects of China's land rush in Australian ruralities and the flesh-and-blood actors behind them. As I visited farms, processing plants, and business offices, I was eager to understand how investors justified their investment decisions; why certain deals had succeeded and others failed; how and by whom investment portfolios were put together; where the money came from; and where the food produced on Chinese-invested farms would end up. I also sought to examine the broader political and institutional landscapes in which investors were operating across China and Australia and the role of the Chinese state as an often-assumed ultimate arbiter of overseas investment decisions. My research also unpacked the ambivalent role of a neoliberal Australian state that, in reregulating Chinese investments, has sought to both encourage and control transnational capital flows into its agricultural sector. Finally, I interrogated the relationship between Chinese agri-investments in Australia and the country's food security goals. The picture that presented itself to me goes against the grain of conventional wisdom. Chinese agri-investments in Australia, this book argues, do little to feed China, simply because the actors behind them have no interest in doing so, even as some of them may claim otherwise. Here, I review the key findings of the book and discuss how they can help activists, scholars, and others working for a fairer and more sustainable food system to develop a more nuanced and realistic stance on China's role in the global land rush.

## Actors and drivers of Chinese agri-investments in Australia

To many casual observers, what comes to mind when thinking about Chinese overseas investments in food and farming are cashed-up, impenetrable, state-sponsored entities carrying out a "grand plan" on behalf of the Chinese government with the aim of feeding China. Yet, in the Australian case, investment presents itself most often in the figure of the private agri-food entrepreneur—a group of self-made Chinese business tycoons who built their industrial fortunes in the wake of China's reform and opening-up policy and who are now discovering agriculture and food as a new frontier for the accumulation of private profits. These business*men* (in the proper sense of the word) are simultaneously *pushed* by the intense pressures of overaccumulation and competition they are facing in their domestic core industries and *pulled* by the promises of a Chinese "dining boom" to invest some of their wealth in Australian food and farming ventures. Investment projects of Chinese agri-food entrepreneurs have accordingly focused primarily on the acquisition of Australian beef and dairy farms for the production of "lifestyle foods" and on practices of place-based valorization that frame the farming environments in which these projects operate as "clean, green, and safe" to carve out protected niches in China's highly competitive consumer market and to justify the premium prices at which investors aspire to sell their Australian food products.

To be sure, agri-food entrepreneurs are not the only Chinese actors investing in Australian food and farming. Indeed, a key concern of this book has been to point out the diversity and multiplicity of investors and investment projects that make up the face of China's agri-investment in Australia. To this end, I have proposed an investor typology that takes into account the fundamentally different investment logics and behaviors separating Chinese agri-food entrepreneurs from private agri-food corporations, state farms, and agribusiness SOEs. A closer look at the blood-and-flesh actors behind the abstract notion of Chinese investment also reminds us how seemingly neat and stable dichotomies such as "public–private" or "domestic–foreign" can become hopelessly confused in the messiness of real-world encounters. As I have shown, many investment projects simultaneously enroll state and private, Chinese and international, financial and commercial capital, combining and re-combining these categories across new forms of investment collaboration and capitalist alliance-building. An investor company like Mengniu Dairy—a previously private agri-food company now majority-owned by a central agribusiness SOE and whose shareholders also include large international dairy corporations—defies the straightjacket of taxonomy just as much as a private agribusiness corporation like New Hope Group, whose investments have been co-financed by high-level financial institutions and private corporations from the global North, channeling capital into the company's investment projects through New Hope Group's own private equity arm.

As for the Chinese central state, the depth and consequence of its involvement vary considerably, from direct ownership in investor companies to indirect facilitation through policy incentives. State involvement also extends to the subnational level. For example, it is fair to assume that county, prefecture, or provincial-level officials, whose own performance evaluations are closely tied to economic development goals, are well informed about the overseas investment activities of businesses under their administration, have endorsed such projects, or even lent material and administrative support, such as facilitating logistics or giving companies preferential access to crucial port or warehousing infrastructure. State actors also coordinate across national borders, often with the aim of creating a friendly investment environment. In the case of Australia, a bilateral trade agreement negotiated between both governments in 2015 was hoped to boost both trade and investment, while provincial investment partnerships were long regarded as a useful tool to attract Chinese capital into the Australian economy. Yet, while state actors shape the broader regulatory and political framework in which investors must operate, it is first and foremost the initiative, commitment, and risk-taking of transnational locals that make or break individual investment deals. It is them who identify appropriate locations to suit a particular business plan, mobilize subscribers for a new agricultural investment fund, negotiate with Australian farmers over prices, or work their transnational business contacts to secure a contract with a Chinese retail chain or logistics company. In sum, then, my research shows that China's land rush in Australia is best thought of as a network of shared interests between wildly heterogenous actors—from risk-taking Chinese business tycoons to business-minded Australian agri-professionals, astute international financiers, ambitious government officials, savvy local deal brokers, and transculturally versed investment intermediaries. These interests coalesce into unexpected, albeit often temporary alliances that crucially shape the manifold ways in which Chinese capital is placed within Australian rural landscapes.

But will such endeavors help to feed China? As this book argues, they won't, simply because they have never been intended to do so by the actors involved in them. As I have shown, food security is of great concern to the Chinese state, but policymakers rely on agricultural production at home rather than imports of food grown on state-controlled farms abroad to feed China. By channeling capital and technology into domestic agriculture, consolidating farmland, and fostering a competitive agribusiness sector, the state has been able to achieve self-sufficiency in key food staples, leaving behind the specter of China's last great famine of 1958–1961. With the exception of soybeans, over whose trade flows the Chinese state has sought to increase control with the help of its state-owned grain traders such as COFCO, much of what the country imports is considered "complementary"—from specialty products to high-quality brands. These imports are popular for their assumed higher food safety and production standards. In China, boosting agricultural production has gone hand in hand with severe damage to the natural environment. Overuse of chemical fertilizers and pesticides and the pollution of soil and water have led to a severe crisis of trust in the safety of domestically produced food. Agricultural products from countries like Australia with a reputation as clean, green, and safe command premium prices among anxious middle-class consumers. By controlling the flow of Australian food products into China's high-end supermarkets, investors seek to capture this premium segment. It is China's food *safety* crisis, then, rather than its food *security*, that investors capitalize on when they acquire farms and food businesses in Australia.

Moreover, it is worth remembering that beef and dairy, the two food products that have received the most attention by Chinese investors in Australia, have not traditionally been part of the Han Chinese diet. Westerners might think of them as staples, but in China, consumption of these foods on a per capita basis is still considerably lower than in Western countries. Despite the food industry's relentless promotion of animal protein as a symbol of the good life, health, and success, most Chinese have yet to develop a taste for cheese or the thick slices of beef Western cultures serve as steak. Yet, consumption patterns are Westernizing rapidly, with ever larger amounts of animal-sourced products but also oils, sugars, and processed foods finding their way onto the plates of Chinese eaters. That this transition is neither beneficial for people's health nor the environment is obvious. To investors of all stripes, however, from the Hangzhou-based agri-food entrepreneur to the private equity manager on Wall Street and the beef company from Queensland, this "dining boom" is the real investment proposition. Chinese investors may occasionally peddle the language of "food security" to gain domestic support for their business endeavors abroad, yet, they have little interest in producing staple grains under declining terms of trade. Instead, what guides their investment vision is to secure the stable supply of "high-quality" animal foods to satisfy the demands of aspirational Chinese consumers anxious about their health and the safety of the food they eat.

## Implications of China's investment drive

How will Chinese investment reshape Australia's agriculture and food sector? The investment projects presented in this book may not feed China, yet they will likely deepen a productivist food production logic that has real social and ecological consequences. Especially where investors seek to control supply chains from farm to table, their need for a stable and consistent supply of food commodities at prices low enough to recoup investment costs will encourage farmland consolidation and intensification of production. To be sure, ensuring stable supply can also be achieved through sustainable investments in farm infrastructure and technology, but investors may also strain scarce natural resources such as water and soils as they increase, say, stocking rates or milk output. Risky financing models may further add social and environmental pressures on farming operations as leveraged buyers scramble to service bank debt or respond to shareholder demands for fast returns.

Generally speaking, industrialized agriculture, including large-scale cattle and dairy farming, comes with big environmental questions. It is a major contributor to climate change, producing greenhouse gas emissions from fertilizer use, diesel-powered agricultural machinery, and cattle digestion. In Australia, industrialized agriculture has also led to a massive environmental degradation of the continent's fragile ecosystems, causing damage to soils, polluting waterways, and exacerbating biodiversity loss (Lawrence & Campbell 2014). By contrast, smaller farms focusing on agro-ecological and organic practices have a much smaller ecological footprint, but the trends toward large-scale, capital-intensive production have pushed many of them out of the agricultural sector as they cannot compete with their consolidated industrial counterparts. The mantra to "get big or get out" has long been a reality reshaping Australian ruralities. Supported by Australia's neoliberal agricultural development paradigm, cashed up investors, whether from China or elsewhere, risk further accelerating this process of rural restructuring. To the extent that investment projects involve the acquisition of farms, they may also contribute to rising farmland prices in Australia's more desirable agricultural regions. Australian farmland prices have been on a steady upward move over the past two decades (Rural Bank 2022), and while it is impossible to determine the extent to which Chinese purchases have contributed to this trend, there is real concern that the growing cost of farmland will keep the next generation of Australian farmers locked out of farming (Naylor 2023). Indeed, conversations with Australian farmers have taught me that many have abandoned the idea of family succession altogether, instead looking for bigger agribusinesses or financial entities to take over their farms. That this only exacerbates the marginalization of small-scale and younger farmers is yet another irony of the forces reshaping the agri-food system.

Deepening Australian food export dependence is yet another dimension that comes along with Chinese agri-food investment. For the Australian government, this is good news. Ever since the liberalization of Australia's agriculture sector in the 1980s and 1990s, Australian policymakers have relied on the touted benefits from global trade to develop agriculture and rural regions. China's large market is a big prize for those Australian farming businesses competitive enough to produce for the export economy, but geopolitical tensions between China and the United States-led Western world make these trade relationships particularly vulnerable to disruption (Zhan 2022). The latest such incident is still fresh on the minds of Australian agri-food exporters. In 2020, a diplomatic spate between the two countries over the origins of the COVID-19 pandemic resulted in a sudden retaliatory ban on Australia's most important agricultural export commodities, including beef, barley, cotton, lamb, lobsters, timber, and wine, leaving agri-exporters scramble for new markets as other countries happily took their market share in China. Even without such vagaries, benefits from trade are distributed unevenly, disproportionately serving the interests of larger corporations while smaller farmers are being left out (Pritchard & Tonts 2011).

But Chinese agri-investment in Australia is not only problematic for its tendency to concentrate corporate power and deepen an ecologically unsustainable agricultural production paradigm. It also accelerates the global shift toward Westernized diets, which are often unhealthier and less sustainable than traditional ways of eating. In China, economic growth coupled with urbanization and a rising middle class have led to a significant change in food consumption patterns. Today, Chinese people do not only consume more food than at the beginning of the country's opening to the West but also eat differently. Sugared soda drinks, fried foods, other kinds of meats beyond China's traditional meat staple—pork—as well as dairy products increasingly appear on the menus of Chinese eaters, while the consumption of healthier grains and legumes is declining (Schumilas et al. 2018, p. 17). At the same time, consumption of pre-cooked and convenience foods is increasing rapidly as changing lifestyles and longer working hours make home cooking a less important feature in people's lives. These trends have been mostly negative for public health. Obesity, diabetes, and stroke—long known as rich-world diseases—are skyrocketing in China (Schumilas et al. 2018). These changes are also bad for the environment. Most livestock farming in China and around the world relies on the production of cattle feed on valuable farmland that could be used more efficiently to grow crops directly for human consumption. Water use and greenhouse gas emissions are other factors negatively impacting the environment. Although its environmental and health costs are widely recognized, the shift toward Westernized and animal protein-based diets is largely considered a natural and inevitable outcome of China's modernization process. Yet, this is not the full truth. Time and again, my interviews have shown how much work goes into "educating" Chinese consumers about the apparent benefits of a high-priced Australian steak or a bottle of fresh Australian milk. Whether it was through their WeChat accounts, marketing campaigns, or cooperation with Chinese online influencers, investors would go to great lengths to associate their animal-sourced foods with images of a modern, sophisticated, healthy, and successful lifestyle. Indeed, investors and the food industry more generally are deeply implicated in the narratives and meanings that are driving dietary change.

The implications I have discussed here stand in stark contrast to the fears most often expressed by Australian media people and pundits critical of China's agri-investment drive. These voices have argued, for example, that Australia would risk losing control over its food production or even face a food security crisis if it allowed Chinese investors to purchase Australian farms and food businesses. These arguments hinge on the assumption that investment from China is fundamentally different from other sources of agri-food capital, posing an essential threat to the neoliberal agri-food order. In contrast, this book has shown that, in many ways, Chinese investment projects are surprisingly similar to investments from other countries and deeply enmeshed in the productivist, industrialized production logic that has shaped the agri-food system globally. Most Chinese investors operating overseas depend on the liberalized, market-based trade and investment regime enshrined in the WTO's Agreement on Agriculture or in bilateral trade agreements. Because these investors rely on market transactions rather than on forms of state-guided food "repatriation" to connect their food production activities abroad with Chinese and other export markets, they are deeply vested in the neoliberal architecture of contemporary agri-food globalization and, wherever possible, have been seeking to use its rules and mechanisms to their own advantage. As I have argued above, Chinese agri-investment is deepening many of the features characterizing the neoliberal development paradigm—from agricultural concentration to corporatization and productivism—and is thus further entrenching a socially unjust and ecologically unsustainable agri-food system. The difference Chinese agri-investment makes is not to be found in the logics of food production, circulation, and consumption but in the increasing number of Chinese investor companies (as opposed to agribusinesses from the global North) that will be able to exploit these logics for their own benefit.

As of this writing, China's investment boom in Australian farms and food businesses has long reached its peak. A global climate of growing geopolitical tensions, disruptions in global value chains, and a return to protectionism make a resurgence of Chinese capital flows into Australian agriculture highly improbable—at least in the foreseeable future. This does not mean that Chinese agri-food capital will leave Australia all together. Established investors with functional farming operations will likely continue running their businesses in Australia, adding on or selling off farmland properties as opportunities arise. Investor interest may also shift further away from farmland and toward downstream links in the food value chain. As an investment expert from a big Australian advisory firm told a local news outlet, "branded and packaged premium products" were increasingly becoming the focus of Chinese investment activity in Australia's agriculture and food sector (Rowley 2020). Yet, many might now look with more skepticism at the promise of a Chinese "dining boom" as the shock of retaliatory trade bans cutting off Australian agri-food imports from Chinese markets is still running deep. Instead, Chinese-run farming businesses in Australia might set their sight on Southeast Asian or other global markets. And for those Chinese agri-food entrepreneurs not yet invested overseas, "friendlier" countries along the Belt and Road or in emerging economies of the global South might present a new, more favorable investment destination. Chinese agribusiness firms remain deeply enmeshed in the global food system, but their brief honeymoon with Australian agriculture appears to be over.

## Old and new responses to China's global agri-food integration

Looking ahead, how should activists, scholars, and advocates of a fair and sustainable food system respond to China's agri-investment drive? In Australia and many other parts of the world, initial responses have focused on the government-led re-regulation of farmland, with the aim of banning or restricting Chinese investors from purchasing farms. These measures and the "land grab" anxieties underpinning them have not only resonated with the Australian public but also appealed to some bottom-up movements and activists. But while restrictions on Chinese land ownership might appear like a logical step to reign in investment flows, they are a highly inadequate response, as has also been noted in other geographical contexts (see e.g., Fairbairn 2020). As I have shown throughout the book, not only does this framing of a Chinese land rush overlook investments in food processing and other parts of the value chain, but it also fundamentally misconstrues these investments as "Chinese" when, in fact, a powerful transnational alliance of corporate agribusiness interests is driving such endeavors. Most importantly, by singling out a Chinese state worried about the country's food security, current responses make invisible the logics of profit and corporate power that are the real drivers shaping the ways in which China is integrating into the global agri-food system.

A more effective response that takes into account the transnational networks and profit interests behind Chinese agri-investments would move beyond a fixation on foreign land ownership and the Chinese state, instead building alliances with movements and bottom-up initiatives within China that propose alternatives to the country's dominant agro-industrial development paradigm. Alternative food networks, farmers' cooperatives, and rural grassroots movements may seem like marginal forces, yet, environmental and broader rural development concerns have created some space for these movements to promote an alternative development agenda. Opposing the dynamics of capitalist accumulation and agro-industrial development, such movements have been highlighting the importance of small-scale, agro-ecological practices that take into account the social, environmental, and health dimensions of food production and consumption (Zhan 2022, p. 61). They provide a powerful counter-example to the productivist and corporatist state policies which, in the name of food security, have depleted China's soil and water resources, hollowed out rural communities, and created a serious food safety crisis.

The Chinese state is aware of the seriousness of these challenges, but it has tried to address them within its industrial model of agricultural development. Support for modern agri-businesses and the expansion of capital and technology are expected to make agricultural production more sustainable; however, similar to experiences in the global North, there are serious doubts about the effectiveness of such a strategy in a context where the short-term pursuit of profits dominates the behavior of food businesses. By contrast, alternative movements focus on reconnecting producers and consumers, strengthening the role of Chinese smallholders, and promoting ethical values over food-for-profit logics. There are significant overlaps with the causes and concerns of such activist movements in China, Australia, and beyond. While China's political conditions and the complicated interactions between the state and civil society have made it challenging for agri-food movements around the world to connect with their Chinese counterparts, strengthening such transnational connections will be crucial to give voice to an alternative vision of China's role in the global food system beyond the promise of premium profits from the Chinese "dining boom."

After decades of rapid agricultural growth and expansion, China is at a critical juncture. It can continue on its current path of agro-industrial development or explore alternatives for a more sustainable agri-food system. Building alliances with those movements within China that call into question prevailing development paradigms can make an important contribution toward an ecologically sustainable and socially equitable food system. For one thing is clear: how China feeds itself will shape not only its own agriculture but also the world's.

## Note

1 I'm borrowing this framing from Lee (2018), whose global ethnography of Chinese investments in Zambia's construction and mining sectors presents one of the most persuasive ethnographic studies on China's global integration recently published.

## References

Burawoy, Michael; Blum, Joseph A.; George, Sheba; Gille; Zsuzsa; Gowan, Teresa et al. (Eds.) (2000): *Global Ethnography. Forces, Connections, and Imaginations in a Postmodern World.* Berkeley, Los Angeles, London: University of California Press.

Fairbairn, Madelaine (2020): *Fields of Gold. Financing the Global Land Rush.* Ithaca, New York: Cornell University Press.

Hart, Gillian (2002): *Disabling Globalization. Places of Power in Post-Apartheid South Africa.* Berkeley: University of California Press.

Lawrence, Geoffrey; Campbell, Hugh (2014): Neoliberalism in the Antipodes. Understanding the Influence and Limits of the Neoliberal Political Project. In Steven A. Wolf, Alessandro Bonanno (Eds.): *The Neoliberal Regime in the Agri-Food Sector. Crisis, Resilience, and Restructuring.* London: Routledge, pp. 263–283.

Lee, Ching Kwan (2018): *The Specter of Global China. Politics, Labor, and Foreign Investment in Africa.* Chicago, London: The University of Chicago Press.

Naylor, Catherine (2023): 'Locked Out': Younger Farmers Struggle to Get a Foothold as Cost of Land Soars. In *The Sydney Morning Herald*, 04/21/2023. Available online at https://www.smh.com.au/national/nsw/locked-out-younger-farmers-struggle-to-get-a-foothold-as-cost-of-land-soars-20230421-p5d29k.html, checked on 2/15/2024.

Pritchard, Bill; Tonts, Matthew (2011): Market Efficiency, Agriculture and Prosperity in Rural Australia. In Matthew Tonts, Muhammed Abu B. Siddique (Eds.): *Globalisation, Agriculture and Development. Perspectives from the Asia-Pacific.* Cheltenham: Edward Elgar, pp. 29–53.

Rowley, Linda (2020): Boom and Bust: Is China Bowing Out of Australian Agriculture? In *Beef Central*, 10/28/2020. Available online at https://www.beefcentral.com/property/boom-and-bust-is-china-bowing-out-of-australian-agriculture/, checked on 2/15/2024.

Rural Bank (2023): Australian Farmland Values 2023. Available online at https://www.ruralbank.com.au/siteassets/_documents/publications/flv/afv-2023.pdf, checked on 2/15/2024.

Schumilas, Theresa; Si, Zhenzhong; Chen, Aijuan; Scott, Stefanie (2018): Transformation's in China's Food System. In Stefanie Scott, Zhenzhong Si, Theresa Schumilas, Aijuan Chen (Eds.): *Organic Food and Farming in China. Top-down and Bottom-up Ecological Initiatives.* New York: Routledge, pp. 16–37.

Tsing, Anna Lowenhaupt (2005): *Friction. An Ethnography of Global Connection.* Princeton: Princeton University Press.

Zhan, Shaohua (2022): *China and Global Food Security.* Cambridge: Cambridge University Press.

# Appendix

# Databank of Chinese investments in Australian agriculture

*Table A.1* Chinese investments in Australian agricultural land as of December 2019

| *Investor company*[1] | *Area of land (ha, total)* | *Type of primary production* | *Year* | *Amount (in AUD)* | *Investment type & current status* |
|---|---|---|---|---|---|
| *DASHANG GROUP* | 115,533 | Mainly livestock production; some fruit orchards | 2015–2017 | 93* | Acquisition |
| *FUCHENG GROUP* | 37,953 | Mainly livestock production; rural tourism | 2015–2016 | 101 | Acquisition |
| *HAILIANG GROUP* | 50,000 | Livestock production | 2015 | 41 | Acquisition |
| *BEIDAHUANG GROUP* | 29,836 | Cropping | 2012 | 52* | Acquisition + additional leases |
| *MOON LAKE INVESTMENTS* | 17,800 | Dairy production | 2016 | 280 | Acquisition |
| *AUSTRALIA FRESH MILK HOLDINGS* | 4,516 | Dairy production | 2015, 2019 | 100* | Joint venture with Australian dairy producers Moxey Farm and Leppington Pastoral. The Chinese partner in the venture, New Hope Group, has also invested in food processing companies in Australia. |
| *HUBEI ORIENT AGRICULTURE* | 11,935 | Cotton production | 2014 | 30 | Acquisition |
| *WEN QINGNAN* | 2,025 | Wool production | 2014 | n.a. | Acquisition |
| *SHANDONG RUYI* | 97,012 | Primarily cotton production; smaller farm involving crop, livestock, and wool production | 2011–2012 | 254 | Joint venture with Australian partner Lempriere holding 20%. In 2019, in accordance with terms imposed by FIRB, Shandong Ruyi sold down its stake to 51%, with Australian farmland investment fund Macquarie Pastoral now holding the remaining 49%. |
| *SHANGHAI CRED* | 1,632,500 | Livestock production | 2016 | 25 | Acquisition |
| *KIMBERLEY AGRICULTURAL INVESTMENT* | 678,100 | Primarily crop production | 2012, 2016 | 160* | Greenfield development + acquisition |

| | | | | | |
|---|---|---|---|---|---|
| *TIANMA BEARINGS GROUP* | 1,348,929 | Livestock production; vineyards | 2011, 2014–2015 | 84* | Acquisition; In 2019, Tianma Bearings put some of the acquired properties up for sale. |
| *UNION AGRICULTURE* | 33,048 | Livestock production and cropping | 2011, 2016–2017 | 67* | Acquisition |
| *XINYANG FERTILISER COMPANY* | 2,300 | Livestock production and cropping | 2016 | n.a. | Acquisition |
| *YIANG XIANG ASSETS* | 205,000 | Livestock production | 2014 | 11.5* | Acquisition |
| *ZHEJIANG RIFA GROUP* | 49,891 | Livestock production | 2014–2017 | 169* | Acquisition. In 2019, Rifa put its entire portfolio of farms up for sale. |
| *DISCOVERY MACADAMIA* | 685 | Nut production | 2016 | 20* | Acquisition |
| *TIANJIN BRIGHT & MENGDE DAIRY GROUP* | 364 | Dairy heifer production (for export) | 2015 | 2.5 | Acquisition |
| *NINGBO DAIRY GROUP* | 280 | Dairy production | 2014 | 13.6 | Acquisition. The planned export and expansion project failed due to local council concerns. |
| *WEILONG GRAPE WINE CO.* | 484 | Vineyards | 2016 | 13.4 | Acquisition |
| *AUSTRALIAN OUTBACK BEEF* | 10,000,000 | Livestock production | 2016 | 280 | Joint venture between Australian majority partner Hancock Prospecting holding 67% and Shanghai CRED as minority partner. |
| *HARMONY AGRICULTURE & FOOD COMPANY (HAAFCO)* | 8,530 | Livestock production | 2016–2018 | 50 | Joint venture in which an Australian partner holds a minority share. HAAFCO has made investments along the entire beef value chain. In late 2019, Australia industry website Beef Central reported that the company had gone into liquidation. The Australian partners continue operating the company, following a major business restructuring. |

(*Continued*)

*Table A.1* (Continued)

| *Investor company*[1] | *Area of land (ha, total)* | *Type of primary production* | *Year* | *Amount (in AUD)* | *Investment type & current status* |
|---|---|---|---|---|---|
| *SHANDONG GEO-MINERAL INTERNATIONAL INVESTMENT COMPANY* | 289 | Aquaculture | 2017 | 1.7 | Acquisition |
| *CHEVALIER GROUP* | 10,910 | Vegetable production | 2013 | 148 | Acquisition |
| *DONGFENG PRINTING* | 580 | Dairy production | 2015 | 24.1 | Acquisition. Dongfeng Printing has also invested in dairy processing. |

*Source:* Compiled and triangulated by the author based on media reports, company documents, and personal interviews.

[1] Table displays actual company names. Note that in the main text all investor companies with which I conducted interviews appear in anonymized form.

* Estimate, no confirmed data available.

*Table A.2* Chinese investment in Australian agri-business as of December 2019

| *Investor company*[1] | *Acquired business* | *Purpose* | *Year* | *Amount (in AUD)* | *Investment status* |
|---|---|---|---|---|---|
| *ABL RED MEAT*<br>Chinese meat importer and wholesaler purchased the business from Australian beef exporter Kenny's Creek, with whom the company has an established supply relationship. | The Mount Feedlot | Beef production | 2015 | 3–4 | Completed and in operation. |
| *AUSNUTRIA DAIRY COMPANY*<br>Acquisition with support of Chinese investment firm CITIC Capital, who is a majority shareholder in Ausnutria Dairy Company. | Australia Dairy Park | Infant formula production | 2016 | 24 | Completed and in operation. |
| *BEINGMATE BABY & CHILD FOOD COMPANY*<br>Beingmate acquired a 51% stake in the factory from its previous owner Fonterra Australia. | Darnum milk factory | Milk processing and manufacturing of dairy ingredients | 2016 | 82 | Terminated.<br>In 2019, Beingmate sold its stake in the processing plant back to Fonterra, who has taken back full ownership of the plant. |
| *BRIGHT FOOD*<br>The company acquired a 75% stake in Manassen from previous owner CHAMP Private Equity. | Manassen Foods Australia | Supplier of branded foods | 2011 | 516 | Completed and in operation. |
| *COFCO*<br>Acquired through a buy-out of Tully's former farmer-shareholders. | Tully Sugar | Processing of sugar cane | 2012 | 136 | Completed and in operation. |
| *CONSOLIDATED AUSTRALIAN PASTORAL HOLDINGS (CAPH)*<br>CAPH is an investment vehicle established by Beijing-based investment company Archstone Investments and its primary supporter, private property developer Shimao Group from Shanghai. The venture acquired a 51% stake in Bindaree. | Bindaree Abattoir | Meat processing and packaging | 2017 | 120 | Completed and in operation. |

(*Continued*)

*Table A.2* (Continued)

| *Investor company*[1] | *Acquired business* | *Purpose* | *Year* | *Amount (in AUD)* | *Investment status* |
|---|---|---|---|---|---|
| *DONGFENG PRINTING*<br>The acquisition involved a formerly shut down dairy processing plant that was refurbished and put into operation again by Dongfeng Printing. | Nepean River Dairy Company | Milk processing and production of dairy products | 2015 | Unknown | Completed and in operation. |
| *HENGYANG CATTLE (FORESUN GROUP)*<br>Acquisition supported by Beijing-based investment firm CDH Investments. | Tabro Meat | Meat processing and packaging | 2014 | 25 | Terminated.<br>Between 2015 and 2017, the investment struggled with adverse business conditions (high cattle prices and low margins for Australian processors), leading to temporary shutdowns.<br>In 2018, a deal was being discussed to sell the plant to Chinese-owned Harmony Agriculture and Food Company (HAAFCO). |
| *HEILONGJIANG GRAND FARM GROUP*<br>Involves primarily a supply agreement with V&V Walsh as well as some smaller investments in the plant's processing capacity but no significant ownership. | V&V Walsh | Meat processing and packaging | 2014 | Unknown | Completed and in operation. |
| *KB FOOD GROUP*<br>The company is a joint venture between Chinese Legend Holdings (90%) and Australia's Kailis Family (10%). | KB Seafoods Company | Processing, wholesaling, a nd exporting of seafood | 2017 | 180–200 | Completed and in operation. |
| *MENGNIU DAIRY GROUP*<br>The acquisition was carried out under the name of Inner Mongolia Fuyuan Farming Company—an investment consortium including Mengniu Dairy as the largest shareholder, Goldman Sachs, and other international investors.<br>The previous owners of Burra Foods continue to hold a 21% stake in the business. | Burra Foods | Milk processing and production of dairy products | 2016 | 300 | Completed and in operation. |

| | | | | | |
|---|---|---|---|---|---|
| *MENGNIU DAIRY GROUP* | Bellamy's Australia | Production of infant formula | 2019 | 1500 | Completed and in operation. |
| *NEW HOPE GROUP*<br>The acquisition was carried out by New Hope Group's private equity arm Hosen Capital through its fund "New Hope Investment Fund I" in conjunction with a number of international investors. | Kilcoy Pastoral Company | Meat processing and packaging | 2013 | 100 | Completed and in operation.<br>In 2018, Kilcoy abattoir was integrated with a string of other acquisitions in meat and seafood processing (Ruprecht Company in the US and Weidao Foods in China) to form Kilcoy Global Foods. |
| *SHANGHAI GROUND FOODS TECH COMPANY*<br>The company acquired Brownes Dairy from private equity group Archer Capital as part of an investment consortium, including a number of Chinese investment companies. Archer Capital had purchased the Western Australian dairy processor in 2011 with a short-term investment horizon.<br>Note: Mengniu Dairy Group holds a minority interest in Shanghai Ground Foods Tech Company. | Brownes Dairy | Milk processing and production of dairy products | 2017 | unknown | Completed and in operation. |
| *TAIHUA FOOD*<br>Purchased in partnership with previous owners. | Churchill Abattoir | Meat processing and packaging | 2014 | 35 | Troubled.<br>Abattoir in receivership since 2018 and looking for new investors. |

*Source:* Compiled and triangulated by the author based on media reports, company documents, and personal interviews.

[1] Table displays actual company names. Note that in the main text all investor companies with which I conducted interviews appear in anonymized form.

*Table A.3* Announced and aborted investments in Australian agricultural land and agri-business as of December 2019

| *Investor company*[1] | *Investment target* | *Purpose* | *Year* | *Amount (in AUD)* | *Investment status* |
|---|---|---|---|---|---|
| *BEIJING AUSTRALIA AGRICULTURAL RESOURCE COOPERATIVE DEVELOPMENT FUND*<br>Public-private investment fund between private company Yuhu Group and state-owned Beijing Agricultural Investment Fund. | Undefined | Undefined | n.a. | 400 | Aborted.<br>The fund had pledged 400 million AUD for investment in the Australian agricultural sector in a highly publicized official ceremony. The agreement fell through for undisclosed reasons. |
| *HUNAN DAKANG*<br>Initial investment consortium comprised of Chinese firms Shanghai Pengxin and Shanghai CRED. | S. Kidman & Co. farm portfolio | Livestock production | 2015 | 282 | Blocked by FIRB.<br>The deal went through in 2016 following a restructuring, with Australian mining firm Hancock Prospecting as the majority shareholder and Shanghai CRED as minority shareholder. |
| *SHANDONG DELISI FOOD*<br>The acquisition would have seen Shandong Delisi acquire a 45% stake in Bindaree Abattoir, while the remaining shares would have remained under previous ownership. | Bindaree Abattoir | Meat processing and packaging | 2015 | 140 | Aborted.<br>Investor did not follow through on commitment to buy a 45% stake in Bindaree. |
| CHINA INVESTMENT CORPORATION (CIC) | Undefined | Interest in dairy production | n.a. | 500 | Unsuccessful.<br>CIC made several announcements to invest in Australian agriculture and, reportedly, made an unsuccessful bid for Australia's largest dairy farm VDL.<br>CIC has not made any direct investments in Australian agriculture, but it has provided financing for COFCO's expansion, including in Australia. |
| *MENGNIU DAIRY GROUP* | Lion Dairy & Drinks | Production of dairy products and other beverages | 2019 | 600 | Blocked by FIRB in 2020 as the deal was found to be against the national interest. |

*Source:* Compiled and triangulated by the author based on media reports, company documents, and personal interviews.

[1] Table displays actual company names. Note that in the main text all investor companies with which I conducted interviews appear in anonymized form.

# Index

Note: **Bold** page numbers refer to tables; *italic* page numbers refer to figures and page numbers followed by "n" denote endnotes.

For Product Safety Concerns and Information please contact our EU
representative GPSR@taylorandfrancis.com
Taylor & Francis Verlag GmbH, Kaufingerstraße 24, 80331 München, Germany

www.ingramcontent.com/pod-product-compliance
Ingram Content Group UK Ltd.
Pitfield, Milton Keynes, MK11 3LW, UK
UKHW020007200926
475702UK00015B/2525

* 9 7 8 1 0 3 2 7 5 5 8 6 1 *